THE SOCIAL LICENSE

This unique book combines a colourful history of Bolivian politics with some of the most advanced quantitative techniques yet developed for socio-political risk analysis. This is the story of how a foreign-owned private sector mining company (Minera San Cristobal – MSC) earned, lost, and regained its social licence to operate (SLO).

Robert G. Boutilier and Ian Thomson, leading experts in stakeholder management theory and practice, transform the concept of the SLO from a metaphor to a management tool. The book traces the development of new concepts and measures in the field of stakeholder engagement while following the narrative of a community struggling with a fundamental change in its identity from a declining, malnourished llama-herding village to one of the richest towns in Bolivia.

This remarkable story will inspire practitioners in the field of stakeholder management; it will provide an invaluable roadmap for professionals working on land re-use projects in the energy, mining, and conservation sectors; it will make stakeholder relations concepts and techniques accessible to students through an engaging and in-depth case study; and it will open your eyes to one of the most fascinating accounts of how two different cultures collided and then came together to address different but aligned goals.

Robert G. Boutilier is a strategy consultant, social researcher, and Associate of the Centre for Sustainable Development at Simon Fraser University, Canada.

Ian Thomson is a practising social consultant, researcher and communicator with more than 40 years of experience in the natural resource industries, most recently as principal of Shinglespit Consultants Inc., Canada.

"An engaging and unique mix of historical context, social science theory, novel data, visualizations and quotes from the front lines where indigenous communities and multinationals negotiate rents, rights and right."

Witold Henisz, Professor of Management at the Wharton School,
University of Pennsylvania, USA

"A readable and thoughtful exploration of the theories and practice of relationships between mining companies and communities. Useful for anyone interested in community development or mine development."

David Clarry, Vice President, Corporate Social Responsibility,
Hudbay Minerals Inc., Canada

"So well written, truly a pleasure to read, not to mention absolutely fascinating."
Pamela Lesser, Faculty of Social Sciences, University of Lapland, Finland

THE SOCIAL LICENSE

The Story of the San Cristobal Mine

Robert G. Boutilier and Ian Thomson

LONDON AND NEW YORK

First published 2019
by Routledge
2 Park Square, Milton Park, Abingdon, Oxon OX144RN

and by Routledge
711 Third Avenue, New York, NY 10017

Routledge is an imprint of the Taylor & Francis Group, an informa business

© 2019 Robert G. Boutilier and Ian Thomson

The right of Robert G. Boutilier and Ian Thomson to be identified as authors of this work has been asserted by them in accordance with sections 77 and 78 of the Copyright, Designs and Patents Act 1988.

All rights reserved. No part of this book may be reprinted or reproduced or utilised in any form or by any electronic, mechanical, or other means, now known or hereafter invented, including photocopying and recording, or in any information storage or retrieval system, without permission in writing from the publishers.

Trademark notice: Product or corporate names may be trademarks or registered trademarks, and are used only for identification and explanation without intent to infringe.

British Library Cataloguing-in-Publication Data
A catalogue record for this book is available from the British Library

Library of Congress Cataloging-in-Publication Data
Names: Boutilier, Robert, 1950- author. | Thomson, Ian, 1946- author.
Title: The social license : the story of the San Cristobal Mine / Robert G. Boutilier and Ian Thomson.
Description: Abingdon, Oxon ; New York, NY : Routledge, 2019. | Includes bibliographical references and index.
Identifiers: LCCN 2018020051| ISBN 9781138579682 (hbk) | ISBN 9781138579699 (pbk)
Subjects: LCSH: San Cristâobal Mine (Potosâi, Bolivia) | Mines and mineral resources—Social aspects—Bolivia—Potosâi—History. | Mineral industries—Social aspects—Bolivia—Potosâi—History.
Classification: LCC TN39.P66 B68 2019 | DDC 338.7/62234098414—dc23
LC record available at https://lccn.loc.gov/2018020051

ISBN: 978-1-138-57968-2 (hbk)
ISBN: 978-1-138-57969-9 (pbk)
ISBN: 978-0-429-50786-1 (ebk)

Typeset in Bembo
by Swales & Willis Ltd, Exeter, Devon, UK

Printed in the United Kingdom
by Henry Ling Limited

CONTENTS

List of figures	ix
List of tables	xi
Author biographies	xii
Preface	xiv
Mutual learning and influence xiv	
Overview of the contents xvii	
Acknowledgements	xxii
List of abbreviations	xxiv

PART 1
Historic context   **1**

1 In the beginning	3

Early days 3
The gift of El Tío 6
The long wait 7
Destiny delivers 11

2 The historical roots of divergent views of fairness	12

Evolutionary theory in the social sciences 13
Institutional theory and rent-seeking 16
A cultural conflict waiting to happen 20

3 Bolivian politics from the Spanish to the neo-liberals	21

The historical resentments of Potosí 21
Economic crisis and neo-liberal reform 23

vi Contents

Consolidating neo-liberal reforms 25
Popular participation and decentralisation 26

4 The anti-foreigner turn   29

The push back against neo-liberalism 29
Emblematic incidents at the time of Buchanan's discovery 31
Opposition to neo-liberalism goes mainstream 33
The rise of Evo Morales 34

PART 2
Retrospective from discovery to operating mine   39

5 Social licence concept and retrospective study method   41

The social licence concept 41
Identification of levels of social licence 46
Methods used for the 1994 to 2008 San Cristobal case study 48

6 From geological discovery to construction: 1994–2004   51

Geological discovery 51
Resettlement 52
Waiting for jobs 56

7 Construction: 2004–2006   59

New management team 60
Big changes, rising anxieties 61
Loss of legitimacy 62
Recovery of legitimacy 65

8 Transition to operating mine: 2007–2009   68

Adjustments to start-up and full operation 68
Water worries 70
Further observations beyond the retrospective study 77
Modernisation and the prophecy about abandoning the old ways 78

9 Re-negotiation of roles and rights: 2010 and 2011   81

Adjustment to arrival of globalisation 81
Regional unrest: multiple issues 82
The 2010 mini-insurrection 85

Mine occupation of 2011 86
Discrimination as either inequity or inequality 96

PART 3
Stakeholder strategies from quantitative measures 99

10 Shift to quantitative risk assessment methods 101

SLSN 101
Quantification of the social licence 102
Quantification of concerns and priorities 107
Quantification of stakeholder influence 109
Changes in methods by year 111

11 Co-evolution of risk hotspots with Bolivian politics and economy: 2009–2015 113

2009: storm clouds on the horizon 113
2011: the occupation 116
2012: horizons expanded to the capital cities 117
2013: the free market shows that it can benefit campesinos too 119
2015: the political emergence of San Cristobal town 120

12 From findings to strategies that work 122

Issues and recommendations by year 122
Dust reduction initiatives 124
Water initiatives 124
Access to health care 126
Communications planning 127
The limits of stakeholder strategies 127

PART 4
Distinctive features and conclusions 129

13 Women and the San Cristobal mine 131

Women and mining 131
Historical overview 131
Women in the mine 134
Perspectives on women in the mine workplace 135

viii Contents

A further perspective 138
Concluding thoughts 139

14 The trouble with llamas   140

About llamas 140
Relocating the llama herds 142
The quinoa factor 148
The situation in 2015 150

15 Concluding observations   152

Story woven from many threads 152
What is the entity that needs a social licence? 157
Summary 159

References   *160*
Index   *165*

FIGURES

1.1	*Los Tres Gigantes* (The Three Giants)	4
1.2	Locations of the three mines in the prophecy	6
1.3	Minera San Cristobal's region of influence	10
2.1	Different principles of justice at the root of the differences between MSC and its Bolivian stakeholders	14
3.1	Cerro Rico, city of Potosí	22
5.1	How the social licences granted by individual stakeholders translate into the impacts on the focal organisation	44
5.2	Hypothesised boundaries between the levels of the social licence (Thomson and Joyce, 2008)	47
5.3	Four-level model of the social licence (based on Thomson and Boutilier, 2011)	47
5.4	Fluctuations in project acceptance at San Cristobal	50
6.1	Map of mine operating area	57
7.1	Achopalla: sacred boulder moved to new town	64
8.1	On-street parking in San Cristobal	79
10.1	Five-year trends in standardised average rated social licence scores and odds ratios of compliments to complaints in open-ended verbal comments	107
11.1	MSC's stakeholder network in 2009 based on ties of strength 4 out of 5	115
11.2	MSC's stakeholder network in 2011 based on ties of strength 5 out of 5	116
11.3	MSC's stakeholder network in 2012 based on ties of strength 4 out of 5	118

x Figures

11.4 MSC's stakeholder network in 2013 based on ties of
strength 4 out of 5   120
11.5 MSC's stakeholder network in 2015 based on ties of
strength 4 out of 5   121
12.1 Per capita frequencies of environmental and water issues
from 2009 to 2013   125
15.1 'No parking' sign in San Cristobal, 2011   153

TABLES

2.1	Context and control differences between equality and equity	15
5.1	Levels of social licence and associated behaviours	48
10.1	Fifteen agree/disagree statements used to measure the social licence at MSC	104
10.2	Labels assigned to sextiles of social licence scores	106
11.1	Legend for node names in network graphs	114

AUTHOR BIOGRAPHIES

Robert G. Boutilier

Robert G. Boutilier is a researcher, author, and an associate of the Centre for Sustainable Development at Simon Fraser University, Vancouver. Robert has conducted workshops on stakeholder relations for managers in over 20 countries and is a regular conference speaker. He has published three books and three book chapters on business management and a dozen scholarly journal articles on topics in issues management, social psychology, and stakeholder relations.

Robert has conducted stakeholder mapping research at over 50 resource extraction and infrastructure projects on four continents in nine languages. He combines his system for measuring the levels of social capital in an organisation's relationships with its stakeholders and among the stakeholders themselves (i.e., the Stakeholder 360®) with a standardised measure of the SLO. Blending these with careful quantification of stakeholders' own words about their preoccupations, he produces strategic recommendations aimed at reducing the company's socio-political risk. More recently he has helped apply artificial intelligence to modelling both traditional and online stakeholder politics.

Ian Thomson

Ian Thomson is a practising social consultant, researcher, and communicator with more than 40 years of experience in the natural resource industries, most recently as President of Shinglespit Consultants Inc. His areas of expertise include stakeholder engagement, social performance guidance and assessment, application of international standards, corporate and operational team training, policy and social context reviews, and guiding multi-stakeholder processes. His early-career years of working on the technical side of natural resource development enable him to ground his consideration of social issues in an understanding of the business and engineering aspects of the industry.

Ian has led development of standards and guidelines for the management of social issues during mineral exploration and mine development programmes. He authored the first version of 'Community Engagement' for the Prospectors and Developers Association of Canada's e3Plus online manual of good practice, facilitated construction of the 'Principles and Guidance for Responsible Exploration' for the Prospectors and Developers Association of Canada, co-developed quantitative metrics for the Social Licence to Operate, and published more than 20 peer-reviewed papers in academic journals.

PREFACE

Mutual learning and influence

Our biases

This book is about the transformational relationship between a mining company and a community. The community is San Cristobal, in the Department of Potosí, Bolivia. The company is *Minera San Cristóbal*[1] (MSC), a subsidiary of Japan's Sumitomo Corporation. The mutual influence extends beyond one community and one mining company. The whole region around the mine experiences economic development, with attendant social and political change. Likewise, the whole mining industry gains new tools for stakeholder relations, with implications for management and finance in the resource extraction industries.

One part of the story looks at the impact of a mining operation on communities. We rely as much as possible on the perceptions of local people themselves. Inevitably, the process of telling a story entails emphasising some aspects and ignoring others. We do not claim to present an 'objective' perspective. Despite our efforts to understand local perspectives, our own perspectives are those of outsiders. However, we try as much as possible to avoid romanticising local life either before the mine or currently.

The other part of the story looks at the impact of the communities on the company and on the management of stakeholder relations in resource projects in general. Here we can more easily identify our biases. We are management consultants. We work on project contracts, mostly for resource companies (primarily mining companies, but we have also worked on oil and gas projects, windfarms, pipelines, and energy projects) and sometimes for financial institutions that monitor the social and environmental performance of companies to which they have lent money. Working on a variety of projects for different clients gives us an opportunity to observe what works and what does not in different contexts. We endeavour to improve the practice of stakeholder relations in the resource industries by applying a blend of practical experience and social science concepts.

The political context of this story is indigenous Latin American. It does not take very much awareness of current events to know that the resource industries are politically controversial in Latin America and elsewhere. Resource companies are accused of everything from destroying the planet through climate change to abusing human rights through duplicity with rapacious governments. Perhaps because of our biases, very little in the following pages is dedicated to justifying positions that could be called anti-mining, anti-resource extraction, anti-consumerism, anti-market, anti-Western, anti-Christian, or anti-globalisation. Nonetheless, the need to understand the predispositions of the communities around a mine requires examining the role that all these perspectives have played, historically and currently. Therefore, we touch on some of these political topics by way of understanding how some of the conflicts between the communities and the company evolved. Moreover, by elaborating the concept of the SLO in stakeholder networks, we have tried to bring more quantitative science to the practice of community relations.

Everyone has political biases, both conscious and unconscious. Perhaps the most distinctive aspect of ours, that we are aware of, is the assumption that communities have power. Communities have not always had very much power, but at least in contemporary Bolivia it is sheer ideological blindness to imagine that companies can bully communities. Both parties have their strengths and weaknesses. Our view is that bad things happen when either party ignores the needs and desires of the other. When communities ignore foreign companies, the Bolivian experience is that the resources end up being exploited in ways that damage the environment, community health, and economic development. Historically, the same damages occurred when companies ignore the communities. Therefore, our overarching orientation in writing this book is to illustrate ways in which companies and communities can work together for mutual benefit.

Divergent cultural views

Because of the nature of their work, mining professionals spend a significant portion of their working lives in remote parts of the world inhabited by traditional subsistence cultures, often indigenous. The juxtaposition of people steeped in sciences such as geology, chemistry, and engineering with uneducated people who survive off the land creates numerous challenges in cross-cultural communication. The starkest contrasts between the culture of science and traditional cultures often involve beliefs about nature and the supernatural.

Many mining professionals have a story to tell about some 'superstition' encountered in a traditional village. Miners sometimes swap these stories over

xvi Preface

drinks, comparing notes about the more creative ways to handle the gulf between the cultures. Most of the stories follow a format in which concrete evidence and factual events validated the scientific view. Nevertheless, there are those few stories in which events and facts validate the supposedly 'superstitious' view. A minority of miners, usually those with more extensive contact with indigenous cultures, have stories of the latter type. In Chapter 1 we recount ours in full, but the next section gives a little foretaste.

Geoscience meets El Tío

Although there was small scale commercial and artisanal mining at San Cristobal in both colonial times and in the 20th century, it was the geologist Larry Buchanan who in 1995 discovered that there was a mineral deposit there that would probably support the development of a very large, world-class mine. The deposit turned out to be right underneath the village of San Cristobal. As the possibility of a mine grew, the need to relocate the village became an issue. In order to monitor how this process was handled, Larry and his wife, Karen Gans, went to live in the village for most of the period during the planning and implementation of the relocation. They also made several subsequent visits to the community. Their experiences are reported in their book, *The Gift of El Tío: A Memoir* (Buchanan and Gans, 2008).

In their book, Larry and Karen report that the discovery had been prophesied, along with a set of social, cultural, and economic changes. The prophecy said that a gift of mineral riches would make San Cristobal residents so wealthy that they would not bother to count their change in the market, that the residents would stop tending their hillside gardens and caring for animals, that they would lose their faith in *El Tío*, the traditional lord of the underground, and that eventually there would be extreme hunger throughout the land, accompanied by cannibalism.

Only the last parts of the prophecy have not yet been fulfilled. The prediction that residents would stop believing in *El Tío* has not yet fully happened, but it is true that young people in San Cristobal do not show much interest in the old gods and rituals and their parents simply do not have the time needed to fully practice the traditional ways of knowing and worshipping. As for abandoning subsistence agriculture, while many of the older generation continue to raise potatoes and other staples on the family plots of land, the younger generation and new arrivals in the community buy all their food from the local market and stores. Only a minority of families in the town continue raising llamas for food or income. Of these, the llama-tending responsibilities are more likely to be borne by the elderly family members or hired shepherds who do not work at the mine. The cultivation of quinoa for export, however, has bourgeoned.

When we ourselves asked about the prophecies in 2013 and 2015, we discovered that there were additional elements not reported by Buchanan and Gans. One involved a prediction of the end of the world following the opening of two additional silver mines in the Department of Potosí, Pulacayo and Mesa de Plata, near San Antonio de Lípez. We also discovered that there were different versions of the prophecy that had apparently changed over the centuries. We examine all this in more detail in Chapter 1.

From our experiences at this and other mining projects in remote areas, we have learned to respect the beliefs of traditional cultures. The best we can offer as a reconciliation of science and traditional beliefs is that different cultures probably shape human potential along different lines. Some cultures bring out the human potential for technological development but suppress the potential for spiritual enrichment and prophecy. Other cultures seem to foster the opposite. The full breadth of human potential just may be greater than any single culture has yet been able to support.

Overview of the contents

The chapters of this book are peppered with incidents of cross-cultural divergence and convergence. The convergences instruct us about the commonality in human nature, while the divergences teach us new ways to view the world and the work of mining.

The four parts of the book

The book is divided into four parts. Part 1 (Historical context) has four chapters that set the cultural and political context while describing a framework for understanding company-community conflicts. In Part 1, we discuss the historical roots of differences between MSC as a corporation and the Bolivian communities, culture, and institutions around the mine.

Chapter 1 focuses on the history of local communities while Chapters 2 to 4 look at the broader historical roots of conflicts and debates in Bolivia and at a few social science concepts that help make sense of them.

Chapters 5 to 9 make up Part 2 (Retrospective from discovery to routine operation). Here we look at the details of the relationships between the communities and the various companies that sequentially owned and developed the mineral deposit from 1994 to 2011. Chapter 5 introduces the formal version of the concept of the social licence and describes the qualitative study methods used to acquire the information reported in Chapters 6 to 9. Chapter 6 covers the ten-year pre-construction period from 1994 to 2004. Chapter 7 covers the construction stage, which lasted from 2004 to 2006. Chapter 8 deals with issues of adjusting to mine operation from 2007 to 2009 but also includes the issue of water, which is a chronic issue that reached its point of maximum controversy in 2009. Chapter 9 focuses on two notable conflicts that occurred in 2010 and 2011 respectively.

Part 3 (Stakeholder strategies from quantitative measures) contains Chapters 10 to 12. This is where we highlight the quantitative techniques we have developed for analysing socio-political risks and how they helped generate strategies for maintaining an SLO. Chapter 10 describes the quantitative study methods developed and refined at MSC from 2009 to 2015. Chapter 11 summarises the findings of

xviii Preface

the qualitative study for five intervals of approximately 15 months each from 2009 to 2015. Chapter 12 covers the same time period with a focus on the strategies developed for raising the level of social licence and the initiatives undertaken to implement the strategies.

Part 4 (Distinctive features and conclusions) contains Chapters 13 to 15. Chapters 13 and 14 touch on two topics that make the relationships distinctive: women mine workers and the territoriality of llamas. Chapter 15 concludes with lessons learned about earning and maintaining a social licence in mining in general.

Chapter by chapter summaries

Looking now at each chapter separately, Chapter 1 helps introduce the cultures of the Altiplano. In addition to describing the unique legal relationship the communities of the region had with the Spanish colonists, we touch upon the changes in economic activities that have occurred. These are all recounted in the context of what we have learned about the spiritual beliefs of local people and the prophecy about mining that they passed down from generation to generation. For approximately 400 years the residents of the Altiplano region of southwest Bolivia have expected the appearance of the mine that now operates near the village of San Cristobal. A shamanistic prophecy foretold not only the mine but the events preceding the end of the world. The prophecy was expressed within the indigenous religious pantheon. The geologist who discovered the mineral deposit, Larry Buchanan, wrote a book (*The Gift of El Tío: A Memoir*, 2008), along with his wife, Karen Gans, about their experiences of living in the village of San Cristobal before the mine was built. Their memoir contains part of the prophecy. We have made further investigations and discovered not only more details but also the apparent evolution of the earliest prophecy into the version that circulates today. In that version, the end is nigh.

Chapter 2 reviews two major perspectives on socio-political conflict: evolutionary theory and institutional theory. They explain how MSC, an international corporation, views justice and fairness from a different angle than the communities around the mine. While each side can understand the other's reasoning, their respective intuitive senses of fairness are biased in different directions by forces rooted in the distant past. The development of the San Cristobal mine provoked questioning of traditional assumptions about everything from corporations and foreigners to subsistence and sustainability. In the process, the principles of equality and equity came to be prioritised differently in a variety of situations. At the end of Chapter 2 we also show how institutional theory can explain the dynamics that determine when and why a country might fall into what has been called the 'curse of natural resources'.

Chapter 3 looks more closely at how Bolivian history since the Spanish Conquest shaped the basic template for political discourses of resentment and victimhood still in use today. Bolivia went through some abrupt changes in economic policy directions in the 1980s and 1990s which set the stage for the election of Evo Morales in 2006.

Chapter 4 examines the specific organisations, movements, and discourses that produced the policy of resource company nationalisation and that brought Evo Morales to power. MSC is still dealing with most of those stakeholders and political currents today in its efforts to continue operating as a private, foreign, resource extraction company in Bolivia.

Chapter 5 introduces Part 2 of the book. Part 2 traces the history of stakeholder relations from the discovery of the mineral deposit in 1995 to the present. Chapter 5 describes the concept of the social licence and the two different methods used to estimate its levels. A retrospective method was used for the period from 1994 to 2011 while a longitudinal quantitative method was used from 2009 to 2016.

Chapter 6 deals with the exploration and pre-construction period, which started with the initial discovery of the mineral deposit (1995) and lasted up to the beginning of mine construction (2004). This includes the period during which the residents of San Cristobal decided to accept resettlement, designed their new village, and made the move, taking their whole colonial church and some sacred boulders with them. The SLO fluctuated a great deal with events like the suspension of construction plans owing to low metal prices.

Chapter 7 describes the construction period (2004 to 2006). When the green light was finally given for construction, a new management team took over. Relations between the communities and the company plunged to an all-time low. The new management team believed they had no time for community relations because the construction schedule was so tight. Relations deteriorated so much that the social licence was withdrawn and construction was halted by a road blockade. The construction management team learned that keeping to their schedule depended on finding time to listen to the community.

Chapter 8 looks at the period from late 2006 to 2009 during which the mine began productive operations. These four years included a rebound for the social licence and a jolting adjustment among community members to the rigid work schedule of an industrial job. Mine workers no longer had time for their community chores and participation in the ceremonies. Events related to the old customs and beliefs began to dwindle, exactly as prophesied.

Chapter 9 examines in more detail the unrest that occurred in 2010 and 2011. There was a period of tension as roles and relationships were re-negotiated to adjust to the new normal. Moreover, the sudden prosperity enjoyed by the communities around the mine produced a sense of unjust inequality among neighbouring communities further from the mine. Meanwhile, the communities closest to the mine chaffed at inequalities in advancement opportunities and access to health services. It was during this period that the deep-rooted cultural differences described in Chapters 2 and 3 came to the surface and manifested themselves in the occupation of the mine in 2011.

Chapters 10 to 12 form Part 3 of the book, which describes the quantitative method we used to assess the level of social licence, canvass stakeholders' concerns, and map the relationships among stakeholders.

In Chapter 10, the evolution of the technique itself is described. It describes (a) how to decide who will be counted as 'inside' the stakeholder network and

xx Preface

(b) the three kinds of interview data that were combined to produce strategies for raising MSC's level of social licence. The qualitative data came from carefully chosen open-ended questions. The social licence measure came from quantitative ratings by stakeholders. The stakeholder network data came from questions about network connections. Together, these procedures form the foundation of a quantitative approach to stakeholder politics.

Chapter 11 summarises the types of socio-political risks that were discovered in stakeholder interviews conducted approximately every 15 months from 2009 to 2015. As the method evolved, the scope expanded from the closest villages, to the region, to the capital cities, and finally to the national news media. For example, in 2009 the biggest risk came from complaints about the dust from the mine that was blowing into the villages and onto agricultural fields. In 2012, the main risk came from national government entities committed to nationalising all mining operations and from trucking contractors pressuring the company to export its concentrate by road instead of by rail.

Chapter 12 describes the stakeholder engagement strategies that were recommended to cope with the socio-political risks described in Chapter 11. Generally, the strategies began with face-to-face relationship building and gradually advanced to media relations and discourse creation or modification. The general progression was from building local support to influencing the interpretation of that support by the electorate and by politically influential stakeholders.

Part 4 of the book is comprised of Chapters 13 to 15. It examines unique challenges faced by MSC and concludes with lessons that other companies can draw from MSC's experiences.

Chapter 13 describes how women came to work in every area of the mine. Although the culture in the region is very traditional, the communities themselves provided the initial impulse that made MSC an industry leader in gender equity. Women went from cleaning and kitchen jobs to driving the gigantic haul trucks in the open pit to extracting the valuable minerals from the rock in the processing plant. However, the arrival of the mine also brought new social challenges for women, which included negative impacts that affect them disproportionately.

Chapter 14 looks at the special problems posed by mixing llama herding with mining. Three conflicting sets of territorial claims had to be resolved: those of the herders, those of the mining company, and those of the llamas. Llamas do not respect the boundaries invented by humans. They are territorial and constantly return to their grazing grounds. However, humans are often just as committed to the land. Questions of proper compensation for giving up grazing land get mixed up with questions of personal identity and the nature of sustainability. Stakeholder issues related to llamas have been some of the toughest problems to resolve.

Chapter 15 concludes with more general observation on gaining and maintaining an SLO. MSC has so far maintained its social and legal licence in a country where nationalisation is official policy. However, it is a truism that governments generally incorporate diverse ministries or secretariats mandated to achieve goals that are at least partially incompatible. Consequently, everywhere in the world it is common for any one policy to make it more difficult for some ministries, or other levels of government, to achieve their goals. The story of MSC highlights not only the importance of including the socio-political discourse of the jurisdiction in strategies for maintaining the social licence, but also the importance of maintaining the licence of the socio-economic sector in which one is embedded.

While many of the stories and contexts described in this book have the unique flavour of the Bolivian Altiplano, the relationships described here have features that are very human and quite universal. These include both the relationships between stakeholders and the company and the relationships among the stakeholders themselves. In effect, the quantification of social licence level in stakeholder networks is the quantification of the most politically relevant aspects of relationships. We hope readers will find insights and techniques they can use wherever they are located and in whichever industry they work.

Robert G. Boutilier   Ian Thomson
Morelos, Mexico   British Columbia, Canada

Note

1 The Spanish word *minera* means 'mining company'. The name of the company would translate into English as The Saint Christopher Mining Company". Throughout this book, we use the anglicized version of the name *San Cristóbal*, which is the same but without the accent on the 'o'.

ACKNOWLEDGEMENTS

In retrospect, the idea of writing a history of the relationship between the San Cristobal mine project and its neighbours first emerged in April 2008, in conversation between Ian Thomson and Margarita de Castro over the ability to apply the then newly recognised normative components of the SLO, legitimacy, credibility, and trust, at the mine. Later that day, two key members of the mine management team were brought into the conversation, Javier Diez de Medina and Juan Mamani, and the first, tentative graph of the history of the relationship was drawn up by pooling our collective information. A few days later, after the graph had been modified and validated by community leaders, we had a reliable framework for the story. However, it was eight years later and the generation of several rounds of quantitative data on the quality of the social licence before there was real confidence in being able to put the whole story into writing.

This book is partly the product of observations made during regular visits to San Cristóbal between 2004 and 2016 by both of us and countless conversations with many people, both employees of MSC and members of the communities. We have drawn on our own files and memories, augmented extensively by information from the public domain and company documents, and many more interviews.

We are most grateful to MSC for permission to use company sources in preparing this book, and for fact checking the text. The company has been generous in not only providing raw data and allowing us to interview members of the management team and staff, but also giving us complete freedom to tell the story as we see it. In this, Javier Diez de Medina, provided continuous encouragement and, together with Juan Mamani and Eva Zamora, willingly responded to our questions and requests for information, while senior managers Dave Assels and Mike Bunch were quietly and constantly supportive.

The story is much more than the mine, it concerns a community that believed in destiny, has experienced profound change and, on several occasions, fought to get what it wanted from the relationship with the company. Many residents willingly engaged in conversation, told us their side of the story and have, indeed, become friends. We have been privileged to know and enjoy the clarity and candour of their perspectives, which we have taken care to respect. Among them we are particularly grateful to Ascencio Lazo, Rudolfo Ramos, Alberto Colque, Segundiño Quispe M., Jose Colque C., Maximo Gonzáles, Valeria Quispe, Pilar Alí, Pilar Yaris, Baldemero Mercado C., Lucrecio Quispe, and Rafael Quispe.

The book is also the story of how the concept of the SLO evolved from a metaphor into a management tool. We fully acknowledge Jim Cooney with coining the phrase in 1997 and our colleagues Susan Joyce, Myriam Cabrera, and Margarita de Castro for their intellectual support in teasing out the normative components, which facilitated the leap to measurement. We are also grateful to Leeora Black for providing the statistical know-how that confirmed the validity of the measuring methodology and provided the final pieces of the puzzle.

We have also benefitted from critical review of early drafts of the text. For this we are most grateful to David Clarry, Alberto Mollinedo, Tena Patten, Michelle Hohn, Leontia Thomson, and Leeora Black. Rowan Helliwell kindly created the sketch maps for the book.

Finally, none of this would have happened without the support and tolerance of our families, to whom we dedicate this book. We humbly recognise that they have put up with us disappearing for hours at a time to create the text, and weeks spent away from home in Bolivia working with MSC and also collecting material for the book.

ABBREVIATIONS

AOU	Act of Understanding
ASC	Andean Silver Corporation
BRICS	Brazil, Russia, India, China, and South Africa
CGIAB	Comisión para la Gestión Integral del Agua en Bolivia
CIS	Catering International and Services
COMCIPO	Comité Cívico Potosinista
COMIBOL	Corporación Minera de Bolivia
COMSUR	Compañía Minera del Sur S.A.
CSR	Corporate Social Responsibility
CSUTCB	Confederación Sindical Única de Trabajadores Campesinos de Bolivia
EAP	Environmental Action Plan
EIA	Environmental Impact Assessment
FPIC	Free, Prior, and Informed Consent
FRUTCAS	Federación Regional Única de los Trabajadores Campesinos del Altiplano Sud
FSTMB	Federación Sindical de Trabajadores Mineros de Bolivia or National Federated Union of Bolivian Mine Workers
GESSBA	Grupo Empresarial de Salud San Bartolome S.R.L.
ILO	169 International Labour Organisation Convention 169 on the Rights of Indigenous and Tribal Peoples
IPSP	Instrumento Público por la Soberanía de los Pueblos or Public Instrument for the Sovereignty of the People
KPI	Key performance indicator
MAS	El Movimiento Al Socialismo or Movement towards Socialism
MINTEC	Minería Técnica Consultores Asociados
MSC	Minera San Cristóbal

NEP	New Economic Policy
NGO	Non-Governmental Organisation
SLO	Social Licence to Operate
SLSN	Social Licence in Stakeholder Networks
YPFB	Yacimientos Petrolíferos Fiscales Bolivianos

PART 1
Historic context

PART 2

1

IN THE BEGINNING

This is another book telling the story of the mine at San Cristobal, in the Department of Potosí, Bolivia. In 2008, the geologist who discovered the mineral deposit, Larry Buchanan, and his wife, Karen Gans, published a memoir about their experiences living in the village of San Cristobal prior to the construction of the mine and their return visits during construction and the initial start-up phase. In 2015, Mariano Baptista Gumucio published an historical panorama, in Spanish, packed with detail after detail up to 2014. Our book is equally panoramic but focuses on the relationships between the communities and the mining company and what can be learned and applied at other mining projects. We apply a variety of social science theories and concepts to understanding the dynamics of the relationships. Above all, we explain how the concept of the social licence to operate was transformed from a metaphor to a practical, measurable management tool during our community relations consulting work at the mine. We start with the historical context of the region and then examine the relations between the company and its stakeholders using, first, a qualitative method, and then a quantitative method. It is both a case study about the challenges of community relations in the extractive industries and a generalisable lesson in community relations techniques.

Early days

Sometime in the second half of the 17th century, rumours began circulating in the community of San Cristobal of a giant silver mine and great riches for the residents. However, the mine and its wealth would arrive long into the future, around the time of the millennium, and come with strings attached (Buchanan and Gans, 2008). The prophecy is retold in the community today, along with many other myths and legends (Consejo Consultivo, 2008) that form part of the collective oral history of the people.

4 Historic context

For almost 400 years, the community of San Cristobal was located in a bowl-shaped depression nestled in the hills that rise steeply above the broad expanse of the Bolivian Altiplano 50 kilometres south of the great Salar de Uyuni. The region is a sparsely populated semi desert known as Nor (i.e., 'North') Lípez where sources of potable water are few and far between. The open, scrub-covered Altiplano sits between 3,600 and 3,800 metres (more than two miles) above sea level while the knot of hills around San Cristobal rises to 4,500 metres (approaching three miles). It is a place of high thin air, cold nights, and warm sunny days. Rains fall, sometimes as snow, between October and April supporting the seasonal cultivation of food crops – quinoa, potatoes, and other vegetables.

Access to San Cristobal was along a dusty track beside a small stream and through a narrow gorge guarded by three tall rock pillars – *Los Tres Gigantes* ('the three giants', see Figure 1.1). Within the bowl, people and animals were protected from the cold winds and close to a permanent source of water. They were surrounded by relatively fertile hillsides with rocks and caves inhabited by spirits. The population lived in harmony with the seasons and followed a characteristically Bolivian blend of animist beliefs and Catholic Christianity.

FIGURE 1.1 *Los Tres Gigantes* (The Three Giants).

In the beginning **5**

There is a distinct lack of documented evidence for the foundation of San Cristobal. However, by combining written records (e.g. Barba, 1640/1817), known dates (construction of the Church in 1620) and the oral history of the community (Consejo Consultivo, 2008), a reasonable sequence of events can be assembled. It seems probable that, around 1605, Spanish explorers led by the Jesuit priest Alonso Barba discovered veins of silver mineralisation within the bowl in the hills close to an existing community known to the residents as Usloque or Osloka (spellings today vary as the name was originally Aymara). This was situated close to a mushroom-shaped rock, venerated by the local people, named Achopalla. A mining camp grew up on the site of the indigenous community, which was renamed by the Spanish; first as *San Cristobal de Achocalla* (spelling is variable in the historic documents) and soon after, *San Cristobal de Lípez* (Barba, 1640). Within 15 years a mining community had become fully established around the silver mines with a fine church, richly decorated with murals, paintings, and silver. The small town of several thousand people also functioned as the commercial and administrative centre for the Altiplano south of the Salar de Uyuni, a region the Spanish called Lípez.

In occupying San Cristobal and assuming control of Lípez, the Spanish colonial administration adopted and incorporated the pre-existing traditional form of indigenous community and local government, the *ayllu*. *Ayllus* are found among the Quechua and Aymara speaking peoples of Bolivia and Southern Peru. *Ayllus* were, and remain, since they have survived to the present day in many parts of Bolivia, essentially self-sustaining units of interconnected extended families that owned land and had reciprocal obligations to each other. The responsibilities of membership in the *ayllu* included communal work for common purposes or work in kind for other members of the *ayllu* and provision of the *mita*, a form of tax that provided public goods, such as maintenance of road networks and irrigation and cropping systems that required inter-community coordination of labour. The latter was co-opted by the Spanish to become a tax due to the Crown, and was taken in part as labour, which subsequently became forced servitude in the mines.

The veins of silver ore at San Cristobal, although locally rich, were thin and discontinuous. Furthermore, the most important mine, Hedionda, was plagued with emanations of carbon dioxide rendering the workings hazardous. Many men are reputed to have died of asphyxiation in the mine (Jacobson *et al.*, 1969). Nevertheless, wealth was created from the silver mines which flowed to the Spanish colonists and, somewhat surprisingly, also the indigenous population. The indigenous people across the district of Nor Lípez pooled their wealth under leadership from San Cristobal, and in 1646 purchased the freehold of their traditional lands back from the Spanish Crown (Quisbert Salinas, 2001), relieving them of paying the *mita* to the colonial administration. The legal acquisition of land title by the *ayllus* of Nor Lípez is the only known example of the recovery of indigenous lands in Spanish colonial history.

6 Historic context

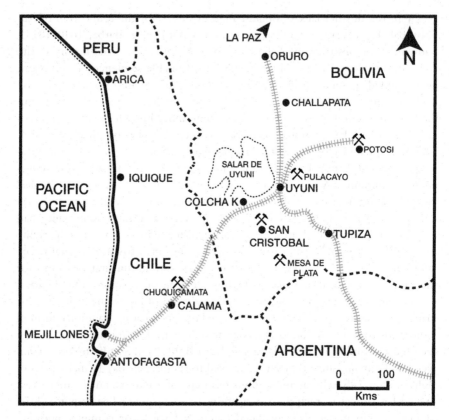

FIGURE 1.2 Locations of the three mines in the prophecy.

The gift of *El Tío*

When rich, thick and persistent silver veins were discovered in 1635 at Mesa de Plata (see map in Figure 1.2), a new population centre emerged some distance south of San Cristobal called San Antonio del Nuevo Mundo, close to today's San Antonio de Lípez. Over the past four centuries, the nearest town and the mining operations there have had various names, including 'Mesa de Plata', 'San Antonio', 'San Antonio del Nuevo Mundo', and 'San Antonio de Lípez' (The Diggings, accessed April 17, 2017).

Despite the population draw of Mesa de Plata, San Cristobal retained its place as an administrative centre for the Spanish in Lípez and mining continued at a reduced intensity. It is probably around this time that the prophecy of a giant silver mine at San Cristobal first emerged. There are several versions currently circulating in the community, which share a core of common elements. All feature the role of *El Tío*.

El Tío (literally, 'the uncle') is the spiritual master of the underworld. He is a cross between a pre-Hispanic animistic god and the Christian devil. *El Tío* is always depicted as a short, hunched man with Caucasian features, a moustache, and a beard. *El Tío* owns the rocks and minerals, but these are also his gift. Not to use them, to not accept his gift, would be an insult. To the miners, he can be both benevolent and malevolent. A benevolent *El Tío* can guarantee the miners will find rich ore; a malevolent *El Tío* will keep the ore hidden and may cause accidents or the death of miners who get on the wrong side of him. Icons of *El Tío* are found at the entrances to mines throughout Bolivia. The icons are given offerings of alcohol, tobacco, and coca leaves to curry favour and as a form of supernatural accident insurance for mine workers.

The essential elements of the story as it is related today are that *El Tío* told a shaman from the community that he had hidden a gift that would be revealed to those that still believed in him around the year 2000. *El Tío* said it would be a gift of silver, the largest and richest in Bolivia, and that it was buried around San Cristobal. He promised that it would bring a new life of wealth to the people. Each of these parts of the prophecy have come to pass.

El Tío also prophesied that there would be so much money the people of San Cristobal would not bother to count their change in the market. The people would live in houses with roofs that shone like silver in the sun. Metal roofs are common in the town of San Cristobal today. The new life would be easy and the people would stop respecting the earth and the gods, including *El Tío*. People would no longer need to work the land or care for animals. These parts of the prophecy have also come to pass.

However, the prophecy also included a caution: the people would be rich, but they would also be hungry. There would be starvation to the point of cannibalism.

The long wait

Although the mines at San Cristobal continued to operate for many years, the focus of the community shifted to commerce based on the movement of goods and people across the Altiplano. San Cristobal was well placed for this, centrally located in Lípez and on the route between the mines of Potosí and the Pacific coast. It was known as the 'window on the sea' welcoming travellers moving between the highlands of Bolivia and the port of Antofagasta, which now belongs to Chile (see bottom left of Figure 1.2). The Spanish also had the need to transport large quantities of supplies from the coast to the mines and take the silver and other metals produced by the mines back to the coast for export to Europe. Horses, mules, and donkeys were imported to function as pack animals, but struggled in the high thin air, had problems reproducing, and suffered severely from the lack of grasses or other suitable forage in the semi desert of the Altiplano. Fortuitously for the Spanish, the dominant indigenous domestic animal of the region, the llama, could be pressed into service as pack carriers.

Llamas are perfectly suited to the role of pack animal. They are relatively easy to train, calm with their owners and handlers, the *llameros* as they are called, and are comfortable carrying side packs on their backs mounted on a saddle-like harness.

8 Historic context

Most importantly, they can live off the land feeding on the shrubs, herbs, and occasional grass found on the Altiplano. Llamas are relatively lightly built and the amount they can carry limited to around 30 kg, which has to be carefully balanced to avoid injury to the animal. They can walk steadily for several hours at a pace of 2 to 3 kilometres per hour across the semi desert but need to rest and be relieved of the weight of the pack they are carrying every few days. The llamas also need water to drink. The net result was that the llama trains followed a meandering path across the Altiplano between permanent potable water sites with camps and settlements one day of llama walking apart.

The people of San Cristobal became key members of the chain of communities that organised and operated the llama trains carrying supplies between the mines of Potosí and Lípez and the coastal ports of Iquique and Antofagasta (see Figure 1.2). As *llameros*, they looked after every aspect of the llamas: breeding, pasturing, training, managing, and leading the pack trains. The movement of goods and supplies by llama train required breaking shipments into many small loads, thus requiring many llamas. Similarly, the need to rest the pack animals meant that any single llama train contained strings of load-bearing animals together with an equal or greater number of animals without loads ready to take over pack-carrying duty. As a result, numerous families and thousands of llamas were deployed in the business of moving materials.

In 1892, transport across the Altiplano was revolutionised by construction of the railway between the port of Antofagasta on the Pacific coast and the city of Potosí (see Figure 1.2). The *llameros* were almost immediately redundant. The rail line follows the plain well north of San Cristobal but south of the Salar de Uyuni. On Figure 1.2, the Salar, a giant salt flat visible from space, is the area outlined with the dotted line, north of Colcha K. San Cristobal was now both isolated from the transportation network and without a productive economic activity, although still the administrative centre for Nor Lípez. People began to leave looking for better opportunities.

In 1912, the *Corregidor* for Nor Lípez was elected from Colcha K (Consejo Consultivo, 2008), a community 60 kilometres to the north-west that was starting to be more populous than San Cristobal. He put in motion changes that resulted in the administrative centre moving to Colcha K in 1917. It was at about this time that San Cristobal also lost its resident priest, ending a 300-year tradition of daily mass in the old church.

There was some reactivation of mining through the 20th century. The Toldos mine, located south of San Cristobal, close to *Los Tres Gigantes*, operated episodically under various owners (Jacobson *et al.*, 1969). The Hedionda mine was rediscovered and brought back into production using innovative methods of air drainage to remove carbon dioxide from the workings (Jacobson *et al.*, 1969). A new discovery at Animas was developed and operated by a co-operative (Jacobson *et al.*, 1969). However, the local population describe these mines as 'one bad experience after another'. 'There were very few jobs for us; they brought in people from outside; they did not treat us with respect.' Both Toldos and Animas ceased operating due to low metal prices in the early to mid-1980s.

Throughout the 20th century, San Cristobal experienced depopulation as families left to find work in the cities of Bolivia or the mines of Chile and Argentina. In 1954, a group of some 20 families moved out and established the community of Culpina K (Consejo Consultivo, 2008, see Figure 1.3). The families chose this location on the edge of the plains, some 17 kilometres due south of San Cristobal, to be close to good llama pastures and cultivatable land and, perhaps more importantly, to be beside the dirt road that now linked the town of Uyuni with Avaroa on the border with Chile.

The same motivations were behind the move in 1980 by a smaller number of families that left San Cristobal to form the settlement of Vila Vila, also beside the road, 12 kilometres to the east. By the early 1990s the old town of San Cristobal had shrunk to a permanent population of 35 families. However, many families that were living and working in the cities, or outside Bolivia, still had an unoccupied, neglected house in the town and considered San Cristobal their real home.

By this time, the three small villages (we will later call them the first-ring communities, see Figure 1.3) that made up the greater community of San Cristobal were physically isolated, very poor, and living a traditional *campesino* lifestyle of self-sufficiency based on small scale agricultural production, largely for personal consumption. In economic jargon, it was a subsistence economy. Access in and out was via an unmaintained system of dirt roads that became largely impassable during the rainy season. The nearest commercial centre, Uyuni, was many hours away. Men left seeking seasonal employment in construction or similar manual labour occupations, returning to plant and harvest crops grown in the family's garden plots. Other income came from remittance payments sent by family members and the occasional sale of a llama for meat. The women, for the most part, managed the home, looked after the llama herds, and tended the garden plots. Younger, unmarried women frequently left to find work as housemaids in the cities. Often, they found husbands in the cities and never returned. Despite the poverty and isolation, the villages were socially resilient and retained a school and a health clinic, albeit with only a low level of basic services. Indeed, the population placed a very high value on education as a way to escape poverty (Joyce, 1997).

From the arrival of the Spanish to the closure of the mines in the 1980s and on into the 1990s, the indigenous population of San Cristobal continued to rely on the co-operative and communal strategies inherited from the *ayllu* tradition despite the pressures of colonialisation, capitalist investment by mining companies, and the replacement of barter with money in the rest of the economy. For example, land was never bought or sold. Rather, it was communally 'owned' with use rights allocated to families. Families were tied together by reciprocal responsibilities. Membership in the group provided support and protection in return for meeting the responsibilities of participation in communal work for the benefit of all, or for other members of the community. Respect and prestige came from taking the responsibilities of leadership on a rotating basis, or from providing the resources for communal feasts and celebrations. Collective identity was further strengthened by knowledge of, and respect for, the gods and spirits that inhabited specific places

10 Historic context

within the lands of the community. These social and cultural characteristics were present in San Cristobal and the filial communities of Culpina K and Vila Vila in the mid-1990s (Joyce, 1997; Buchanan and Gans, 2008).

Sometime before the mid-1980s a slightly different version of the prophecy started to circulate widely across the provinces of Nor Lípez, Sud Lípez, and Enrique Baldivieso (i.e., the south-west corner of Bolivia). In this version, which became accepted as traditional knowledge, the legend and prophecy of *El Tío* was linked to the collapse of mining at Mesa de Plata in the 1680s and the abandonment of the town of San Antonio de Nuevo Mundo in 1700. According to the legend, *El Tío* left Mesa de Plata when the mine shut down. He went to live at Chuquicamata, Chile. On Figure 1.2 it is near the rail line to Antofagasta, just north of the town of Calama.

The Chuquicamata mine brought with it the wealth of what became the largest copper mine in the world for most of the 20th century (see map on Figure 1.2). However, *El Tío* said that he would return to Mesa de Plata at the end of the world. The first sign of the beginning of the end of the world would be the start of a mine at San Cristobal in the year 2000, followed just before the end of the world by the

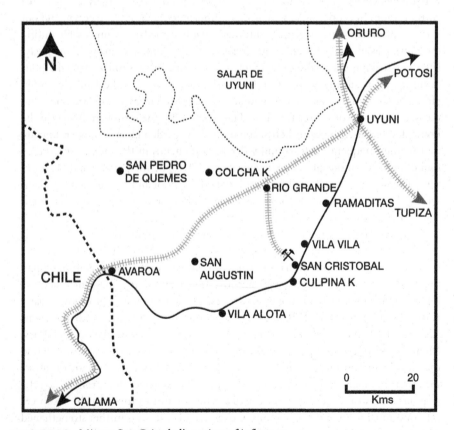

FIGURE 1.3 Minera San Cristobal's region of influence.

start of a mine at Pulacayo, north-east of the town of Uyuni, Bolivia. The final sign would be the start of a new mine at Mesa de Plata, near the abandoned town of San Antonio del Nuevo Mundo (J. Mamani, pers. comm., May 2015).

A Canadian company named Prophecy Development Corp[1] has all the permits and plans ready for the Pulacayo mine but has not yet announced a start date for construction. Bolivia's state-owned mining company, COMIBOL, is the current owner of Mesa de Plata.

Destiny delivers

In January 1995, geologist Larry Buchanan, working for Apex Silver Mines of Denver, Colorado, USA, spent a long day prospecting around San Cristobal (Buchanan and Gans, 2008). He quickly recognised that the hills surrounding the town are the remains of an ancient volcano and that the bowl in the hills is the site of a caldera, the eruptive centre of the volcano. Across the hillsides, he found the widespread presence of mineralised rocks. Veins and disseminations of mineralised material could even be seen in the walls of the houses and outcroppings in the streets. Buchanan was standing on top of what would become the largest silver discovery of the 20th century.

How could that be? How could Buchanan see something that prospectors, geologists, and miners had not seen in more than two hundred years of looking? Buchanan considers it to have been more than luck: he believes that *El Tío* was on his side (Buchanan and Gans, 2008). He also knew immediately that to develop a mine, San Cristobal would have to be moved – houses, church, cemetery, sacred rocks and caves, and all the people. We take up that thread of the story again in Chapter 6, but first there is more cultural and historical context to be understood.

Note

1 www.prophecydev.com. 'Prophecy' was part of the company's name before it acquired Pulacayo.

2

THE HISTORICAL ROOTS OF DIVERGENT VIEWS OF FAIRNESS

This chapter examines a couple of contemporary theories that help understand how the roots of conflicts between mining companies and the communities can be traced back centuries, if not millennia, before the Spanish Conquest. They are evolutionary theory and institutional theory. These theories will help contextualise conflicts that we examine later between MSC and some of its stakeholders. In Chapter 3 we look at the causes rooted in the centuries since the Spanish Conquest up to the decades preceding the election of Evo Morales as President of Bolivia in 2006. In Chapter 4 we examine in more detail the forces that brought Evo Morales to power along with the policy of nationalising resource companies.

Institutional theory and evolutionary theory are not theories of development or underdevelopment. Unlike dependency theory or neo-liberal theory, they do not attempt to explain patterns of poverty or wealth. Rather, they explain different trajectories in the development of social institutions related to maintaining social justice in different societies in general.

Evolutionary theory evokes processes that began thousands of millennia in the past and form part of the evolution of the human species. Evolutionary theory is applied here to explain divergent preferences for principles of fairness.

Our application of institutional theory starts with historical differences in governance institutions that emerged mere centuries ago, before the Spanish Conquest. Institutional theory explains cultural divergences in institutions for distributing wealth according to meritocratic principles versus principles of favouritism, clientelism, and loyalty to the elite. Both theories concern culturally conditioned differences in perceptions of justice and fairness. We argue that divergent principles of fairness were deep-rooted exacerbators of conflicts between MSC and some of its stakeholders.

Institutional theory has also been used to explain the phenomenon of the 'curse of natural resources', which includes dynamics that are very relevant to understanding the conflicts that MSC had with some stakeholders. The institutional theory explanation of 'the curse' focuses on the extent to which a country's institutions encourage entrepreneurs to expend resources either seeking rents or developing productive innovations.

Evolutionary theory in the social sciences

Evolutionary biology, Dunbar's number, and equality versus equity

An estimated 100,000 years of living in tribal groups of approximately 150 members (i.e., 'Dunbar's number'; Dunbar, 2011) has left humanity with a preference for living in communities in which everyone knows everyone, in which everyone contributes and shares, if not equally, at least to the best of their abilities, and in which everyone's future is tied to the welfare of the group. In short, tribalism is part of our evolutionary heritage (Crouch Zelman, 2015). Indeed, in his book, *Moral Tribes*, Greene (2013) makes a convincing case for how a tribe-centred sense of justice helped humans overcome selfish urges and practise co-operation for the common welfare of all.

To help us adapt to such a social environment, it appears we have also developed an innate sense of fairness and group loyalty (Ellis, 2013). Living in small groups makes it possible to monitor the extent to which everyone is making their fair contribution, and conversely the extent to which individuals may be taking a 'free ride', benefiting from the labour of others without making their own contribution. As humans began living in larger groups, such monitoring became impossible. Therefore, the problem of dealing with injustice grew more acute. Hierarchies topped by kings and dictators who promised to maintain social order frequently turned out to be unreliable solutions because there was no accountability placed on the top of the hierarchy.

The European Enlightenment and impartial meritocracy

A breakthrough occurred in Europe during the Enlightenment. Rather than eliminate hierarchies, the principle of justice on which they operated was changed and the top of the hierarchy was made accountable to lower echelons, in theory, through democratic institutions (Fogel and North, 1993). Figure 2.1 and Table 2.1 summarise the differences between justice processes appropriate for living in small tribal groups and justice processes appropriate for living in societies comprised of millions. These imply divergent broad tendencies in views of justice, fairness, binding commitments, and the well-being of the collective society.

Contrasting principles of justice

The relevance of evolutionary perspectives can be seen in the boxes with the white backgrounds in the two rightmost columns of Figure 2.1.

14 Historic context

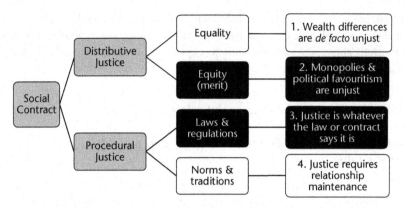

FIGURE 2.1 Different principles of justice at the root of the differences between MSC and its Bolivian stakeholders (MSC preferences in black background, Bolivian preferences in white background).

Like many rural communities in the developing world, the Altiplano communities of Bolivia have been shaped by a long history of subsistence agriculture. They have adapted to a steady state economy where economic growth is noticeable on a time scale of generations, not years. For entire lifetimes, the size of the economic 'pie' is fixed and the only question remaining concerns how it will be divided. In this context, the focus of justice naturally falls on the distribution of costs and benefits in the social group. Altiplano communities ended up enacting the reasoning that because everyone's co-operative effort is needed for the bare survival of the group, the principle of equality leads to the best outcomes for all. Everyone contributes their best efforts and everyone shares the benefits equally.

The black background boxes in the two rightmost columns of Figure 2.1, by contrast, show how fairness and justice is more often sought in large, formal organisations like governments and corporations. The emphasis is on distributing rewards based on merit, which consists of abilities and effort. Special abilities and hard work together should be rewarded more. Legal endorsement of this idea goes back at least to the civil service examinations of Confucian China but became more widely promoted in 17th century Europe with the rise of nation state bureaucracies and corporate administrations. It was a progressive rejection of promotion and hiring based on aristocratic privilege.

The two rightmost columns in Table 2.1 show qualities of the two principles of justice that were contested in MSC's relationships with its closest communities. The rows show the ideal contexts in which each operates and the types of abuses and abuse control mechanisms each one typically uses. Equality works well in a small social group where everyone knows everyone else because that knowledge is what prevents parasitic 'free riding'. In economic terms, free riders are those members of a group who take their equal share of the benefits without making their share of the contribution to producing the benefits.

TABLE 2.1 Context and control differences between equality and equity

	Equality	Equity
Ideal context	Family, small village	Meritocracy, ideal bureaucracy
Type of abuse	Free riders, parasites	Nepotism, favouritism
Control of abuse	Social norms, social pressure	Human resources policies and procedures

The equity principle is ideally suited to the corporation, or any organization, patterned on the ideals of the impartial bureaucracy that were described by one of the fathers of sociology, Max Weber (Weber, 1983). The hierarchical structure of the organisation means that benefits are unequally distributed. The justification for the inequality of benefits is the inequality of contributions. Those higher up should be making a contribution that is either greater in quantity or rare and more sought after in terms of quality. Any kind of favouritism or nepotism would violate this requirement.[1] To ensure that greater benefits are deserved, the organisation institutes formal, performance-based and certification-based requirements for hiring and promotion. In the contemporary corporations, these are administered by the Human Resources department.

Equality versus equity as foundations of fairness

For centuries, the communities of the region survived by sticking to a strict code of behaviour: don't lie. Don't steal. Don't be lazy. It condenses the philosophy that everyone's survival depends on everyone fulfilling their responsibilities and working for common good. Everyone contributes equally and receives equally. Prosperity is a community achievement and is enjoyed by the whole community equally. Free riders are those who violate the code by either contributing less than others or taking more. Typically, they are given extra responsibilities as a last chance to redeem themselves. If they continue to be lazy or dishonest, they are ostracised (J. Mamani, pers. comm., May 2015). In the Altiplano desert, an ostracised individual stands very little chance of surviving. Equality is a life or death issue.

The corporation, by contrast, operates on the principle of equity. Equity means that those who contribute more, or whose contributions are of a higher value, get rewarded more. In the corporation, it is fair for the general manager to earn more than a cafeteria worker. Persons who engage in nepotism or favouritism can be fired, which is the corporate equivalent of ostracism. The consequences of being fired are usually not lethal but can drastically affect one's immediate income and can continue to affect one's economic prospects for life.

Note how unequal pay is automatically unfair when equality is the sole principle of fairness. By contrast, equal pay, regardless of contribution, is automatically unfair when equity is the sole principle of fairness. In practice, there are few systems that operate exclusively on either equality or equity. There are, however,

16 Historic context

many systems that show a bias in favour of one versus the other. In Chapter 9 we examine how the tensions between equality and equity deepened the conflicts that emerged in 2010 and 2011 between communities and governments, between communities and MSC, and among communities themselves.

Institutional theory and rent-seeking

Institutional theory and the differences between England and Spain

Part of understanding the differences that contributed to conflict between MSC and its stakeholders depends on understanding the different institutional histories of the parties involved. As a capitalist corporation, MSC's institutional roots go back to the emergence of an independently wealthy merchant class in Europe. The first corporation was the Dutch East India Company, established in Amsterdam in 1602, during the European Enlightenment. The corporation was part of an emancipatory process in which the aristocracy and the Church were forced to share power with a new merchant class that claimed legitimacy on the basis of individual effort and merit. By contrast, what wealth accumulation that had occurred during the Aymaran and Incan empires was very centralised and controlled by an aristocracy that, like the European aristocracy of the Middle Ages, claimed legitimacy through special connections with an unseen spirit world. In the 16th century, the indigenous aristocracy was replaced by a Spanish aristocracy that continued to operate on pre-Enlightenment principles.

According to one of the founders of institutional theory, Douglass North (1990), historical events in 17th century Europe, set England and Spain on different courses that were distinct and irreconcilable. The Spanish Crown was an early coloniser and implemented a system that had not been modified very much by the Enlightenment, which was just beginning to sweep through Protestant Europe. The shift that took place during the European Enlightenment included:

- A rejection of clientelistic authority, including the authority of the Church.
- An embrace of the rule of law and protection of property rights from the state.
- A spread of meritocracy, applying the principle of equity impartially.
- Recognition, in the Late Enlightenment, that meritocracy has limited legitimacy without equal opportunities to gain merit (e.g., education, employment experience).
- A recognition of the need for verifying and certifying credentials and performance in order to make meritocracy work.

Under feudalism, both the Spanish and the English monarchs attempted to fund their regimes through confiscatory taxation. The crucial parting of the paths occurred when the English landowners, who were being taxed, successfully limited the power of the Crown. The details of the process go by the name of the

Glorious Revolution of 1688. The net effect was that the English monarchy was eventually forced to guarantee property rights. This, paradoxically, gave the monarchy more money than it could have gained through confiscation. First, having guaranteed property rights, the new English King, William III, was able to borrow more than his predecessors because the lenders now felt secure that their property rights would be respected and that therefore they would be repaid. Second, the dominant merchant banks of the day moved operations from the Dutch Republic to London. Thus, the ethos that inspired the invention and fostering of the world's first corporation took root more deeply in England.

The Spanish kings, by contrast, were quite able to confiscate and consequently enjoyed a monopoly on the wealth extracted from the Americas. To help pay for their high military expenditures, they had a grand clientelistic system that rewarded nobles for loyalty and service to the Crown. Culturally, this had the effect of resisting the more egalitarian sentiments that became popular in Protestant Europe at the time. It also maintained the steep power-distance (Basabe and Ros, 2005) gradient in the culture and put the whole Spanish empire on a path towards rewarding rent-seeking over productive innovation.

Non-Enlightenment institutions (like those imported by the Spanish Conquest) basically encoded loyalty to the patron as the principle of justice and institutionalised the boundaries between clients and non-clients along racial lines. This created the overlap between race and social class. The classist state that followed Bolivian independence simply continued down the historical path of clientelism practised by the Spanish monarchy. Consistent with this path, mining in Bolivia is still officially the exclusive right of a state-owned monopoly, COMIBOL. It is no wonder that the appearance of a foreign entity based on the British path of private property rights for private corporations would encounter some resistance based on rejection of its essential operating principles.

The natural resource curse and incentives for rent-seeking

The nationalisation of resource companies is a classic characteristic of countries that fall into what economists and political scientists call 'the curse of natural resources', or the 'resource curse' for short. There are two hallmarks of the curse, one economic and one political.

Economically the curse involves a select portion of the population benefiting from the sale of extracted resources while the masses remain poor and the non-resource economy experiences very slow growth. Certain resources are more likely to make a country more prone to the curse (i.e., petroleum, precious metals, and especially, foreign aid in cash form) (Brautigam and Knack, 2004; Knack, 2001).

Politically the curse involves politicians depending on sales of the commodity to foreign corporations (if the extraction company has been nationalised), or taxes from foreign corporations (if the foreign corporation does the extraction), rather than on income tax proceeds from the mass of the citizens. The politicians no longer need the population to be prosperous and therefore tend to spend government

18 Historic context

revenues on support-buying schemes and projects to benefit key blocks of potential supporters. In political science, this support-purchasing dynamic is called 'clientelism'. The broader population whose support is not purchased, for their part, pays very little in taxes and therefore has no stake in holding the government accountable for how it spends. Democracy tends to deteriorate.

The phenomenon has been analysed by some of the world's top economists, including Nobel Prize winners (Humphreys *et al.*, 2007). The dynamics that scholars have identified as causing the curse appear similar to those that MSC faced. We briefly describe the dynamics that the academic literature has pinpointed and then in Part 2 trace the same processes among MSC's stakeholders.

Based on comparisons among many countries that export natural resources, the key dynamic that seems to differentiate those that get the curse from those that do not is the strength of their institutions designed to prevent political entrepreneurs from appropriating portions of the wealth produced by the natural resource extraction. When wealth is appropriated without any contribution of work or innovation, the process is called 'rent-seeking'. In the economic theory, 'rents' are incomes derived from the exercise of rights or power rather than from productive activity. There is much debate about the line between productive activity and rent-seeking, but the clearest examples are things like inflated incomes from monopolies, cartels, exclusive permits, and patents. Rents can be obtained by coaxing governments to grant exclusive rights to one group. For example, in many cities taxi companies or unions expend enormous effort to gain the exclusive right to serve an airport. That non-productive effort is called rent-seeking.

Research has shown that the institutions that are essential for preventing the resource curse are those that prevent corruption and protect property rights (Kolstad, 2009). These come under pressure from well-organised groups that promise politicians political support or 'contributions' in return for a slice of the resource 'pie'. Reciprocally, politicians sometimes initiate the transaction by 'buying' support from key groups that can influence the political process. In the worst cases, the politicians lead military groups that use a combination of money and coercion to capture the cash flows from the natural resources. In most cases, however, the turning point lies in the cost/benefit calculation made by entrepreneurs about where to apply their efforts and talents.

If institutional incentives lead the majority of entrepreneurs to choose the rent-seeking course, the country falls into the curse. In pursuing this course, entrepreneurs devote their creative energies to activities like pressuring and politicking for 'compensation', 'rights', 'concessions', monopolies, or patronage employment in order to capture a portion of the revenues produced by the resource extraction (Bjorvatn and Naghavi, 2011). These activities are essentially redistributive insofar as they do not create new wealth, but rather redistribute existing wealth. This feature of rent-seeking is what accounts for both the slow economic growth and the weakening of institutions (e.g., Democratic Republic of the Congo, Guinea, Sudan, Venezuela) (Mehlum *et al.*, 2006).

Historical roots of divergent views of fairness **19**

By contrast, if the incentive structure created by a society's institutions convinces the majority of entrepreneurs that it would benefit them more to pursue the wealth creation course, they will eschew rent-seeking and, instead, develop new products, production processes, and markets. This approach became established in British institutions and their progeny around the world when the industrial revolution combined with guarantees of property rights and the institution of the private corporation to make innovation a key wealth-generating strategy for entrepreneurs. It was not the only wealth-generating strategy used by the British during their imperial epoch. Exploitative mercantilism was the dominant strategy for most of the period. However, the encouragement of productive entrepreneurship was an additional element that made the British approach distinctive and that was maintained, practised, and amplified in former colonies and societies affected by them. Giving entrepreneurs more incentives to create economic growth generated jobs and moved more people out of poverty and into the middle class. We cannot forget that there are also important roles for government and civil society institutions in allowing this to happen. In such systems, more citizens pay income tax and therefore feel the urge to hold the politicians accountable for public spending. Absent clientelism and rampant rent-seeking, governments feel more pressure to enact policies that will further expand the middle class and broad-based economic growth. In this way, the curse has been avoided in resource-dependent countries like Australia, Botswana, Canada, Chile, and Norway.

Preview of the dynamic at MSC

As we will see in Chapters 9 and 11, some of MSC's stakeholders were confronted with the choices that face entrepreneurs who are deciding between rent-seeking and wealth creation. To briefly illustrate the relevance of these concepts without going into details, here are some examples.

On the rent-seeking side, some stakeholders repeatedly made comments about the 'social debt' that MSC owes to the inhabitants or the region and the amount of compensation that MSC should pay for alleged damage to the environment. During the 2010 mini-insurrection in the Department of Potosí, a few protesters overturned MSC's railcars. They were using non-productive tactics in a bid to get a monopoly on the transportation of ore. Into 2012, some of the transportation co-operatives tried to organise opposition against MSC in an attempt to coerce the company into favouring them in the award of contracts. It turned out that they were smuggling organisations that were intent on using MSC contracts as a cover for their illegal activities. After the leaders were convicted and jailed, the remaining transportation co-operatives were eager to learn new administrative skills in order to expand their markets internationally, thereby reducing their dependence on MSC contracts.

On the wealth creation side, there were many calls for regional economic development and mentions of several specific innovations, like ISO certification,

20 Historic context

that would permit access to new markets internationally. Many of the comments related to assistance for producers involved new production or marketing ideas. Generally, the rent-seekers withheld the social licence or granted it at a minimal level. The wealth creators were more ambivalent, and some granted a high level of social licence.

A cultural conflict waiting to happen

The consequences of Dunbar's number, biases towards different principles of fairness, difference in historical paths of institutional development and their implications for the prevalence of rent-seeking strategies all point in the same direction. The rural culture of Potosí and the corporate culture of an international company were worlds apart when they met. It is not that their differences were so vast as such. After all, they did indeed find mutually acceptable ways to work together. Rather it was that the roots of those differences went so deep. That depth made it more probable that neither party was aware of its own biases when the differences of opinion first arose. However, today both parties understand more about who they are themselves. The encounter created wisdom.

Note

1 Those who express outrage at executive pay levels that are many multiples of the pay levels of the lowest paid employees are not necessarily calling for a shift to the equality principle. To the contrary, they are often calling for more stringent meritocracy. They simply question the relative value of the contributions being made by the executives and accuse boards and executives of practising favouritism towards members of their own social class or clique.

3
BOLIVIAN POLITICS FROM THE SPANISH TO THE NEO-LIBERALS

History matters today because the choices we find ourselves facing today have been shaped by the evolution of our organisations and institutions in the past. The way today's perceptions and options are limited by what we have inherited from the past is called 'path dependence'. Institution theory explains how path dependence works in the co-evolution of economies and political institutions. This chapter and the next chapter illustrate how stories, identities, and institutions developed in the past serve to carry forward particular sets of options but not others. We also look at how perceptions of what is just and unjust were woven into stories of identity in Bolivia and the Department of Potosí. The accounts given in these chapters make the contemporary political context in Bolivia much more understandable.

The historical resentments of Potosí

The mini-insurrection of 2010 in the Department of Potosí was a manifestation of diverse grievances all tied together by history. Soon after they invaded and conquered the Andes in the 16th century, the Spanish discovered a mountain of silver, named *Cerro Rico* (see Figure 3.1), in what is the present-day city of Potosí. Even after five centuries of mining, there were still in 2015 some 14,000 miners who entered the mountain every day to extract silver. The deposit was so rich that the Spanish set up a royal mint in the city of Potosí. At its height, it was one of the most populous cities in the world, larger than London. Many legends of its fabulous wealth abound, including the true story of the time city officials dug up all the paving stones in one street, plated them with silver, and put them back in place to commemorate a special ceremony.

Local residents, however, received very little of the wealth that was taken from their territory. Throughout the five centuries, the elites prospered while everyone else in Potosí lived in poverty. Even after national independence, it was official

22 Historic context

FIGURE 3.1 Cerro Rico, city of Potosí.

government policy to take wealth from Potosí to provide services for eastern Bolivia. This created an historical resentment that is very much alive today and an important part of the political dynamics. MSC was easily slotted into the category of just another foreign power taking riches out of Potosí and leaving locals in poverty. More generally, Potosí residents hold a grudge against the rest of Bolivia for not providing them with government services proportional to the wealth their department contributes to the country. Indeed, the resentment has been codified in songs and poems and passed from generation to generation.

Given the location of the Cerro Rico in the city of Potosí, it is not surprising that the resentment is concentrated most intensely there. However, distinct versions are expressed by those representing two different kinds of organisations. The 'grassroots' organisations are those that evolved historically from the traditional Aymara and Incan *ayllus*. Now they bear names that include words like 'original', 'workers', and 'union'. The organisations that have non-indigenous roots include post-secondary educational institutions, business associations, and government bodies.

The worker and indigenous organisations want foreign companies like MSC to pay more royalties. They also want to see more services provided by the national government. In terms of mining practices, those in the city of Potosí want a continuation and expansion of the co-operatives, despite their environmental damage and unsafe working conditions. Outside the city of Potosí, there is a strong tendency to romanticise the rural life of living off the land. People who raise animals such as chickens or llamas have a sense of shared identity, no matter what else they may do in the community for extra income. Leftist discourses mention 'pollution' as a health threat, but also as a symbol of modernisation, urbanisation, and injustice.

Representatives of government, business, and some university organisations, by contrast, see higher royalty requirements as a disincentive to development through their tendency to drive out investment. They would prefer the type of contributions that MSC has made with the first-ring communities around the mine. They want partnerships that open opportunities for sharing knowledge and promoting value-added exports. The tourism potential of the city of Potosí is often mentioned as an under-developed resource. However, in terms of mining practices, most city leaders equate mining with what they see at the Cerro Rico. Some say mining should be stopped because of its pollution and unsafe conditions. Of course, the mining co-operatives that work in the Cerro Rico oppose them. Only a minority of the residents of the city of Potosí seem aware that mining does not have to be polluting or unsafe like Cerro Rico. For this minority, MSC is described as 'a new kind of mine' because of the cleaner, safer practices it has introduced.

The miners' union, indigenous organisations, and various co-operatives were central actors in the 1952 national revolution. The movement they kept alive for several decades finally blossomed into the democratic election of an indigenous President. Hopes were high that Evo Morales would set right the perceived injustice suffered by Potosí, but when several issues flared up at the same time in 2010, the resulting frustration erupted in the mini-insurrection.

Economic crisis and neo-liberal reform

When Larry Buchanan walked across the hillsides above San Cristobal in January 1995, finding silver mineralisation everywhere he looked, he was not the only geologist seeking riches in Bolivia, nor was he the first to have visited San Cristobal. There was evidence of the recent presence of other geologists all over the place in the form of broken rocks and sample tags left by several different companies. Evidently, they had been looking for gold and had missed the signs of silver mineralisation (Buchanan and Gans, 2008; Baptista Gumucio, 2015). All of them were participating in a rush of foreign investment into Bolivia: a time of rapid change and deep controversy within the country. In this section, we describe the political, economic, and social backdrop to the discovery, exploration, and development

24 Historic context

of the San Cristobal mine, paying particular attention to factors that had a direct bearing on the project. The full story begins in the early 1980s with the reforms that initiated a cascade of economic and social change across Bolivia that continued into the 21st century.

Many Bolivians over the age of 50 look back at the 1980s with decidedly mixed feelings. It was a time when the country could count more Presidents than years of independence and for a few years the largest import by volume was reputedly freshly printed bank notes. It was also a time of massive, rapid change.

The financial crises that rolled through Latin America in the early 1980s, as foreign debt exceed earning power in country after country, reached Bolivia in 1983. Following many years of mismanagement by successive military-backed governments, the Bolivian economy was in tatters. To maintain liquidity, the civilian government of Hernán Siles Zuazo, appointed by the military in 1982, was obliged to print money, which led to inflation. As inflation ramped up through 1984 into triple digit numbers, the Vice-President of the country resigned and Siles Zuazo became politically isolated. Moreover, he was harried by frequent strikes called by increasingly militant unions. In desperation, he called for early elections.

As hyperinflation erupted, the country turned to a known entity and in 1985 elected Victor Paz Estenssoro for his fourth term as President (1985 to 1989) in the first truly democratic process in many years. Paz Estenssoro, at the time in his late 70s, moved quickly to implement a series of readjustment policies which collectively became known at the New Economic Policy (NEP). Action was essential as inflation reached a breathtaking 23,000 per cent in 1985, the price of tin, a major foreign currency earner, collapsed and oil prices also dropped. The Bolivian economy was in free fall.

Much of the design and almost all of the implementation of the NEP was carried out by the Minister of Planning, Gonzalo Sánchez de Lozada (later to become President of Bolivia), with the support of Harvard economist Jeffrey Sachs. Essentially, the NEP called for the dismantlement of the state capitalism that had prevailed for the previous 30 years in favour of a neo-liberal economy built on (a) domestic and foreign private investment, and (b) the privatisation of former state assets. The country was now technically open to foreign investors.

With the labour unions actively repressed to assure government authority, the mines of the state-run company, COMIBOL, were closed down or placed on care and maintenance. Overnight, the workforce of COMIBOL was reduced from 30,000 to 7,000 in order to cut the government payroll. Many of the now unemployed miners and their families relocated to the eastern foothills of the Andes settling in the Chapare district to become farmers. Others set up co-operatives and continued mining. Many of the co-operatives turned to small mineral deposits while others illegally occupied and re-entered a number of the COMIBOL mines.

The displaced miners who reached Chapare found Evo Morales – known almost universally as Evo – leading the *campesino* (rural workers) union. Evo had moved there in 1978. The soil and climate conditions in Chapare are ideal for growing coca, the source of cocaine. Most of the new arrivals gained a measure of economic security in supplying the rapidly expanding, albeit illegal, international drug trade. As leader of the '*cocaleros*', Morales campaigned against US and Bolivian programmes to eradicate coca as part of the War on Drugs. He denounced the 'war' as an imperialist attempt to destroy Andean indigenous culture. The leaves of the coca plant have held religious and cultural significance for the people of the Andean highlands for millennia. For centuries, Andean people have chewed coca leaves and made coca tea to help reduce the ill-effects of the lack of oxygen living at altitude. Today, Bolivian supermarkets sell coca tea alongside packets of Earl Grey and English Breakfast tea.

By 1988, the NEP had brought inflation under control. The social costs, however, were substantial. Because the economy had not yet grown meaningfully, there were many displaced mine workers and much poverty, both rural and urban. In analysing the situation, economists Morales and Sachs (1988) predicted that the emergence of three dynamics would shape political, social, and economic discourse through the 1990s and into the 21st century:

- economic and social inequality;
- ideological disputes between neo-liberal and socialist visions for the economy, and;
- geographic differences and rivalries between western and eastern Bolivia.

Western Bolivia is comprised of highlands while eastern Bolivia includes some agriculturally rich lowlands. The west includes the Altiplano and Andean Mountain ranges where mining forms the backbone of the economy. The western region is home to some 64 per cent of the population and includes many poor and difficult-to-access villages. Western Bolivia includes the cities of La Paz, Oruro, Potosí, and Cochabamba. By contrast, eastern Bolivia has some 36 per cent of the national population, is relatively rich, and possesses a diversified economy based on oil, gas, and industrial-scale agriculture centred on the city of Santa Cruz.

Consolidating neo-liberal reforms

In 1989, the country elected Jaime Paz Zamora as President on a platform based on an unlikely alliance with a former political adversary, General Hugo Bánzer. Officially referred to as the 'Patriotic Accord' both leaders announced their forgiveness of past enmities as a way to consolidate democracy. While this pleased many citizens, particularly in the cities, others were far from happy and wished for a socialist, state-run system.

The Presidency of Jaime Paz (1989 to 1993) was successful in sustaining the reforms initiated by the Paz Estenssoro administration and achieving a reassuring level of stability within the country. International mining companies were encouraged by this stability and apparent commitment to neo-liberal policies that support private enterprise, foreign investment, and open markets. They began exploring in Bolivia. Through this period, La Paz-based *Minería Técnica Consultores Asociados*

26 Historic context

(MINTEC), under the leadership of geologists Jonny Delgado and Scotty Bruce, actively promoted the mineral potential of Bolivia and offered services to companies wishing to enter the country.

Globally during that period, rising metal prices led to an expansion of mining investment. In Bolivia too, there were significant foreign investments in the mining sector during the Jaime Paz Presidency. These included Battle Mountain Gold's purchase of a 35 per cent interest in the Inti Raymi gold mine from Zeland Mines, a Bolivian company. Similarly, Rio Tinto took a one-third interest in Compañia Minera del Sur S.A. (COMSUR), Bolivia's largest private mining company, owned by Gonzalo Sánchez de Lozada and his family.

The Inti Raymi gold mine, located on the Altiplano some 40 kilometres northwest of the city of Oruro, had commenced operations in 1982 as a mid-sized heap leach gold mine. With the financial and technical capacity provided by Battle Mountain, the mineral reserves were increased and the mine expanded to a bulk tonnage, open pit, and vat leach operation. The expansion required resettlement of the community of Chuquina, and a trade of mineral resources in which mining co-operatives that had worked the mineralisation that became the Inti Raymi mine gained title to concessions at Iroco, close to Oruro. A notable outcome was the formation of the Inti Raymi Foundation, created to provide 'sustainable' support for the resettled population (Loayza *et al.*, 2001). The commercial success of Inti Raymi caught the attention of other international mining firms. By 1991 there were at least a dozen more from Canada, Australia, the USA, and England actively exploring or evaluating investment possibilities in Bolivia. Most of these companies were looking for gold mineralisation.

Popular participation and decentralisation

Gonzalo Sánchez de Lozada (known to everyone as Goni) won the 1993 presidential elections on a platform of further economic and social reforms that were designed to help the population of the western Bolivian highlands and Altiplano. Goni's victory in the popular vote was aided by his running mate, and subsequent Vice-President, Víctor Hugo Cárdenas, an indigenous Aymara from the Lake Titicaca district west of La Paz. Cárdenas was the first indigenous person to occupy such a high office in Bolivia.

Under Goni the Constitution was re-written to establish Bolivia as a multi-ethnic and multi-cultural nation: indigenous rights were enshrined. The central socio-economic initiative of the Goni administration was the *Ley Participación Popular* (Popular Participation Act), which decentralised the country by creating more than 300 municipal governments empowered for local governance. Nor Lípez was split into two municipalities, Colcha K in the east and San Pedro de Quemes in the west. The law introduced direct municipal elections for the local people, authorised local decision making on municipal spending, and guaranteed funding from the central government on a per capita basis. Other programmes initiated by the Goni government included classroom teaching in

Politics from the Spanish to the neo-liberals **27**

the local indigenous language, universal medical coverage for pregnant women and children under the age of five, and a universal old-age benefit. The leading economic reform, entitled Capitalisation, allowed the major state-owned companies to joint venture with private investors, both national and international.

Within the Capitalisation programme, the privatisation of the oil and gas sector was immediately successful in attracting foreign investment. International companies such as Enron, Shell, Petrobras, and Repsol invested through an auction process that animated the industry. Almost immediately, an initiative emerged to export gas via a pipeline to Brazil.

There was little investor interest in the COMIBOL mines. On the other hand, the high geological potential of the highlands of the Andean Cordillera and Altiplano plus the welcoming stance of the Goni government attracted the interest of the exploration arm of the mining industry. By 1995 it was estimated that at least 30 major and junior companies were operating in the country. Optimism was high and as a further effort to attract investors, MINTEC organised a major international mining convention in La Paz attended by several hundred people from around the world. Goni, who was regarded as a mining man through his family ownership of COMSUR, gave the keynote address.

One of the companies that came to Bolivia for the MINTEC-sponsored convention and stayed to look around was the Vancouver, Canada-based Pan American Silver. In 1999, the company optioned the San Vicente mine from the state-owned mining company COMIBOL. San Vincente is located in the southern part of the Department of Potosí, close to the border with Argentina.[1] San Vicente is a very large, old mine that exploits a complex network of silver-zinc-lead bearing veins. Pan American Silver carried out a programme of exploration drilling and ore reserve definition. They built a positive relationship with co-operative miners working adjacent parts of the mineral system. The company identified a substantial body of mineralisation and, on this basis, signed an exploitation agreement with COMIBOL. The agreement allocated 62.5 per cent of the resulting cash flow to a new entity that was 95 per cent owned by Pan American.

During Goni's mandate (1993 to 1997), the country experienced strong economic growth in the eastern lowlands driven by agricultural exports and the resurgent oil and gas sector. In the west, however, the economy was less dynamic. While there was stronger economic activity in the cities of La Paz and Cochabamba, the 'boom' in mineral exploration did not translate into new or renewed mine operations with associated employment in places such as Oruro and Potosí. Likewise, there was no rise in minerals exports or tax revenues for local government. More particularly, the rural, indigenous Quechua and Aymara populations saw very little financial benefit from the economic reforms. Rural poverty throughout the western highlands and Altiplano remained an intractable problem. Consequently, migration from the countryside to the cities increased through the 1990s as *campesinos* searched for gainful employment. Many people found new homes, but not much work, in El Alto. El Alto is the city adjacent to La Paz, which grew over the decade to become larger than La Paz itself.

28 Historic context

It was in this context that Larry Buchanan discovered the potential of the mineral deposit at San Cristobal. Some areas of Bolivia were seeing growth while others that experienced no improvements in economic conditions felt that the national policies were all for the benefit of someone else. A huge number of displaced COMIBOL workers harboured resentments against the neo-liberal reforms initiated in the 1980s by Paz Estenssoro and continued by Jaime Paz and Goni. The national administration of Goni was also not experiencing much financial benefit from the boom in mining exploration either. Nonetheless, decision-making power and government services were penetrating the Aymara and Quechua-speaking rural areas. In short, educational reforms, governance reforms, and economic reforms were creating rising expectations, but for most, incomes were not rising.

The fact that incomes were not rising saved Bolivia from fulfilling the preconditions for a revolution, according to Brinton's (1965) theory of rising expectations. The theory says both expectations and incomes must be rising, some incomes much more than others, for a revolution to occur. The fact that only one of the conditions was fulfilled may account for why Evo Morales' rise to power was through the ballot box rather than through revolution. In any case, the San Cristobal mine was discovered at a time when indigenous communities in Bolivia were beginning to feel empowered and were seeking improvements in their standard of living. In the next chapter, we look at the specific organisations and personalities who had a stake in mining exploration during that period.

Note

1 The location is more famous as the last stand of Butch Cassidy and the Sundance Kid.

4

THE ANTI-FOREIGNER TURN

The push back against neo-liberalism

Opposition to the reforms introduced by Paz Estenssoro (1985 to 1989) was muted, initially overwhelmed by the need to confront the financial crisis and later marginalised by the success of the reforms. Nevertheless, a significant portion of the population wanted a return to a state-controlled economy. The presidential campaign of Jaime Paz Zamora (1989 to 1993) included promises to 'roll back' the neo-liberal reforms introduced by Paz Estenssoro. His failure to do so disillusioned many in the population, particularly in the western part of Bolivia. Opposition to the neo-liberal economic model, especially to foreign investment in mining, started to grow and solidify.

Several mining projects became controversial. The development of Inti Raymi by Battle Mountain Gold during 1989–1991 involved the relocation of the village of Chuquina and the co-operative miners. A vocal opposition to the process emerged in Oruro based on fears of environmental harm and criticism of the way the rights of the people involved had been handled. The most active critic was the Oblate priest attached to the Pastoral Social of the Catholic Church in Oruro. He used Radio Pio XII, owned by the Church, to broadcast his message across the Altiplano in Quechua, the main language of the region's indigenous population.

The rights-based criticism became stronger in 1991 when Bolivia became a signatory to the International Labour Organisation Convention 169 (ILO 169) on the Rights of Indigenous and Tribal Peoples. The national government signed the agreement in response to pressure from the indigenous tribes in the eastern lowlands of the country. However, the Quechua and Aymara-speaking people of the Altiplano and Andean Highlands also claimed indigenous status and, therefore, specific rights guaranteed under ILO 169. With the signing of the Convention, ILO 169 became attached to the Bolivian Constitution. This created a difficult situation

30 Historic context

in which the indigenous population were guaranteed various rights, including that of free, prior, and informed consent (FPIC), but without any enabling legislation that allowed them effective access to these rights. This was new territory and, whilst the Church and the civil society organisations working with indigenous groups made sure the local population was informed of the situation, most of the mining companies remained quite ignorant of the existence of ILO 169.

Opposition to the neo-liberal reforms was led by the union movement, which favoured a socialist model for the country. With the decimation of the miners' union as a consequence of closing the COMIBOL mines, CSUTCB (*Confederación Sindical Única de Trabajadores Campesinos de Bolivia*) became the principal union actor at the national level. In addition, social and environmental activists came to the country to work with the various organisations critical of, or openly opposed to, the neo-liberal policies and presence of foreign companies, particularly the mining companies. Among them was a young Belgian woman, Chantal Roelants, a confident, colourful, and outspoken individual with a socialist perspective. Roelants quickly became known variously as the '*Gringa Verde*' for her environmental activism and the '*Gringa Cholita*' for her habit of wearing the traditional dress of the women of the Bolivian Highlands: *pollera* (pleated skirt) with many petticoats, colourful shawl, and bowler hat.[1]

Roelants joined FRUTCAS (*Federación Regional Única de los Trabajadores Campesinos del Altiplano Sud*) the *campesino* (rural worker) collective representing the people of Nor López where she worked closely with Francisco Quisbert Salinas. FRUTCAS was, and remains, based in the town of Uyuni located on the south-east margin of the great Salar de Uyuni some 90 kilometres north-east of San Cristobal.

Quisbert is an author, communicator, radio commentator, and committed socialist. In the early 1990s he was also an executive of FRUTCAS.[2] He coordinated opposition to the neo-liberal policies of the central government. In particular, he believed foreign investment in mining threatened the rights of the local indigenous population and the security of the environment. The central elements of his message were (a) the historic ownership of the land purchased back from the Spanish in 1646 (Quisbert Salinas, 2001), (b) FPIC rights granted to indigenous people by ILO 169, and (c) respect for *Pachamama* (the earth goddess of Andean cosmology).

Despite the many positive aspects of the Goni Presidency, strong divisions of opinion existed. In the Andean Highlands and the Altiplano regions, there was strong opposition to Goni's neo-liberal policies. Some saw foreign investment as positive because the country lacked capital and because outside financing offered much-needed economic growth. Others saw it as negative, mostly for the lack of improvement in incomes and the threats to indigenous rights. Both sides pointed to Inti Raymi to illustrate their arguments. In the absence of foreign investment in operational mines, the activities of the foreign, non-producing, mineral exploration companies came under scrutiny.

During 1995, CSUTCB created the group *Instrumento Público por la Soberanía de los Pueblos* (IPSP or Public Instrument for the Sovereignty of the People)

The anti-foreigner turn **31**

that subsequently morphed into *El Movimiento Al Socialismo* (MAS – Movement towards Socialism) under the dynamic leadership of Evo Morales. The consequence was a consolidation of power and influence that effectively united political opinion from the centre left to the far left in Bolivia.

Emblematic incidents at the time of Buchanan's discovery

Critics of international mining investment in Bolivia came from the ideological left, led by (a) the union movement, who backed a system with both co-operatives and state-owned mines,[3] (b) the Catholic Church, concerned with rights, equity, and the protection of the indigenous peoples, and, (c) environmentalists, who pointed to the toxic legacy of 300 years of mining in the country. All three used radio extensively to disseminate their concerns to the rural population, creating a climate of fear, uncertainty, and ambiguity towards the presence of mineral exploration teams in the region. Many exploration projects ran into difficulties and the frequency of social conflicts increased through the early to mid-1990s. Projects were slowed, stopped, and, on occasions, prevented from starting, by opposition within host communities. Three such incidents have become emblematic within Bolivia: Challapata, Amayapampa and Porco.

Challapata

Conflict at Challapata broke out in December 1993 and reached a climax in January and February 1994 with a blockade, physical confrontation, and the death of at least one individual. A Canadian company had been exploring an area north of the town of Challapata, immediately adjacent to an extensive area of irrigated farmlands, for two years prior to the conflict. In November 1993, the company announced that preliminary studies showed the existence of a large body of gold mineralisation. Based on this data, the company believed that there was an economic resource that could be exploited through a large open-pit operation mine with cyanide-leaching methods. This announcement was immediately concerning to the communities given the close proximity of the proposed mine to the irrigated lands and perceived risk of contamination to ground and surface water.

During the last months of 1993, representatives of communities requested information from both the company and the government about the mining project, but they could get no satisfactory answer to their questions. Given the silence of the company and authorities, in January and February of 1994 the communities of Challapata mobilised. They blocked the road between Oruro and Potosí, which goes through their territory and constitutes the main artery flowing towards the south of the country. The farmers also occupied the exploration area and sacked the facilities built by the company. The company was forced to cease its exploration and remove its staff from the area, thus paralyzing the mining project indefinitely (Madrid Lara *et al.*, 2012).

32 Historic context

Amayapampa

The conflict at Amayapampa broke out in December 1996 towards the end of the Goni administration. Exploration of the old gold mines at Amayapampa and Capacirca by a Canadian company was initially peaceful. However, over a two-year period, there was a gradual deterioration in the relationships between the company and the local population, miners at the Amayapampa mine, and the co-operative working the Capacirca sector.

Difficulties developed between the union leadership at the mine and the company. The problems arose, at least in part, from the history of labour organisations and conflict in the region. As the project continued, it became evident that the miners were being pressured by outside groups which opposed the North American company's activities. Local concerns about working conditions and environmental risks were overtaken by the broader political discourse of control and wealth flowing to foreign, private investors. Manipulation by political interests became clearer and strengthened as the national presidential election approached.

The traditional authorities had presented an initial list of demands to the company. As the presidential election neared, however, they were pushed aside by regional figureheads inflaming the unrest for political purposes. Soon, national congressmen were denouncing the company. What had been a somewhat conflictive but contained and local situation, became first regional and then national; and highly politicised. Regional-level leaders mobilised other mining and rural agricultural communities to oppose the company and support the takeover of the mine by the local people. The company faced the occupation of its mine and the economic pressure of an extremely tight time frame for the development of the property. The company pressured the national government to restore law and order in the region. The government responded by sending in the military.

The army took over the mine site on December 23, 1996, killing at least nine people during a day-long confrontation which spread beyond the mine site to other communities in what became known as the 'Christmas Massacre'. In the wake of the conflict, the company withdrew. The project became a symbol of rejection of foreign investment and remained inactive for the next 12 years.

The Porco tailings spill

A little earlier in 1996, on August 29, a tailings dam collapsed at the Porco mine, a zinc-lead-silver producer operated by COMSUR, south-west of the city of Potosí. The resulting spill of more than 400,000 tonnes of noxious material flowed into the Pilcomayo River system creating a plume of contamination for many kilometres downstream. In addition to the immediate contamination of the river, the spill heightened awareness throughout Bolivia of environmental risks associated with mining. Although there was no local conflict associated with the incident, the negative consequences of the spill were immediately incorporated into the language of those critical of mining. They highlighted the aspect of foreign ownership, noting the minority interest in the company held by Great Britain's Rio Tinto. The Porco spill added to the base of opposition to foreign investment in Bolivia.

Opposition to neo-liberalism goes mainstream

The 1997 presidential elections saw Hugo Banzer sworn in for his second term, and the first leader in Latin America to return to power democratically after earlier ruling as a military-backed dictator. A strong man who emphasised law and order, Banzer was faced with managing a weakening national economy and a decline in foreign investment, particularly in the mining sector. In an attempt to strengthen the economy, Banzer moved to privatise the domestic water supplies in the cities of Cochabamba and La Paz. There was immediate outcry against this initiative from the political elites on the left, but a much more material response came from events on the ground.

In September 1999 an international consortium, *Aguas del Tunari*, won the concession to provide domestic water and sewage services to the city of Cochabamba and exclusive rights to the water sources upstream in adjacent valleys. The *Aguas del Tunari* consortium was made up of a British subsidiary of Bechtel known as International Waters (55 per cent), Abengoa Spain (25 per cent), and four Bolivian companies (5 per cent each). As a condition of the contract, *Aguas del Tunari* had agreed to pay the $30 million in debt accumulated by the existing government-owned water enterprise, finance an expansion of the water system, and build a dam to increase water storage capacity. To pay for these obligations, the new owners announced, and then implemented, an increase in the cost of water to domestic users.

The English and American officials running the consortium appear to have been unaware of the social, cultural, and economic realities of Bolivia. The increase in cost to households was an average of 35 per cent or about $20 per month. That was an extraordinary sum of money for the many families that lived on just $100 per month. For them, the increase was more than they spent on food. To add insult to injury, the manager of the consortium (an expatriate) announced that 'if people don't pay their water bills, the water will be turned off'. In December 1999, demonstrations and protests broke out against the rate increase, the consortium, and the privatisation of the water system. In January 2000, the poor were joined in protesting the situation when middle class homeowners and businesses saw exactly how much their water bills increased.

As the government attempted to repress opposition to the privatisation, violence occurred repeatedly. In February and April of 2000 there were several days of intense confrontations between the self-identified *'guerreros del agua'* (water warriors) and the police. Matters reached a head in the first week of April with a civil strike and further demonstrations in Cochabamba. On April 8, the Banzer government declared a 'state of siege', which led to a day of intense clashes between the water warriors and the police. City authorities advised the expatriate managers and officials of the consortium that they could not guarantee their safety.

34 Historic context

The expats understood that they were a visible minority and would be targets of violence. They fled the city. The Banzer government then declared that the consortium had abandoned the project and that therefore the contract with them had been voided. On April 10, the government signed an agreement with the leader of the water warriors to return the Cochabamba water system to municipal control.

Hugo Banzer resigned the Presidency in August 2001 due to ill health. Jorge Quiroga assumed the Presidency to see out the term against a background of economic decline and widespread social unrest. In 2002, Goni was elected President for a second term.

The rise of Evo Morales

When Goni took office, he was faced with an economic and social crisis inherited from the Banzer administration. Economic growth had plunged from the 4.8 per cent at the end of his first Presidency to 0.6 per cent in 1999 and had recovered to only 2 per cent for 2002. The fiscal deficit was running at 8 per cent.

In January 2003, a group of union leaders, united under the leadership of Evo Morales, formed the 'People's High Command' (*Estado Mayor del Pueblo*) to contest the neo-liberal economic model, which, from their perspective, was not working for the people. A new wave of heightened protests began. Main roads were blocked. Towns and cities were brought to a standstill. Some groups aired long-standing grievances against the government, notably the *cocaleros* protesting the programmes of coca eradication funded by the USA. Others targeted entirely local issues, protesting against decisions of the now self-governing municipalities. In February 2003, a standoff between police demanding higher pay and army units called to protect the presidential palace ended suddenly in violence, shooting, and deaths in the streets of La Paz.

Early in 2002, the administration of President Jorge Quiroga had proposed building a pipeline through Chile to the port of Mejillones to enable export of natural gas to markets around the Pacific. However, to this day antagonism towards Chile still runs deep in Bolivia, a result of the loss of access to the coast in the War of the Pacific (1879–1884) with Chile. A concerted campaign began against the Chilean option in favour of either routing the pipeline through the Peruvian port of Ilo, or keeping the gas in Bolivia and using it to promote industrialisation. Quiroga postponed any decision, leaving this highly controversial issue to his successor, Goni, who had expressed a personal preference for the Chilean route.

Through 2003, demands increased for the government to return to the corporatist state model and nationalise Bolivia's hydrocarbon resources. Protesters in the western highlands demanded Goni's resignation. In the eastern lowlands, people marched and demonstrated in the city of Santa Cruz in support of gas exports and a movement to declare independence from the rest of Bolivia. In late September 2003, north-west of La Paz, a confrontation between protestors and the army led to six deaths, including two soldiers and an 8-year-old girl.

The anti-foreigner turn **35**

A few days later, in early October, media reports described President Goni as having decided to export Bolivia's gas to Mexico and the United States through a Chilean port. In response, protesters blockaded the main highway linking El Alto with the adjoining city of La Paz. That spread to other key access points creating a near complete siege of La Paz.

After three days, fuel and other essential supplies were dangerously low in La Paz. On October 11, Goni promulgated Supreme Decree 27209, ordering the militarisation of the gas plants and the transport of hydrocarbons. As a result, police and military troops, fully armed with heavy machine guns and supported by tanks, were sent as a security force to open the way through El Alto for diesel and gasoline cisterns to transport fuel into La Paz. Protesters tried to block the convoys at several locations along their route. At some point, police and government troops started shooting indiscriminately resulting in 67 civilian deaths and 400 injuries, according to official reports. El Alto residents believed the official reports to underestimate both the number killed and injured. The Catholic Church and civil society organisations described it as a 'massacre' by government forces.

While blaming the violence on 'narco-sindicalists', Goni proposed a National Dialogue. He promised a national referendum on gas exports but was confronted with demands for his resignation. Faced with rising anger at the deaths, and with loss of support from his Vice-President and coalition partners, Gonzalo Sánchez de Lozada resigned from the Presidency on October 17. He flew to the United States on a commercial flight early the next day.

In an atmosphere of deep crisis, Carlos Mesa assumed the Presidency in October 2003. During 2004, Mesa held a national referendum on five points of national gas policy. The result was clearly in favour of nationalisation but only moderately in favour of the pipeline through Chile and a proposed policy regarding the use of government income from exports. The 2004 municipal elections confirmed a shift in popular opinion as MAS emerged as the largest national political party with almost a third of the councillors elected. In May of 2005, congress raised taxes on foreign companies from 18 per cent to 32 per cent. Evo Morales and his MAS party criticised this as much too small an increase. In June, Morales led protests and road blockades that cut off food supplies to several major cities, effectively shutting down the country. Mesa resigned the same month. Eduardo Rodriguez, chief justice of the Supreme Court, was sworn in as interim President with the primary task of quickly organising an election by the end of the year.

In early 2006, Evo Morales was sworn in as President. He was elected in the first round of voting with an absolute, popular majority having campaigned on a platform of nationalism, anti-imperialism, and anti-neo-liberalism. Once in power, policies of the Morales government were based on a development model that prioritised *vivir bien* – 'living well' (Farthing and Kohl, 2014). This approach aimed to promote social harmony, consensus, the elimination of discrimination, and wealth distribution. There was also an emphasis on environmental protection and the need to respect *Pachamama* (mother earth). As such it strongly reflected elements of

36 Historic context

traditional Andean indigenous cosmovision and social organisation rather than the Western norms that had prevailed since 1986 (Farthing and Kohl, 2014).

Morales proposed a liberal, mixed economy in which the state would have a strong role. One of his first actions as President was to take increased control of the oil and gas sector through Supreme Decree 2870 under which the division of corporate revenues was reversed such that the companies paid 82 per cent of profits to the state and retained 18 per cent. This was a popular move and although technically not a form of nationalisation was referred to as such by the Morales government. Under this so-called nationalisation, the state oil and gas company, YPFB (*Yacimientos Petrolíferos Fiscales Bolivianos*), also took control of all sales and marketing of hydrocarbons in Bolivia. The private sector retained control of oil and gas production but had to sell their production to the state company. Having gained direct control of revenues from a key sector of the economy, Morales had the ability to fund promised (and much-needed) social and infrastructure projects. Revenues from the mining sector also increased as global metal prices rose in what has come to be known as the period of the 'commodities super cycle' driven by demand from China. For the first time in many years the economy began to expand.

Further structural changes brought in by Evo Morales included a new Constitution, finally approved in 2009 in a national referendum, which established Bolivia as a Plurinational State. The Constitution emphasised Bolivian sovereignty of natural resources, the separation of Church and state, prevented the establishment of foreign military bases, and permitted limited regional autonomy. It conferred the right of every Bolivian to water, food, free health care, education, and housing (Farthing and Kohl, 2014). The concept of Plurinationalism also recognised the rights to self-determination of the various indigenous nations within the single state of Bolivia. The immediate consequence was to increase the power of the indigenous majority of the population.

The initial years of the Morales Presidency were characterised by relative calm in the western, highland and Altiplano regions of the country, pride among the indigenous population, and a reaffirmation of national identity. There was, however, ongoing tension with the eastern, lowland areas of Bolivia where there was significant support for the neo-liberal economic model, which better suited the extensive agribusiness that dominates the economy, particularly in Santa Cruz. There were also episodic initiatives for the eastern departments to declare independence, led by Santa Cruz. However, Morales was able to withstand these pressures and reach a working political understanding with Santa Cruz and the other eastern departments (Farthing and Kohl, 2014).

Within the ruling party, MAS, there were almost continuous calls for nationalisation of the privately owned mining companies. Morales resisted these pressures stating that, at least for the near term, Bolivia needed the investment and technical skills of foreign mining companies to fully exploit Bolivia's natural resources in an economically efficient and environmentally satisfactory manner (Farthing and Kohl, 2014). Nevertheless, foreign investors were wary of Morales'

The anti-foreigner turn **37**

socialist policies and intimidated by the restructuring of the hydrocarbon sector and nationalisation of some mining properties. While global mining investment soared through the remainder of the 2002 to 2012 super cycle, very little came to Bolivia.

Despite the apparent political difficulties presented by the policies of the Morales government, in 2006, USA-based Coeur Mining signed an agreement to develop and operate the San Bartolome mine located on the slopes of the Cerro Rico, within the city limits of Potosí. After necessary technical studies, mine construction began in 2007 with the commencement of full production in 2008. The mine is still operated by Minera Manquiri, a Bolivian company wholly owned by Coeur Mining. However, Minera Manquiri does not own its property outright. Rather, it leased the mining rights from several Potosí mining co-operatives that, in turn, held mining rights leased from state-owned COMIBOL.

As of this writing, foreign mining in Bolivia consists of five operations. Pan American Silver continues to operate the San Vicente Mine and Coeur Mining still operates the San Bartolome Mine. Glencore purchased COMSUR from the Sánchez de Lozada family in 2012, and continues to operate a number of mines under the corporate name Sinchi Wayra. The mines of these three companies are all directly or indirectly joint ventures with state owned COMIBOL. The San Cristobal mine and the Don Mario mine are the only ones wholly privately owned. San Cristobal is owned by Japan's Sumitomo Corporation. Don Mario is owned and operated by Vancouver, Canada-based Orvana Minerals. The foreign investment mining boom of the neo-liberal 1990s has been reduced to these surviving, and prospering, companies.

Notes

1 This was in an era before acts of 'cultural appropriation' were purported to be a form of cultural imperialism.
2 See http://le-pari-bolivien.blogspot.ca/p/encadre-la-vie-bolivienne-de-guillaume.html for more detail on Chantal Roelants and her husband Guillaume.
3 Many Bolivian co-operatives are indistinguishable from private companies in the way they operate.

PART 2

Retrospective from discovery to operating mine

Part 2

5

SOCIAL LICENCE CONCEPT AND RETROSPECTIVE STUDY METHOD

In this section, we look at the history of the San Cristobal community and its surrounding region as revealed in a retrospective study that tracked the perceived levels of social licence granted by the communities to the company. The year 1995 marked the discovery of the mineral deposit that is now the basis of the operating mine. Ian Thomson and his colleagues conducted a thorough retrospective study of the communities from 1995 to 2008. They applied the concept of the licence to their data in order to trace the ups and downs of the relationship between the company and the community.

This chapter explains our view of the licence and the methodological details of the retrospective study. Chapters 6 to 8 describe the events and stakeholders during the major periods covered by the study. Chapter 9 follows up with our own retrospective account of the conflicts that occurred subsequently in 2010 and 2011.

The social licence concept

Metaphor with the legal licence

The Google Ngram service counts the usage of words and phrases in books published from 1800 to 2008. In the 19th century and most of the 20th century, 'social licence' (or 'license') meant breaking social norms, or not feeling compelled to observe social norms. Thus, in 1818 John William Cunningham, Vicar of Harrow on the Hill (Cunningham, 1818), used the term to describe behaviour that failed to show proper reverence for the Sabbath.

In contemporary usage, the phrase 'social licence' applies to the level of acceptance or approval of an organisation's activities. This meaning invokes a metaphor with the legal licences needed by mining companies to begin their projects.

42 Retrospective from discovery to operating mine

Apparently, the modern meaning of the term was coined independently by two different people at almost the same time. Moore (1996, as cited in Hall and Power, 2016, p. 2) used the term in a two-page comment in a paper industry magazine. He argued that paper companies should exceed government environmental regulations in order to keep their social licence with the public. In March 1997, Jim Cooney, then Director, International and Public Affairs for Placer Dome Inc., used the term in a meeting with World Bank officials in Washington. He used it as an analogy with the legal licence. Unlike Moore, his focus was not on environmental stewardship but rather on community well-being. Cooney observed a widespread failure of governments to take account of, and protect, the interests of communities as part of the process of granting legal licences for mining. Therefore, to compensate for government failures, which produce community opposition later, Cooney recommended that mining companies seek a social licence directly from communities (Cooney, pers. comm., 2011).

In May 1997, World Bank representatives used the term, in Cooney's sense, at a conference on mining and communities in Ecuador. From there it spread quietly through the mining industry. The first known publication to use the term in this sense was an article by Susan Joyce and Ian Thomson (the second author of this book), published in 1999 in the *Mining Journal*. It was entitled, 'Earning a social licence' (Joyce and Thomson, 1999).

Implicit in Cooney's metaphor was the idea that communities, or more broadly, networks of stakeholders, have the power to obstruct projects, even if those projects have been approved by government. The concept is sometimes disparaged in government and legal circles because it implicitly acknowledged that lawmakers are sometimes doing nothing more than waving around worthless pieces of paper. To put it another way, a noticeable number of politicians, lawyers, and government experts are irked by the political power of activists to unilaterally overrule laws and regulations. Despite the distaste expressed by such professionals, it remains a fact that communities, activists, and stakeholder networks can exert power equal to or greater than that wielded by those who grant legal licences.

Definition incorporating stakeholder perceptions

In the most general contemporary sense, the social licence can be defined as *the level of tolerance, acceptance, or approval of an organisation's activities by the stakeholders with the greatest concern about the activity.*

In the original context of an individual mine or mining project (including exploration projects), the social licence is rooted in the beliefs, perceptions, and opinions held by the local residents and other stakeholders of the mine or exploration project.

As a purely mental phenomenon, the social licence is therefore 'intangible'. However, that does not mean it is unquantifiable. Black (2013) presents a set of agree/disagree questions that can measure the social licence for mining projects and an analysis of the reliability and validity of the measures can be found at www.socialicence.com. Because it is based on beliefs, opinions, and perceptions, the social licence is also dynamic and non-permanent. Beliefs, opinions, and perceptions are subject to change as new information is acquired or when new social influences come to bear. Hence the social licence must be earned and maintained daily (Thomson and Boutilier, 2011).

Stakeholder theory (Freeman, 1984) defines stakeholders as those who can affect the focal organisation (e.g. the mining company) or those who can be affected by it. Stakeholder concerns, of course, come from an intention to affect the activities of an organisation, or an experience or anticipation of being affected by those activities. The definition of the social licence proposed here incorporates the definition of stakeholders by acknowledging that the grantors or withholders of the social licence may self-declare. It is not only those who are affected or can potentially affect who can grant or withhold a social licence. The social licence can also be granted or withheld by those who are not affected but who nonetheless want to have an effect upon the focal organisation. For example, an ideologically or religiously motivated group may decide that the organisation's activities represent something they wish to eliminate, even though they are not impacted themselves. They are self-declared stakeholders and therefore can grant or withhold the social licence according to their own beliefs, perceptions, and opinions.

The definition of the social licence proposed here implies gradations in the level of support granted. No support is a withheld social licence. The terms 'tolerance, acceptance, or approval', however, indicate degrees of support or suspicion about the organisation's activities. This has been the topic of some theoretical and empirical study that we discuss in the subsequent section of this chapter labelled 'Identification of levels of social licence'.

Social licence as platform for stakeholder politics

The definition of social licence used here is not the only one that has been proposed. A group of researchers centred in Brisbane has developed measures based on the level of acceptance or approval by the general public (Moffat and Zhang, 2014; Moffat *et al.*, 2014; Zhang *et al.*, 2015). Although their findings concur that trust and perceptions of fairness are key determinants of the level of social licence, they do not put any special importance on stakeholder organisations. Instead, they use random sample public opinion surveys to measure their version of the social licence. This speaks to a fundamental difference in assumptions about who has political power. The public opinion approach assumes that the general public rules. The stakeholder opinion approach assumes that the public might influence stakeholder organisations, but that organisations and organised groups carry the day.

A social licence granted by a stakeholder network is not the same as a social licence granted by the general public. However, there are circumstances in which the two are indistinguishable. For example, in a jurisdiction where the public knows and cares about a project and where the government knows and cares about what the general public thinks, the two approaches should suggest the same strategies. Public opinion will affect the social licence granted by stakeholders like politicians and regulatory authorities. Through those kinds of channels, the stakeholder approach would also reflect public opinion.

In other circumstances, however, the general public has no knowledge of, and therefore no concern about, the activities of the organisation needing a social licence. Moreover, where the government mostly ignores the public, perhaps in favour of pleasing a powerful elite, public opinion seldom affects the social licence. Alternatively, where a powerful elite has the skill and means to control public opinion, a government might feign taking public opinion into account while actually paying more strict attention to the opinions of the elite. The social licence is often granted or withheld by a group that is more select than the general public. A majority of the general public can more easily become the most influential stakeholder when the public in question is quite small (e.g. a village nearby the organisation's activities) or when the organisation's activities actually do affect the majority of the public (e.g. a government plan to raise taxes or to eliminate a public service). Even then, however, the public's concerns are usually expressed through broadly representative stakeholder organisations like village councils, taxpayer organisations, or beneficiaries' groups.

Social licence versus access to resources

An important distinction must be made between, on the one hand, the social licence granted by each stakeholder group or individual and, on the other hand, the net effect on the focal organisation of the interactions among those stakeholders. Because the term 'social licence' is often applied to both phenomena, confusion arises about who can say they have withheld or granted 'the' social licence to an organisation. This confusion becomes dissonant when it appears that a minority of stakeholders have prevented an organisation from continuing its activities.

Figure 5.1 attempts to untangle the basic social licence from the more complicated political process in which it is embedded. The stack of rectangles on the left represent the social licences granted by each stakeholder. They can vary in levels according to the how the beliefs, perceptions, and opinions of each

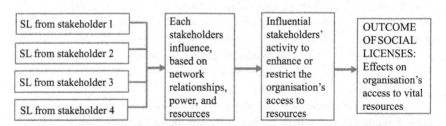

FIGURE 5.1 How the social licences granted by individual stakeholders translate into the impacts on the focal organisation.

stakeholder affect the stakeholder's tolerance, acceptance, or approval of the focal organisation's activities.

The core social licences represented by the stack on the left of Figure 5.1 feed into the next rectangle on the right. This rectangle is recognition that not all stakeholders are equally influential. One of the best predictors of influence is the stakeholder's position in the network of relationships among stakeholders themselves. As an empirical matter, those with more power, resources, and influence generally (a) are essential links in more communications pathways throughout the network (i.e., measurable as 'betweenness centrality'), (b) have more relationships overall (i.e., measurable as 'degree centrality'), and (c) are more well connected to more well-connected others (i.e., measurable as 'eigenvector centrality').

The second rectangle from the right in Figure 5.1 acknowledges that power and influence do not accomplish anything without action. Some influential stakeholders simply will not choose to act. Although there can be many reasons for this, the result is always that the level of social licence granted by the stakeholder has very little effect on the focal organisation. The corollary is that even a relatively small group of stakeholders with a minority opinion can have a great deal of influence if they do act. So-called 'activists' understand this intuitively. Indeed, the dynamics of 'minority influence' have been studied by social psychologists for decades (Moscovici, 1980; Gardikiotis, 2011). A consistent and persistent minority can often impose its views on a larger group.

The rightmost rectangle in Figure 5.1 is the outcome for the focal organization in terms of the ease or difficulty it has in accessing vital resources. The resources go well beyond land and water. They include human skills, technology, markets, financing, reputation, and legal permits. A focal organisation can lose access to resources for many reasons (e.g., natural disasters, economic upheavals). The withdrawal of the social licence by influential, active stakeholders is only one of many possible causes. Nonetheless, when withheld social licences on the left side of Figure 5.1 lead to a loss of access to resources at the right side, it is common to say the organisation has lost its social licence.

There are two places in Figure 5.1 where common usage of the term 'social licence' creates confusion.

First, on the extreme left, it is certainly possible to measure the social licences granted by all the stakeholders and then average them all to get one 'social licence' number. However, that number assumes all stakeholders are equally influential and active. To get one number that better reflects the political reality, the stakeholder's social licence scores would have to be weighted by measures for the middle two rectangles.

Second, on the extreme right of Figure 5.1, it is assumed that the loss of access was caused by a withdrawn social licence among influential and active stakeholders. Even when this is true, stakeholder boasts that they have withdrawn the organisation's social licence, ring false for two reasons.

First, such claims make it sound like the social licence is a one-time event. They imply that the loss of access will not galvanise supporters to act. Given the social psychology of majority and minority influence on opinions in social networks and the political science of coalition formation and decline, it would be more accurate to say that the social licence has 'dipped into the withdrawn range' this week. Next week, alliances may shift, and new information or interpretations of information may appear and cause the social licence to be regained.

Second, sometimes the triumphalist tone of stakeholder claims to have withdrawn the social licence[1] seem to imply that the stakeholder has a quasi-legal right to exercise a veto. A more empirically accurate description would say that those stakeholders with enough political sophistication and dogged determination can momentarily block the focal organisation's access to resources, provided the supporters of the organisation's activity do not surpass them in these qualities. A momentary political victory should not be confused with a legal right to exercise a veto. Of course, listeners with an understanding of how issue framing can be used as a subterfuge for converting political victories into legal entitlements would not be confused by such statements.

Identification of levels of social licence

The three-level model

Informal conversations between Ian Thomson and his colleagues Myriam Cabrera, Margarita de Castro, and Susan Joyce provided confirmation of the patterns and the rationale for a hypothesis regarding the levels of the social licence. First presented to the public as a keynote address at the annual convention of the Prospectors and Developers Association in March 2008 (Thomson and Joyce, 2008), it was proposed that the social licence is comprised of the stakeholder perceptions of the legitimacy and credibility of the mine or project and the presence or absence of true trust. Furthermore, these elements are acquired sequentially and cumulatively as the social licence improves. The mine or project must be seen as legitimate before credibility is of value in the relationship, and both must be in place before meaningful trust can develop. Furthermore, the process can operate in both directions: trust can be lost, as can credibility and finally even legitimacy. The concepts were summarised in a stair-step model (Figure 5.2) that also offered the hypothesis that without legitimacy a project faces rejection, that with legitimacy acceptance would emerge, and that with credibility, approval became a probable outcome.

Four-level version

As Figure 5.3 shows, our current model proposes four distinct levels of the social licence. A lost or absent social licence is the withdrawn or withheld level. The lowest granted level is acceptance or bare tolerance. The next higher level is approval. Finally, over a longer period, psychological identification with the project or the

Social licence retrospective study method 47

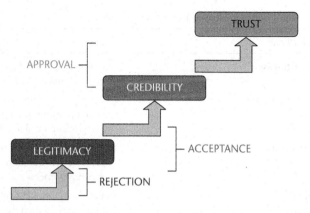

FIGURE 5.2 Hypothesised boundaries between the levels of the social licence (Thomson and Joyce, 2008).

industry can occur. For example, residents may describe their community as a mining town, just as Hollywood is identified with movies and Silicon Valley is identified with computers.

For most practical purposes in the extractive and infrastructure industries, the social licence is an expression of the quality of a relationship, as perceived by the community. Given this, it is possible to identify potential indicators of the nature of the relationship as listed in Table 5.1. Demonstrations and blockades strongly suggest that the social licence is being withdrawn or withheld. On the other hand, the community petitioning government in support of a mining project is reasonable evidence of something more than mere acceptance.

FIGURE 5.3 Four-level model of the social licence (based on Thomson and Boutilier, 2011).

48 Retrospective from discovery to operating mine

TABLE 5.1 Levels of social licence and associated behaviours

Level of Social Licence	Frequently Observed Behaviours
Withheld/withdrawn	Shutdowns, blockades, protests, violence, sabotage, legal challenges
Acceptance/tolerance	Lingering/recurring issues/threats, watchful monitoring, presence of antagonistic outside NGOs
Approval/support	Company seen as good neighbour, pride in collaborative accomplishments
Psychological identification	Political support, co-management of projects, united front against critics

The extremes of social licence levels are easy to identify. In the middle ranges there is more room for ambiguity about attitudes towards the project within the host population. After listening to community members in countless interviews at numerous projects over a number of years, patterns started to emerge in the use of words when people described how they felt about a company or project. We often heard the words 'legitimacy' and 'credibility' used to describe turning points in relationships between communities and companies.

While based on extensive field observations, the model and hypothesis were, to that point, untested. The opportunity to put these ideas to a test came later in 2008 during a visit to the recently constructed mine at San Cristobal, Bolivia.

Methods used for the 1994 to 2008 San Cristobal case study

Participant field observation, historic documents, and interviews with residents

Ian Thomson was actively involved with the development of the San Cristobal mine as a consultant for the commercial banks that financed its construction. The banks needed the project to be compliant with the Equator Principles, which specify standards for environmental and social performance. Thomson was responsible for monitoring progress and assuring that compliance. This work involved regular visits to the project beginning in 2004 and numerous interviews with residents of the communities affected by the project to validate statements by the company and to determine exactly what was going on, and in some cases, why. Thomson also had access to historical plans and reports in company files.

Social licence retrospective study method **49**

His colleague, Susan Joyce, had conducted the first social investigation at the project in 1997 and returned while working with the International Finance Corporation of the World Bank in 2000 and 2001. During 2001, Margarita de Castro had been retained by the company to update plans for the post resettlement of San Cristobal. De Castro had subsequently returned as a consultant to the company in 2006 to provide further support. There was thus access to personal and documented accounts of the interaction between the mining company and host communities over an extended period of time. The observations of the consultants and data from the files were further augmented by insightful contributions from Juan Mamani, who had been working continuously on the San Cristobal project since 1998. Mamani, a Quechua speaker, had first come to San Cristobal as a surveyor at the time of negotiations over land purchase and resettlement, and subsequently risen to the post of MSC's Superintendent for Community Relations and Sustainable Development.

Retrospective approach

In April 2008, Thomson, de Castro, and Mamani met at the mine site to discuss the idea of reconstructing the history of the relationship between company and community, and by implication the social licence of the San Cristobal project, from day one to the present (2008). With the active involvement of Javier Diez de Medina, Manager of Social Responsibility at the mine, a preliminary graph was developed based on readily available reports, field notes, and collective recollections of the attitudes of the population at various times. It was found to be reasonably easy to recover the phrases and expressions used by the community, hence a plot of perceptions of legitimacy, credibility, and trust was assembled. No attempt was made at that time to try and apply the concepts of community acceptance and approval, although this may be interpolated.

The preliminary plot was then given to a number of community leaders who adjusted the shape of the plot to accord with their memory of the situation at any given time. The resulting timeline of the quality of the relationship between the San Cristobal mining project and the host community is shown in Figure 5.4. Importantly, it was agreed that the quality of the social licence had varied over time and that key inflection points could be related to specific events that strongly influenced community perceptions of the company.

Over the next three chapters we recount details of the history of the relationship depicted in Figure 5.4 based on the information described above, augmented by (a) interviews with company and community informants conducted in 2015 and (b) published studies and accounts in the media. In the following chapters, numbers identified with a hashtag (#) refer to the numbers on the timeline shown in Figure 5.4.

50 Retrospective from discovery to operating mine

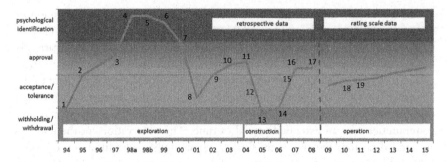

FIGURE 5.4 Fluctuations in project acceptance at San Cristobal (see text for events corresponding to the numbers on the line).

Note

1 ecojustice.ca, 2013. www.ecojustice.ca/pressrelease/environmental-groups-tell-review-panel-to-reject-northern-gateway-pipeline/.

6

FROM GEOLOGICAL DISCOVERY TO CONSTRUCTION

1994–2004

Geological discovery

The story begins in 1994 with Denver, USA, businessman and mining promotor Thomas Kaplan founding Cayman Island-based Andean Silver Corporation (ASC) to develop mining projects in South America. ASC's Bolivian subsidiary, ASC Bolivia LDC, entered into a partnership with MINTEC, a Bolivian mining consulting company which held the option to purchase mining concessions in and around San Cristobal. With this partnership, basic legal legitimacy was achieved (#1 on Figure 5.4). Geologist Larry Buchanan was hired to lead exploration in Bolivia. In January 1995 Buchanan discovers the giant ore-body. MINTEC scrambled to consolidate the land holdings by optioning more properties in and around San Cristobal. By mid-1996 the land parcel was secure and MINTEC assigned all the properties to ASC Bolivia. In August 1996, Apex Silver Mines Limited was established as a US corporation with the purpose of purchasing and developing silver, zinc, and lead extraction projects worldwide. Its first project was to finance drilling activities at San Cristobal.

Buchanan's initial visit to San Cristobal is remembered in the community as being very respectful. The prospecting team asked permission to enter community lands and hired an individual as guide and to help collect rock samples. Other early encounters between the company and community were similarly recalled as respectful and positive, particularly the opportunity for direct interaction between community leaders and Jonny Delgado, the President of MINTEC, who was in charge of the overall exploration programme.

MINTEC established a base of operations in the old Toldos mine camp with offices, a commissary, and accommodation for its professional staff and contract personnel. Over the next year and a half hundreds of holes were drilled and sufficient information acquired to be confident that the mineral resource was large and

52 Retrospective from discovery to operating mine

rich enough to sustain a financially feasible mine. The quality of the relationship continued to improve due to the availability of work for local residents and frequent contact between community leaders and Delgado. Community leaders recall how they would talk with Delgado late into the evening sharing stories and visions of the future. They also recall that Delgado treated them with respect and willingly incorporated cultural activities important to the community into the MINTEC work plan, which helped them come to believe that he could be trusted. They became friends.

Initiation of the drilling programme drew the attention of individuals and groups critical of mining. In particular, Francisco Quisbert, assisted by Chantel Roelants, used the FRUTCAS (Federación Regional Única de los Trabajadores Campesinos del Altiplano Sud)-owned radio station in Uyuni to broadcast messages declaring that a mine at San Cristobal would inevitably be a source of environmental contamination and social harm. The tailings spill at the Porco mine and the alleged impacts on health at the Inti Raymi mine were among the examples used to paint a profoundly negative picture of the future. Further messages highly critical of mining came from radio station Pio XII, owned and operated by the Catholic Church. Collectively, they tried to convince the residents of San Cristobal that the company was systematically lying to them and that they should reject mining because it would bring pollution and destruction. They urged the local residents to resist and push out MINTEC.

Community leaders, who could have opposed the presence of the company and forced its withdrawal, actively approved of the exploration programme moving ahead. In a sense, San Cristobal chose MINTEC to explore the wealth discovered by Buchanan. However, while it is important to note that the relationship was at this point highly dependent on the quality of the personal interaction between Delgado and the leadership of the community, the company was becoming a credible actor in the eyes of a majority of the population (#2–3 on Figure 5.4)

Resettlement

By the end of 1997, the company was confident that it had defined a potentially economic body of silver, zinc, and lead mineralisation and moved to initiate a full feasibility study. When briefed, community leaders did not believe Delgado's account of a big mine being built in the near future. Nevertheless, this information spread rapidly through the community and reached family members in distant regions. A migration back to San Cristobal began in response to the lure of work at a mine. Geologist Larry Buchanan and his wife Karen Gans took up residence in San Cristobal. Gans started teaching in the school. Many residents saw this as an expression of solidarity with the community.

In April 1998, the company initiated negotiations with the San Cristobal community for the resettlement of the village. Later in 1998, ASC Bolivia acquired the name and all the assets of MINTEC. The community was largely unaware of this change since continuity of personnel was maintained. Delgado continued representing corporate interests in interactions with the community as President of the restructured company.

The community became divided upon absorbing the news that, if there was going to be a mine, the population would have to move and the existing physical structures in the village of San Cristobal would have to be destroyed. Sentiment was split between those who were willing to move and those who could not countenance leaving the place they called home. The group supporting the move was dominated by younger people who wanted work and saw the mine as a positive opportunity and the relocation as a necessary way of gaining that opportunity. The people who were against moving were predominantly older and female with deep emotional attachments to the place. For these individuals, destruction of the old town and relocation to make way for a mine also meant destruction of the spiritually significant rocks, caves, and sacred places. For them, the loss was not worth the trade-off against jobs.

The question of relocation and resettlement in new houses constructed by the company was debated extensively within the community at a series of open assemblies. Gradually a broad consensus was reached, although a minority endorsed it half-heartedly. The older members of the community agreed to the move so that the younger people, their sons, daughters, and grandchildren, could have a better future. To develop a clear idea of what they wanted as part of any agreement with the company, the community was able to draw on the skills and experience of individual leaders such as Ascencio Lazo, Alberto Colque, and Rodolfo Ramos.

As noted by Muriel Hernández and Fernández Moscoso (2014), both parties entered the process of negotiations with clear objectives and a willingness to be open to the other. For example, the company was sensitive to community requests to incorporate cultural rituals, both Catholic and Andean, important to the local people into the negotiation process and the layout of the new town. (see, Buchanan and Gans, 2008; Baptista Gumucio, 2015). Similarly, the community listened to proposals from the company and carefully assessed how they would advance the process. Both parties look back on the experience as something that brought them closer together.

Early in the negotiations, the company indicated a willingness to set up two mixed committees made up of representatives of both the community and the company, with the community holding a majority of the positions. This move effectively empowered the community to lead in two significant areas of investigation and decision making: (a) determining who is eligible to be resettled and compiling an inventory of communal and individual assets affected by the resettlement, and (b) planning the new settlement. The latter task involved identifying the location of the new village of San Cristobal, deciding the character of the houses to be built, organising the geographic layout, and setting up the fundamental institutions.

54 Retrospective from discovery to operating mine

This process of empowerment created a strong sense of ownership by the community and a belief that they were partners with the company in the development of the mine (#4–5 on Figure 5.4). Language used at the time included, 'The Company has the money and technology to build the mine, but we have the land and without our willingness to move, there would be no mine'. Further enhancing the sensations of empowerment and equality was the fact that negotiations for resettlement were held between the company senior management, led by Delgado, and community leaders. Both formal and informal discussions took place, which created a high level of mutual confidence and understanding. In the oral tradition of the Quechua-speaking community, Delgado's word was as good as any written contract. The community came to trust Delgado, and by extension the company, believing that it would always honour its commitments and never knowingly harm or disadvantage the people of San Cristobal.

At this point, the partnership between the community and the company was very much in accordance with the principle of justice as equality and the associated enforcement system for fairness based on mutual monitoring and norm adherence (see Figure 5.4). Instead of hierarchy, there was complementarity based on specialised skills, knowledge, and interests. Perhaps not coincidentally, the community viewed this era as the high point in relations with the company. For the company, although the relationship was moving well in the right direction, it was not yet producing mutual financial benefits.

The relocation committees functioned very well, according to reports from both the company and community. Based on the inventories and surveys, it was agreed that 140 new houses would be built to accommodate the families eligible for resettlement, plus communal buildings such as schools, a hospital, an administration building, and necessary infrastructure. To the surprise of the company, the community selected a site 8 kilometres south-east of the old village on the edge of the open, wind-swept plains rather than the location in a sheltered valley recommended by the company's consultants. Moreover, after travelling to inspect various types of housing at locations throughout the Altiplano, the committee chose concrete panel wall construction with corrugated iron roofs that closely resembled the institutional housing found in a mining camp. The company had recommended a design based on traditional adobe construction.[1] Despite the protestations of Jonny Delgado, the community voted to accept both the location and design of houses selected by the committee. The vote was not unanimous, however. A small minority, almost entirely women, voted against the resettlement. They did not want to move away from their old homes.

On June 9, 1998 an agreement for the resettlement of San Cristobal was approved by vote at a general assembly of the community. It included three commitments by the company that would have long term implications for the quality of the relationship between the parties. They were the following:

a) All residences will have the basic services of potable water, sewage drains, and electrical energy installed.

b) The company will:

give priority for contracts to residents of San Cristobal of active age and quality as workers for the development of the mining project during the periods of exploration, construction, and exploitation: to make this effective, the company will give them practical training courses to adequately use their skills and work strengths, abilities and work habits from the list provided by the community authority.

c) The company will create a Foundation and an agro-industrial company to benefit the social and economic interests of the community. The company provided US$2 million to fund creation of the Foundation (the San Cristobal Foundation) and to seed the agro-industrial company. A number of specific projects were listed as obligations of the Foundation.

In parallel, agreements were signed for the relocation of the cemetery and for construction of a replica of the old church within the new community.

In November 1998, construction of New San Cristobal began. In March 1999, the first disagreement surfaced. Men from the community marched against the company over the treatment of local people by the contractors hired to supervise aspects of the construction programme. The brief dispute was settled in favour of the community members, with relationships intact.

The cemetery was relocated successfully with the full participation of the Church and community. Similarly, the replica church was built in the community and the interior of the old church transferred to the new location, to international acclaim, by specialists in the restoration of Spanish colonial architecture.

In July 1999, the residents of San Cristobal moved from the old village to the new site and took occupancy of the houses allotted to them. Within weeks a collective awareness arose that the houses were not going to be a success (#6 on Figure 5.4). The women, who had been essentially excluded from the process of selecting the design and construction of the houses, found serious deficiencies. The concrete panel walls provided very little insulation against the cold when compared to the adobe construction they had lived in previously, rendering the houses both uncomfortable and very expensive to keep warm. Similarly, they were drafty, quickly became dusty, and were very difficult to keep clean. The biggest problem, however, was the layout of the kitchen and lack of an oven large enough to bake traditional breads. A frantic building programme burst out across the village with traditional wood-fired adobe ovens constructed in the 'garden' area behind each house. However, as explained later, the residents 'could not raise any complaint with the company over problems with the houses. They had been approved by the community' (J. Mamani, pers. comm., May 2015).

Under the Constitution of Bolivia, all unoccupied lands are the property of the State and are used at the discretion of the government. As such, the company could gain the use of surface rights for the mine and associated facilities directly

56 Retrospective from discovery to operating mine

from the State without any reference to the users of the land. In the case of the San Cristobal project, the company took the position that the communities of San Cristobal, Culpina K, and Vila Vila had traditional use rights to the lands and *de facto* used areas close to the villages for agricultural production and occupied extensive areas for grazing llamas. Accordingly, the company entered into negotiations with all three communities to provide compensation for loss of access to land to make way for the mine, mill, offices, camp, and related facilities, and in the case of Culpina K, the land of the closed depression known as Wila Khara (see map in Figure 6.1), which would be used to store tailing from the mine. Once again, the process of reaching agreements was facilitated by the active involvement of members of the relevant communities in every aspect of the process, including identification of land parcels and 'ownership' structures and requirements to mitigate impact on llama herds. Compensation in all cases reflected the communal ownership of the land by benefiting the whole affected community, or at least a significant majority of it.

Waiting for jobs

The residents of San Cristobal had come to expect that construction of the mine would start as soon as the community had moved to the new village and jobs would be available. This belief had prompted the return of yet more families in the months immediately after the relocation to New San Cristobal. These families built their own houses on the east side of the new town using adobe construction. A similar return was experienced at both Culpina K and Vila Vila.

The mine and jobs failed to appear immediately upon resettlement. The company was trying to raise financing for mine construction in a poor market while finalising a full feasibility study and waiting for approvals from the national government after submitting a comprehensive Environmental Impact Assessment (EIA). None of these matters were communicated to the local population. As a result, concerns about the shortcomings of the houses were joined by greater misgivings about the absence of progress with the mine, the lack of work, perceptions of being discriminated against for the few jobs with the company, and the number of commitments in the San Cristobal resettlement agreement that remained unfulfilled. At the same time, criticisms started to surface in Culpina K that they had signed a 'poor deal' with the company. With frustrated expectations on the part of the communities and an absence of information, confidence in the company declined. Doubts as to the credibility of the promises made earlier emerged in conversations among and between families (#7 on Figure 5.4).

In 2000, a major corporate restructuring took place. MSC was formed in Bolivia as a wholly owned subsidiary of Apex Silver Mines and all the assets of ASC Bolivia were transferred to the new company. At the time, many aspects of the resettlement and land acquisitions agreements remained outstanding and there was no sign of the mine and the jobs promised by the company. The change of name was first seen as indicating that the mine will start very soon. However, this optimism

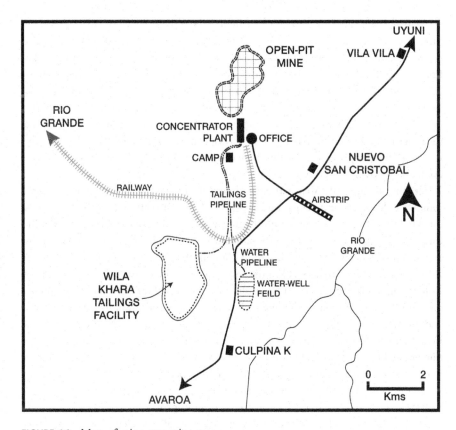

FIGURE 6.1 Map of mine operating area.

was completely crushed by the physical absence of Delgado from the MSC Bolivia management team. Delgado had decided to return to Spain for the benefit of his family and, although he had agreed to retain the title of President, in future he would only visit the country occasionally. The man who had given his promise of compliance with the agreements and in whom the communities had developed great trust was no longer there. Trust was lost and credibility in the company to deliver on any of the promises made declined.

Aware of the need to sustain a positive relationship with the communities the Bolivian management team, under the leadership of Executive President Carlos Fernandez, launched a limited programme of infrastructure improvements at the project site. Nonetheless, very little of the associated work went to local residents. Their perceptions of the company remained negative. The Bolivian government issued the environmental permits needed for the project to proceed to construction in 2001. However, community sentiment dipped further that year when MSC announced that it was putting the project on indefinite hold owing to a combination of low metal prices and high electricity prices. Sentiment in the communities became quite negative (#8 on Figure 5.4).

58 Retrospective from discovery to operating mine

Management at MSC in Bolivia realised that, to avoid the risk of social conflict, it was necessary to provide some form of employment and deliver on the commitments in the community agreements. The resources of the San Cristobal Foundation were employed to build a hotel, a solar greenhouse for the cultivation of vegetables, and other infrastructure projects to provide some employment. With funding from the Andean Development Corporation, a comprehensive series of projects in tourism, agriculture, and capacity building were launched. Regular meetings between senior management at MSC and community leaders became the norm, as did the presence of MSC managers at community open assemblies. The company recovered credibility.

Culpina K and Vila Vila participated actively in the agricultural improvement (quinoa cultivation and llama husbandry) and tourism programmes. Culpina K quickly began to expand quinoa production with the objective of creating a significant cash income from the crop. An initiative was implemented to attract tourists by creating novel streetscapes and interesting architectural forms. The project, known as '*Pueblos Modelos*' (model communities), was launched under the leadership of Bolivian artist Gaston Ugalde. The results were a blend of traditional-looking buildings and striking new forms in Culpina K such as a ziggurat, monumental archways, and metallic 'trees'. These confirmed opinions that Ugalde was the most important living artist in Bolivia, the Andean Andy Warhol. However, his creations were not universally liked by the local population. People in San Cristobal were less interested in the tourism and agricultural projects but entered the training and capacity-building programmes enthusiastically as preparation for employment in 'our mine'.

MSC also supported other projects such as improved roads, water supplies, and drainage systems for the expanding populations at San Cristobal and Culpina K. This provided employment and long-term benefits to the population. People saw MSC as a credible actor, genuinely interested in the best interests of the local population. Perceptions of MSC further improved (#9 on Figure 5.4).

In 2004, with improved metal prices and availability of financing from a consortium of banks, MSC was able to move forward with development of the San Cristobal mine. In August 2004, Fernandez travelled to all the communities and, at a series of open meetings, announced that construction would start immediately on an access road from the Chilean border to the west and the town of Uyuni to the east (see map in Figure 1.3). Construction of the mine would begin as soon as the access road had been completed and materials could be delivered to site. Credibility rose into the 'approval' level with this news (#10 on Figure 5.4).

Note

1 When asked much later why the committee had chosen the concrete panel wall construction over adobe, a community leader involved in the process answered: 'because the soil at the new site is totally unsuitable for making quality adobe' (R. Ramos, pers. comm., May 2015).

7

CONSTRUCTION

2004–2006

Following the announcement of the start of construction, MSC suggested that the communities carefully consider how they wished to interact with the outside workers who would arrive to help build the mine. The resulting 'rules' developed by Culpina K and San Cristobal suffered from a lack of real understanding of mine construction and were soon essentially abandoned.

Community leaders were also requested to prepare a list of individuals eligible for employment as members of the families registered as residents of San Cristobal, Culpina K, and Vila Vila. These became the master lists of persons that would be hired 'preferentially' by the company and its contractors. Positive anticipation of the long-awaited arrival of full time employment at the mine lifted credibility in the company to a new high (#11 on Figure 5.4).

Within Apex Silver, President Tom Kaplan announced his decision to step aside now that the mine was becoming a reality. The Board of Apex Silver appointed Jeff Clevenger, a man with proven mine development experience to replace Kaplan, along with a US-based senior management team filled with mine builders and operators. Notably, none of them had prior experience in Bolivia.

Simultaneously, MSC began assembling a team to manage construction and also let the first series of contracts for the construction of the road. Graham Buttenshaw, a highly qualified engineer with extensive experience in mine construction was appointed General Manager in November 2004. Shortly afterwards Carlos Fernandez left the company and Jonny Delgado resigned as President, ending what little contact and influence he had with the company and the communities.

For the parent company, Apex Silver, the long-term plan was for MSC to operate the mill and all other processing operations while the ore extraction aspects of mining would be contracted out, as would camp management and services. By late 2004, contracts had been signed with Washington Group for ore mining and with Catering International and Services (CIS) for camp management, catering, and services.

60 Retrospective from discovery to operating mine

New management team

By January of 2005, Buttenshaw had put a construction management team in place. It was made up almost entirely of expatriates (Australians, Canadians, and US citizens), none of whom had direct prior experience in Bolivia. Only one person remained who had participated in the exploration phase and negotiations for resettlement and who was familiar with the commitments made to the communities. As a Bolivian, he had little influence on the thinking of Buttenshaw and others for whom the objective was to build the mine to specifications on time and on budget. For all reasonable purposes, the management team was ignorant of the commitments and their social significance as fundamental to the relationship between MSC and its host communities.

Community leaders were disappointed about losing Fernandez and the relationship that had been built with him over the prior four years, but any misgivings were superseded by the prospect of employment. However, the newly arrived management team had not communicated the long-term plan to contract some operational aspects of the mine to Washington Group and CIS to the communities. As a result, when notices of work were posted by CIS and Washington Group inviting applications people, particularly in San Cristobal, sat back waiting for MSC to announce an invitation for people to work at the mine, where they knew they would have priority. By the time this confusion cleared, both Washington Group and CIS had hired a significant number of people, including individuals from other regions of Bolivia. The communities felt deceived and frustrated by the MSC management team.

Because the number of openings at Washington Group and CIS were limited early in construction, community members sought employment with other contractors. Here they encountered further frustration when they were rejected as unqualified for jobs in the trades. The training received earlier under the programmes provided by MSC had not been certified, and without certification was of no value in securing jobs. A further issue was social in nature. The local people found themselves to be the butt of jokes, the subject of jibes and racist remarks.

Men, and women, particularly those from San Cristobal felt marginalised and discriminated against at their mining project and on their land. They were angry and further frustrated because it seemed that management was indifferent to their situation. The situation was made worse by Buttenshaw refusing to meet with community leaders, delegating this to a two-person community relations team that was rapidly overwhelmed by the number and complexity of problems confronting them. From the community point of view the situation was intolerable. The company was not complying with the agreements made in 1998/9 and was doing nothing to mitigate the problems. Indeed, it was apparent that the senior manager was unaware of the commitments beyond that of employment. There was a rapid loss of credibility in the company and doubts as to the legitimacy of the way in which the new management was acting (#12 on Figure 5.4).

Construction 2004–2006 **61**

Nevertheless, the local population remained committed to the mine and wanted it to succeed. As such they resisted attempts by outside organisations, notably FRUTCAS, to convince them that mining would be a mistake. The commercial banks financing the project became concerned at the potential for disruption by outside elements when the documentary '*Les Trésors Maudits de l'Altiplano*' (The Cursed Treasures of the Altiplano) produced by Dominique Lenglat was broadcast on television in France during October 2004. The documentary followed Francisco Quisbert (of FRUTCAS) as he visited a number of mining locations on the Altiplano. It included segments highly critical of the mine development at San Cristobal. The banks were reassured by the news that when Quisbert came to the village of Culpina K in January 2005, he was rebuffed and physically removed by a group of residents. Local leadership took the position that the communities supported the mine; that the oversight of environmental concerns was in their hands; that outsiders who supported the operation were welcome, but that agitators who opposed the mine were not. Nevertheless, a movement against the mine, based largely on a perceived threat to the quality and quantity of potable groundwater, became active in Uyuni and among the small communities at a 'second-ring' distance from San Cristobal, such as Ramaditas (see map in Figure 1.3). Criticism and activism against the San Cristobal mine, much of it provoked and/or coordinated by FRUTCAS, continued throughout construction and influenced thinking among some members of the three host communities.

Big changes, rising anxieties

In May, 2005, MSC hired a woman with experience in mining to join the community relations team. The women in the communities were very pleased because they now had a potential contact that would understand their problems. However, employment issues, notably complaints of discrimination were escalating and now included complaints against the Human Resources staff of MSC. Pre-stripping of the open-pit had begun and groups of residents started to walk from San Cristobal up to the crest of the hills overlooking the bowl where they used to live to view progress. Many were horrified at the scale of the excavation underway. They had not understood how large a modern open-pit mine can be. For older members of the community, the point of reference had been the tunnels and openings of the Toldos and Animas underground mines. A number of older women were seen crying at the loss of the landscape that had been home for them.

The two-person community relations team came under significant stress, mostly because it lacked a plan of action and any team members with relevant experience. MSC hired a very highly qualified individual in July 2005 to provide leadership and direction to community relations and also to handle any issues related to land. A coherent, comprehensive plan for community relations and sustainable development was quickly prepared and put into action in August 2005. Unfortunately, the new head of community relations made a very poor impression on the local people

62 Retrospective from discovery to operating mine

who almost immediately labelled him as arrogant and racist. MSC brought in two outside consultants to cover specific areas of action. Tension was rising between the communities and MSC. The only source of legitimacy remaining was employment. Even this aspect was perceived to be under threat when, in July, Washington Group hired former employees of the Inti Raymi mine in contravention of an agreement made with the previous management team. Following a demonstration and vigorous negotiations, the matter was resolved in favour of the local workers.

Tensions were also rising within the communities. In San Cristobal, the individuals who had gained employment with Washington Group, and particularly those trained to operate the large haulage truck and other heavy equipment, self-declared as the 'real' miners. They were also the highest paid individuals and represented the emergence of an economic elite that challenged the traditional elites who gained status from age and experience. People working for CIS were the object of scorn as were others that worked supporting the contractors.

Mine employees were also spending money more freely. Confident of the continuity of employment, they started to purchase goods that were beyond the financial means of non-employees. The first open evidence of this phenomenon was the appearance of large numbers of motorcycles on the streets of the three villages. The germ of a service sector also first appeared at this time: a kiosk operated by an enterprising woman selling food in the square at San Cristobal in the evenings as workers came off shift.

Loss of legitimacy

On October 11, 2005, a bulldozer pushed a roadway through agricultural land to provide access to the area where a water-well field was to be drilled (see map in Figure 6.1). This act was seen as illegal by both San Cristobal and Culpina K as both the road and the well field were outside both the construction area agreed to with the communities and the land ceded under the land acquisition agreements (#13 on Figure 5.4).

The response was immediate. The company lost its social licence because it lost its legitimacy in the eyes of the community.

Men and women marched to the construction site and blockaded access for 48 hours while frantic negotiations took place to resolve the issue. At this point MSC management realised that there were no agreements in place for the well field, the access road to the well field, or the right of way for the rail spur to carry ore concentrates from the mine to the main rail line running to the port of Mejillones in Chile. Negotiating a full set of agreements became a priority, and subsequently drew in the community of Rio Grande since the rail spur would run through their community lands (see map in Figure 1.3).

A few days later, the woman community relations specialist was fired by MSC for helping a community member write a letter to the company. This act was seen by management as a conflict of interest. In response, a large group of women from all three communities marched on the company to demand her re-instatement.

However, the march was overtaken by the men who voiced a larger range of complaints related to employment, conditions of work with the contractors and sub-contractors, and, most particularly, claims of incompetence, discrimination, and failure to keep promises by the head of the MSC community relations group. There was a specific demand for the dismissal of the head of community relations, who the communities had come to dislike personally. There were also complaints of non-compliance with the community agreements. The demonstration and blockade with threats of violence persisted for 48 hours during which there were negotiations between the company and community leaders.

This was the nadir of company-community relations. Many in the community saw the company as violating social norms of equality (Figure 2.1). Moreover, the company's behaviour confirmed the worst stereotypes of foreigners and neo-liberalism that were then being propagated by Evo Morales, his MAS, party, and allied government opponents. For community members, all of their concepts of fairness were being violated.

At the request of the community leaders, Jonny Delgado was flown in to help reduce tensions and negotiate a solution. Trusted by the communities, he was able to broker an agreement that the head of community relations must leave and the company would review working conditions with the contractors. The remaining community relations personnel resigned in frustration.

Two points of significance emerged at this point. First, the USA-based senior management of Apex Silver were shaken by the two, closely spaced demonstrations and blockades, which they erroneously saw as law and order issues. It was not until much later that they came to understand that negotiation through confrontation is a cultural norm in Bolivia. Nevertheless, at the time, the US-based management of Apex Silver were alarmed at the character of the confrontation and actively considered the idea of having armed guards. Fortunately, this proposal was subsequently withdrawn. Second, these episodes also marked a beginning of a difficult period for the community relations team. The company came to think that the community relations team was working for the community, while the community thought it was working for the company.

During November 2005, three new people were hired as community relations specialists. Unfortunately, all three lacked materially useful experience with mining and none had worked on a mine construction project. Into 2006, tensions continued over employment, land issues, dust, and, with increasing frequency, water and the security of the Wila Khara tailings storage facility. Residents of Culpina K became increasingly fearful that the tailings impoundment would leak, contaminating the potable groundwater used by the community (see map in Figure 6.1). Despite meetings and briefings from the company on the management procedures that were to be applied to mitigate these risks, and additional geotechnical studies that confirmed the integrity of the closed basin, these fears persisted.

January 2006, saw the appointment of a new manager for Human Resources, who was also given responsibility for Community Relations and Sustainable Development. Despite a lack of experience in these areas, he was sensitive to the complexity of the challenges and willing to listen. He also instituted regular meetings with community leaders. Relations recovered a little. Significant tensions remained, however, and were sustained in part by dysfunctional aspects of the community relations team. It was marked by competition for influence, poor coordination, and weak interpersonal relationships with community leaders.

As pre-stripping of the open-pit became well advanced, many residents of San Cristobal, particularly the elderly and most of the women, became concerned for the fate of the sacred stones that had been important features of the spiritual life of the community. In February 2006, there was considerable relief when the greater part of Achopalla and its companion stone were brought down to New San Cristobal and subsequently erected in a memorial park (see Figure 7.1). A ceremony of farewell and forgiveness was held that helped stabilise emotions and ameliorate the sense of loss of the old settlement.

At the same time, however, residents of the three villages were increasingly concerned that they would not get the promised jobs at the mine. They saw construction advancing with operations due to start within months but no sign of any training for employment. Surrounded by qualified individuals contracted to construct the mine, they saw themselves losing out to people with proven skills, experience, and trade certificates. In San Cristobal, there was fear that outsiders will benefit from 'our' mine – repeating a pattern dating back to Spanish colonial times.

FIGURE 7.1 Achopalla: sacred boulder moved to new town.

Tensions boiled over at the end of March 2006, with demonstrations and confrontations on consecutive days. The confrontation included physical violence as well as causing a further 48-hour blockade and work stoppage during construction. The principle issues concerned employment. The company described the brief conflict as 'labour related'. The demonstration was precipitated by the decision by MSC to bring in an outside security company. This was seen by local people as a provocation and a reason to protest. They feared they would be discriminated against by the outsiders and lose access to the area around the mine site. To this was added a demand for the removal of two middle managers seen as disrespectful or unreliable by the community, and a litany of complaints about working conditions with contractors and sub-contractors. Anxious to avoid further violence, the company agreed to remove the two middle managers in question.

This event demonstrated the need for an effective grievance mechanism to process the complaints, which had been lacking to that date. More importantly, this was a social conflict related to sensations of injustice and inequity on the part of the three communities. Deep frustration existed because written commitments in the contracts from the negotiations around resettlement and land acquisition were not being kept. The unwritten agreement to be partners in the mine had been betrayed. Community opinions of the company reached an all-time low.

By this point in the construction phase, complaints of discrimination had become almost constant. Indeed, there was ample evidence of frequent discrimination against local people in the work place, which verged on abuse, and was most prevalent among the subcontractors. Much of this arose from the strong regional rivalries that exist within Bolivia. In particular, people from Santa Cruz regarded the rural people of the Altiplano as ignorant and primitive and treated them accordingly, creating tension when these attitudes were expressed by managers and supervisors. By the same token, the local population saw themselves as masters in their own house, working in 'their' mine, and frequently treated 'outsiders' in an equally discriminatory and abusive way. Typically, this treatment was aimed at co-workers. The lack of support from MSC in dealing with the problem was the much greater issue for residents of the three communities.

Tensions were also present in the communities in the form of continuing struggles for power and influence. The leadership of Culpina K was challenged and displaced at the same time as the confrontation with the company. Wealth was increasing with trucks and SUVs replacing motorcycles. New elites were emerging and asserting themselves on the basis of wealth and possessions.

Recovery of legitimacy

Relations with the community began to improve just months after Evo Morales became President of Bolivia. In August 2006, the company organised a Job Fair at which all the potential employment opportunities with the company were on display. The Fair was only open to local residents and all were invited to apply for the jobs that interested them. Both men and women attended the Fair and

66 Retrospective from discovery to operating mine

signed up eagerly. The company had deliberately structured manpower requirements and shift patterns to maximise employment opportunities. It had also contracted a Chilean organisation to screen applicants and provide training. Most importantly, the criteria for eligibility for employment were kept deliberately simple – to be eligible for employment required basic literacy: to be able to read and understand the health and safety instructions. The Chilean organisation then interviewed all applicants and assessed them on the basis of interest and aptitude for particular tasks. Training and jobs were assigned on this basis. Individuals lacking in literacy skills were given literacy training and allowed to re-apply once they had reached the minimum skill level. The communities were very pleased to see this approach to employment and considered this as fully meeting the relevant commitment in the community agreements. MSC had recovered at least some credibility (#14 on Figure 5.4).

Water was, and remains, a constant issue. Families continued to return to the three villages in search of work at the mine, putting stress on available water supplies and sewage treatment facilities. Community leaders petitioned the company to upgrade facilities in compliance with the obligations assumed in the agreements. Preoccupied with the construction, the company was slow to respond. The waste water treatment system for the construction workers camp became overloaded during peak occupancy and failed repeatedly, allowing an unknown quantity of raw sewage to flow into the watercourse below the camp. MSC made modifications to the water treatment plant and changed the way in which grey and black water streams were processed, resulting in an improvement in the quality of water discharged. Discharge water quality was reported by MSC to be within legally acceptable norms. However, the situation remained socially unacceptable because of the persistence of fetid, black, organic-rich sediment (remnants of the sewage sludge discharged the previous year) and residues in the water that made it unpalatable for llamas.

In September 2006, MSC experienced a shake-up in its ownership and financing. Sumitomo Corporation of Japan joined the project by taking a 35 per cent ownership stake. At the same time, the commercial banks that were funding the project and that were concerned at the high levels of social tension, put pressure on MSC to change its management and approach. During September 2006, a new leader of the community relations and sustainable development team was appointed. Juan Mamani, an indigenous Bolivian, Quechua-speaking and familiar with the local people and culture, was immediately welcomed by the communities. His hire was accompanied by the arrival of Javier Diez de Medina as a consultant who brought in a number of innovations appreciated by the local population. Simultaneously, the problematic community relations personnel left, which made room for the initial hiring of what has become the long-term team.

Buttenshaw took a planned leave of absence and was replaced by an acting manager willing to interact directly with community leaders. Regular meetings between MSC management and community leaders were restored. The acting manager also met with community members from Culpina K on site at the Wila

Khara tailings facility to discuss their concerns. People started to believe that the company was really listening to them again and treating them with respect.

With construction nearing completion and training of workers underway, some community leaders began to think about the longer-term future after the mine closes. In San Cristobal a small group, self-identified as the *Soñadores* (Dreamers), began meeting and developed a number of concrete ideas which they brought to the company and the community of San Cristobal. From this grew the concept of a leadership group from the four communities directly linked to the mine: San Cristobal, Culpina K, Vila Vila, and Rio Grande. With the support of MSC the *Consejo Consultivo* was formed.

The message from MSC was one of empowerment. The *Consejo Consultivo* would provide leadership in ideas and initiatives for the long-term well-being and sustainability of the communities. The metaphor provided was of a large truck. The truck represented the population of the four villages. The *Consejo Consultivo* was the driver who decides where to go and how to get there. MSC would provide some gas (money) to get the journey started and would be available with spare parts (legal and technical assistance) as needed. However, it was up to the *Consejo Consultivo* to decide when it wanted help from the company. For many in San Cristobal, the sensation of being partners in the mining project had finally returned. There were many commitments still outstanding from the community agreements, but in the eyes of the people, the company was once again truly a credible actor (#15 on Figure 5.4).

A third event was also expressive of the rapidly improving relationship between MSC and its neighbours. Community leaders in San Cristobal became concerned that a small number of women heads of single parent families were falling behind in access to employment and income, rendering their children more vulnerable. The community approached the company with a direct request to find the best-paying jobs possible for these women. MSC agreed to the proposal and subjected the women to the same screening process applied to all other applicants, offered literacy training to the few that needed to gain additional skills, and then placed them in jobs for which they were judged to be most suited. This example of collaboration was perceived as yet further evidence that, now that the chaos of construction was receding, the company would work with the community to resolve problems.

8

TRANSITION TO OPERATING MINE

2007–2009

The San Cristobal mine was designed to be a highly mechanised open-pit operation with a flotation mill processing 40,000 tonnes per day of mineralised material producing silver-zinc and silver-lead concentrates to be shipped to Japan, Europe, and other world destinations via the port of Mejillones on the coast of Chile. At the outset, the plan was to operate the mine as three units: physical mining under contract to Washington Group; mineral processing, recovery, and sale of concentrates as a wholly owned aspect of the mine; and, camp and catering contracted to a specialist company. On the way to achieving this plan, several adjustments had to be made by both the company and the stakeholders.

Adjustments to start-up and full operation

With employment at the mine secure, tensions between the company and community continued to decrease. Buttenshaw returned from leave of absence at the end of 2006 more open, understanding, and willing to continue the pattern of regular meetings with the community. By early 2007, the mine was beginning to function as an integrated operation and the process of optimising all aspects of the production cycle was underway. Residents of the three villages started to adjust to the rhythm of shift work. Further changes in management saw the Human Resources manager replaced by a Bolivian already well known and respected by the communities.

Development agreements with first-ring communities

In August 2007, the mine declared production start-up. Throughout 2007, the company negotiated a series of agreements with San Cristobal, Culpina K, Vila Vila, and Rio Grande that defined roles and responsibilities into the future with

Transition to operating mine **69**

respect to initiatives related to social and economic development and infrastructure, including the nature of the relationship with the *Consejo Consultivo*. This further stabilised relationships and improved confidence in MSC within and between the communities.

The latter part of the year saw renewed labour tensions with Washington Group and a series of strikes and stoppages that turned violent. Many of the problems that arose during construction remained the cause of friction. Community leaders appealed to MSC to intervene, which led to necessary negotiations and realisation by all parties that a clear distinction could usefully be made between labour issues and strictly social and community matters. The relationship was starting to evolve towards one based on institutional factors rather than individual contacts, persons, and personalities.

A major milestone was reached in November 2007. Monthly assemblies were held as usual in San Cristobal, Culpina K, and Vila Vila and, for the first time in more than two years there were no complaints or votes against MSC. Community feelings towards the company were uniformly positive. Full credibility had been regained (#16 on Figure 5.4).

Llamas, dust, and in-migration

Although operations began in late 2007, full production was not achieved until 2008. Washington Group was discharged from contract mining in 2010 and operations were consolidated into two units (mine and processing plant) that were administered by MSC.

Also in 2007, the relocation of llama herds away from the open-pit and tailings facility began. Problems arose almost immediately, which in turn created new tensions both with MSC and among families of the communities (see Chapter 14). Similarly, with the tailings facility now functioning, there were renewed concerns about the integrity of the impoundment, the risk to groundwater, and, for the first time, dust contamination.

Through 2007 to 2009, dust had become an issue at the mine and mill site as well. There were concerns about the contamination of llama grazing areas and agricultural land as well as worries about the possible impacts on the health of workers. However, dialogue and negotiation continued and, while people were concerned, they believe they were being listened to. Credibility in the company began to solidify.

In-migration of families continued through 2008, putting pressure on MSC to hire individuals declared to be eligible. The in-migration also created pressure to upgrade water and sewage treatment facilities to cope with the expanding population.

The retrospective study described in the section of Chapter 5 entitled, 'Methods used for the 1994 to 2008 San Cristobal case study' did not go beyond 2008. However, the effort to track levels of community social acceptance of the MSC continued both formally and informally. In the remainder of this chapter we include informal observations of how the social licence fluctuated all the way through to 2009.

70 Retrospective from discovery to operating mine

Water worries

Concerns about water are a permanent feature of life in an arid region like Nor Lípez. However, around 2009, three reports were published that brought criticism of MSC's water use to heights not seen before or since. For that reason, we review the whole chronology of water issues in this chapter dealing with the 2007 to 2009 period.

Specifics of the arid environment

Immediately south of the mine at an elevation of almost 4,500 metres on the summit of Irucancha is a view point constructed by MSC as one of the commitments under the resettlement agreement with San Cristobal. The view point was built to allow tourists to see into the mine workings. It also offers a full 360-degree view of the region around San Cristobal. To the north, the scene is dominated by the vast, bright whiteness of the Uyuni salt flats (i.e., '*El Salar de Uyuni*'). To the east, the jagged peaks of the eastern Cordillera of the Andean mountains are clearly visible. To the west and south, the vista is of the Altiplano with its sweeping, open planes with white patches of salt flats between broken hills. Way off on the western and southern horizon, the conical peaks of snow-capped volcanoes are visible along the western Cordillera and the border with Chile. The landscape is bare, dun-coloured, and treeless. It is a semi-desert where surface water is usually saline. The few places where fresh water can be found are highly valued for use by people and animals.

Nor Lípez is classified as a cool desert with well-defined wet and dry seasons. It is characterised by warm days of bright sun, cool clear nights, and strong winds, particularly in the afternoon. Precipitation in the form of rain and snow comes with moist air drawn in from the Atlantic Ocean during the months from November to March. Overall precipitation varies with altitude, falling preferentially on the hills across the Altiplano, and decreasing systematically from east to west. Daily monitoring over a nine-year period reveals an average annual precipitation of 239 millimetres (a little less than 10 inches) at and around the San Cristobal mine site. The data also confirm local knowledge that precipitation is unpredictable with noticeably wet (e.g. 355 millimetres in 2011) and dry (e.g. 121 millimetres in 2016) years. Everyone is deeply conscious of the impact this variability has on the productivity of their crops and the well-being of llama herds. Furthermore, the strong sunlight of the Altiplano, together with the low humidity of the desert and persistent strong winds result in extreme rates of surface evaporation. At San Cristobal, the average annual water loss to evaporation is 2,251 millimetres. The net result is an average moisture deficit of around 2,000 millimetres (close to 80 inches) per year, which easily explains the presence of salt flats and areas of saline efflorescence in soils.

In Nor Lípez, fresh water is scarce and precious. For people and animals, it is a matter of life and death. For MSC it is a strategic resource that must be managed with care.

Water for the mine

Water consumption at the mine is a highly sensitive issue from an environmental and social point of view and remains an ongoing concern for local and national stakeholders, particularly for the surrounding communities. This should not be a surprise. A rule of thumb for metal mines which, as in the case of San Cristobal, produce a sulphide concentrate as the final product for sale and export, is that to process each tonne of ore requires one cubic metre of water.

The project description and accompanying technical chapters in the 2000 EIA documents for the San Cristobal mine called for processing water to be sourced from a deep subterranean aquifer located some 10 kilometres south-west of the mine site (see map in Figure 6.1). After being used to produce silver-bearing zinc and lead concentrates, the water would be pumped as slurry with pulverised waste rock to the Wila Khara tailings disposal facility. There it would be lost to evaporation (Knight Piesold, 2000).

In the EIA (Knight Piesold, 2000), this water source, now known as the Jaukihua Aquifer, was characterised as highly saline and not suitable for direct human or animal consumption, or even for irrigation without treatment. In practice, it is not only saline but also moderately corrosive on low quality steel. Its corrosive character became evident when the metal casings in early development water wells collapsed during testing, ahead of mine start-up, and had to be replaced with higher quality steel. The replacement of the well casings was a costly exercise that also resulted in a water shortage during the early stages of start-up.

From the beginning of construction, the mine came under heavy criticism for allowing water to simply evaporate from the tailings facility. Coupled with the cubic metre per tonne quantity of water required for mineral processing, these processes seen as a wasteful way to use a scarce resource. Furthermore, the EIA mentioned a risk of drawing down the near-surface fresh water aquifers used by local residents. In response to these issues, the mine took early steps to reduce water usage.

When full production was first achieved in late 2007, the mine was processing 40,000 tonnes per day of ore, which required some 40,000 cubic metres per day of water for processing. MSC had become the largest industrial user of water in Bolivia. However, beginning in mid-2008, the mine began recycling water from the Wila Khara tailings confinement back to the mill for re-use in the concentrator plant. This was achieved by constructing a sump pond in the tailing facility, a pumping station, and a pipeline back to the plant site. Shortly afterwards, MSC adopted a policy of promoting technical studies and innovation to reduce the intake of aquifer water in all aspects of the mine operation.

Today, in addition to recycling water from the tailings facility, all rainwater and drainage water from the open-pit is collected and redirected for use in the mill. Similarly, waste water from the camp site and commissariat, which formerly was discharged into an adjacent stream after treatment, is now recycled for use in dust control on the mine roads. Technical innovations include a modification to the

72 Retrospective from discovery to operating mine

tailings thickeners that increases water recovery, for which an international patent has been obtained. As of 2015, the mine has a zero-discharge policy and does not release any waste water outside of the area of operations.

Cumulatively, these initiatives have drastically reduced the need to draw water from the Jaukihua Aquifer. At the same time, mine throughput has increased to more than 50,000 tonnes of ore per day. The net result is the need to pump 'new' water from the Jaukihua well field has declined substantially and is now, on average, close to 0.5 cubic metres per tonne of ore processed, a 50 per cent reduction over the situation at the beginning of 2008.

Despite these technical achievements, MSC continues to come under criticism and close scrutiny from stakeholders because of the quantity of water used in mineral processing and, as described below, because of the fears and beliefs of communities in many parts of the provinces of Nor Lípez, Sud Lípez, and Enrique Baldivieso (i.e., essentially the south-west corner of Bolivia, see map in Figure 1.2).

Water for the communities

The agreements signed between the company and San Cristobal, Culpina K, and Vila Vila for resettlement and land acquisition all included requirements to build domestic water supplies and waste water treatment systems for the communities. In the case of San Cristobal, the agreement required the company to provide 200 fully serviced building lots plus services for a school, hospital, and other utilities. Planning and construction of the water supply and waste water treatment system was based on a projected population of approximately 1,000 persons. The potable water was to come from the *Aguas Claras* springs in the hills north of the village (Knight Piesold, 2001). The population of San Cristobal at the time of the resettlement was 450 individuals in 140 houses with 130 pupils in the school.

With Culpina K, the agreement was more specific in designating the Kaysur spring, located 8 kilometres north of the village, as the water source to be developed.

For all the communities, the desire and expectation was for a gravity-fed water supply and treatment system that would be reliable, inexpensive to operate, and easy to maintain. For its part, the company anticipated handing over responsibility for domestic water supply and waste water management to the municipality of Colcha K once royalty and tax monies started flowing to the municipal government from the operating mine.

Documents and statements included in the EIA for the mine (Knight Piesold, 2000) and in the subsequent Social Management Plan (Knight Piesold, 2001) indicated that the company fully complied with the terms of the agreements. However, by 2004 with the population of San Cristobal estimated at 1,000 individuals in 200 houses, strains were appearing in the water systems. Due to the level of immigration by returning family members, the supply of water to Culpina K and San Cristobal was nearing its maximum capacity. In practice, the majority of the returning families and individuals moved in to live with parents or other family members. Hence the rate of population increase was greater than that of house building.

Transition to operating mine **73**

In 2005, the sewage processing system at San Cristobal failed, having become overloaded due to population growth. It had to be expanded. Through 2006 and 2007, water demand grew in tandem with population growth as families continued to return to the local communities in search of work in construction and, ultimately, at the mine. Water supplies became severely stressed. MSC found it necessary to arrange a supply of 'top-up' water for San Cristobal and Culpina K. This additional water was brought to the villages by road in tanker trucks.

At the same time, concerns grew in Culpina K that groundwater wells supplying the village would become contaminated by seepage from the nearby Wila Khara tailings disposal site and that over time all wells would run dry. The fear was that the water table would be drawn down by the company pumping groundwater to supply the mine. In response to the concerns in Culpina K, MSC conducted further hydrogeological studies. The study process confirmed the security of the tailings impoundment and involved the community in monitoring the tailings impoundment and the quality of the water in the village wells. Over time concerns for contamination from the tailings diminished. By 2014, concerns had largely disappeared. On the other hand, concern for the potential drawdown of the near-surface water table (a risk noted in the Knight Piesold (2000) EIA) continued undiminished and became central to the argument for obtaining water from a source that would be stable over the long term.

With stability of employment and regular income, families started moving out of shared housing and building their own homes. By mid-2009, daily per capita use of water in San Cristobal exceeded that in the city of La Paz. At the time, the company thought this would be a temporary situation and that seasonal shortages could be offset by supplies brought in by tankers to meet daily demand. However, the building boom continued, albeit at a reduced rate, into the next decade because existing families expanded and improved their homes and the population of the village continued to grow. Regardless of what was written in the various agreements, the communities considered MSC responsible for guaranteeing an adequate supply of water under their traditional understanding of reciprocity in the relationship, which was essentially, 'We moved and gave up land for your benefit so you are obligated to look after us'. More explicitly, this was seen as an obligation in perpetuity that could not be transferred to the municipality or any other authority normally responsible for public infrastructure.

In the following years, MSC came under intense pressure to solve the water supply issue for San Cristobal and Culpina K as these two villages continued to expand owing partly to in-migration and, more visibly, as a consequence of a very healthy baby boom. By 2015, the population of San Cristobal had increased to an estimated 2,000 individuals with 1,000 pupils in the schools. In response, the company, in concert with the communities, initiated a search for alternate permanent sources of water while continuing to supply both San Cristobal and Culpina K with water by tanker from sources outside of the immediate area. MSC reluctantly found itself acting as a surrogate government and set up a unit within the Community Relations/Sustainable Development group

74 Retrospective from discovery to operating mine

to handle infrastructure needs. Meanwhile, there was an increasing flow of tax monies to the local municipality, which should have been taking responsibility for municipal infrastructure, but which for the time being lacked the capacity to do so. MSC proposed to offset any shortfall in existing water supplies to San Cristobal and Culpina K by drilling wells and installing pumps but there was significant pushback from communities. The residents wanted a gravity supply system. Nevertheless, wells were drilled to access sources of potable groundwater and pumps were installed to transport the water to individual households. This was accepted on the understanding that the wells represented a strictly interim solution to the water problem.

Vila Vila also experienced population growth but because it was a smaller community did not experience the same extreme levels of water stress encountered by San Cristobal and Culpina K. Modifications to the existing water supply were sufficient to provide for the expanded population.

The search for sufficient water to supply San Cristobal and Culpina K into the future was ultimately successful in 2013 when a source was found that would offer both sufficient quantity of potable water and a gravity supply to the two communities. However, this source was in the lands of another community and construction of an intake and aqueduct required an agreement with this community and potentially another as well. At this point the direct involvement of the municipality of Colcha K became essential. It was the local government common to all of the communities involved and thus the umbrella authority for any agreement to access the water and build pipelines. However, at the time, the municipality continued to lack the capacity to take action.

In 2014, with the help of MSC, the municipality of Colcha K started to gain the capacity to manage its own infrastructure projects. At the same time, the leadership in San Cristobal and Culpina K came to accept that the long-term security of water supplies lies with the municipality. In this environment, MSC moved to support the development of the distant water source with design and engineering studies. At the time of this writing, negotiations are well advanced between the municipality and the various communities to allow the development of this distant water source. It is now anticipated that funding for the new water supply system will come from the municipality, which will assume long-term responsibility for the management and maintenance of the source and the pipeline to San Cristobal and Culpina K.

Water and the region

Almost as soon as Larry Buchanan identified the vast potential of the mineralisation at San Cristobal, the project became the locus of controversy. At various times, there have been active movements to nationalise the mine, to have it transferred to local 'cooperativas', to get access to revenues from the mine, to expand employment at the mine, and to deal with assorted social and environmental impacts of the mine. However, the most enduring controversy has been around the potential impacts, perceived and actual, of the mine on water.

During the early life of the project, as exploration advanced and the resettlement of San Cristobal took place, there was a concerted campaign against mine development led by FRUTCAS with a particular emphasis on the risk of severe environmental harm. This included warnings that mining would pollute the water and cause multiple health problems including birth defects and deaths. Away from the core communities of San Cristobal, Culpina K, and Vila Vila, people became fearful that the mine, however distant, could cause them harm. There was, after all, plenty of visible evidence of contamination, acid drainage, and poisoned water around the numerous mines throughout western Bolivia abandoned when the tin industry collapsed only a few years earlier.

With the deferral of further development in 1999/2000, the controversy died down only to re-emerge in 2004/2005 when the company announced the start of construction. FRUTCAS again raised concerns about water pollution by the mine.

Very soon thereafter another concern about the mine's impact on water was added: climate change. By 2006, Nor Lípez and adjacent provinces were entering the fifth year of a drought. People were witnessing fresh water springs drying up in many places. They believed that the winters were getting warmer and that the southern Altiplano's legendary winds were becoming weaker and less persistent. *Campesino* observations of changing weather patterns based on traditional knowledge were now supported by scientific observations: climate change was real. From this reality, a new controversy emerged and came to dominate conversations and politics about the mine. The question became, 'what is the impact of the mine on existing and future water supplies?'

The opponents of capitalist globalisation took note and quickly constructed a new discourse to blame the impacts of climate change on this specific mine. Fransico Quisbert linked up with Oscar Olivera, who had led the Water War in Cochabamba, to disseminate the idea that the mine was not only a source of contamination but that it was also going to destroy water sources and cause desertification of the region. Quisbert, through FRUTCAS and Olivera, operated through the non-governmental organisation (NGO) *Comisión para la Gestión Integral del Agua en Bolivia* (CGIAB, The Commission for the Integrated Management of Water in Bolivia). They started to question the reliability of the scientific studies behind the EIA for the mine and declared that there had not been full disclosure to the impacted communities.

From declarations, the controversy was soon augmented by independent studies. An early example is the work of Jorge Molina, a professor at the University Mayor de San Andres in La Paz, Bolivia. His 2007 study (Molina, 2007) on water in the southern parts of the department of Potosí included an analysis of the situation at San Cristobal. Molina had access to the San Cristobal EIA and, while agreeing with much of the work, was highly critical of the modelling of draw-down and recharge of the Jaukihua Aquifer, which he considered grossly underestimated the amount of drawdown and overestimated the rate of recharge. Molina also drew attention to the fact that there was no fee, tax, or royalty paid for the use of this water.

76 Retrospective from discovery to operating mine

Other studies emerged over the following two years (e.g., López, 2009; López and Ferrufino, 2009), which further questioned both the reliability of the EIA and the existing regulations that allowed San Cristobal to use what were, in Bolivian terms, and in a semi-desert environment, vast quantities of water. Although some studies acknowledged that the water was not suitable for drinking, bathing, or irrigation, they raised the more worrying fear that this rapid and significant drawdown of a deeper aquifer would inevitably affect groundwater closer to the surface. That, in turn, might exhaust the supply to wells and springs used by local people. The discourse resonated with the observations and concerns of residents in Culpina K.

FRUTCAS and CGIAB, in collaboration with other NGOs, arranged various fora and conventions at which water was the subject of discussion and San Cristobal invariably the focus of presentations and analyses. At the same time, a growing number of communities across Lípez were attributing declining or lost flow of water in wells and springs directly to the opening and operation of the mine at San Cristobal. This included communities and settlements hundreds of kilometres, and beyond mountain ranges, from San Cristobal in locations where, from the perspective of geoscience and hydrogeology, it is physically impossible for the mine to have affected underground and surface water bodies. For example, loss of water supplies was one of the complaints against the company raised by the people of San Pedro de Quemes in the 2010 conflict with Minera San Cristobal. Pressure on the mine increased even further when FRUTCAS and CGIAB brought in Robert Moran, an international consultant based in the United States, to evaluate the situation at San Cristobal. His report (Moran, 2009) confirmed much of the earlier work by Bolivian investigators but also raised the level of controversy by stating categorically that the mine definitely would affect surface springs and wells in the area. Equally significantly, the title of his report, *Mining Water*, allowed people to infer that the mine was using fossil water, trapped underground for millennia and that the mine was depleting permanently, for free.

Public awareness of water issues, climate change, and their relationship to industrial activity increased at this time as a result of media reports of the April 2010 World People's Conference on Climate Change and the Rights of Mother Earth. This meeting was hosted by the Morales government in Cochabamba. The final communiqué (People's Agreement) from the conference was highly critical of the capitalist system, which was described as directly responsible for climate change. In response, delegates to the conference proposed:

> the recovery, revalorization, and strengthening of the knowledge, wisdom, and ancestral practices of Indigenous Peoples, which are affirmed in the thought and practices of "Living Well," recognizing Mother Earth as a living being with which we have an indivisible, interdependent, complementary and spiritual relationship
>
> *World People's Conference, 2010*

Needing to respond to criticism and wishing to move the controversy away from a trajectory towards violent confrontation, the company opened a dialogue with FRUTCAS and subsequently established the basis for working together in a multi-party Environmental and Economic Development Commission to address regional environmental issues (principally water) and to pursue economic development opportunities. Acknowledging that the claims in the Moran report raised serious concerns, one of the first initiatives was a broader, independent study of water in Lípez with an emphasis on water use by the mine. The multi-party study was designed to have legitimacy and credibility through strong Bolivian participation. It was led by Niltetsu Mining Consultants but featured the direct involvement of FRUTCAS and support from Bolivian academic experts, consultants, and government specialists. It was financed by Japan Oil and Gas Corporation and Sumitomo. The study group completed a series of intensive investigations between October 2010 and June 2011. The final report, published in 2012, dismissed the idea that the mine was using fossil water. Moreover, it established that the Jaukihua Aquifer is recharged from the adjacent uplands and is open to the south-west where it adjoins a larger valley aquifer, which no one uses. The report also contradicted Moran's claims of effects on surface water. It was found that the Jaukihua Aquifer is too small, in comparison with adjacent aquifers, to affect surface waters, water wells, and springs beyond the immediate area of the Jaukihua basin. The springs that are locally important to San Cristobal, Culpina K, and Vila Vila cannot be affected by the drawdown because they are supplied by bedrock sources in the hills behind them (Minera San Cristobal, 2014).

Following release of the report, criticism from FRUTCAS, CGIAB, and others on water use by the mine diminished, although the topic continues to surface from time to time as communities across Lípez experience the growing impact of climate change in the form of diminished fresh water supplies. Water continues to be a highly emotional issue across the Altiplano and throughout the highlands of western Bolivia. Most recently, there have been claims that falling water levels in Laguna Colorado, located several hundred kilometres south-west of San Cristobal near the border with Chile are the result of 'excessive water use by the mine': a geological and hydrological impossibility. The question of payment for water uses has also resurfaced several times as part of political posturing but to date has failed to gain sustained traction with governments or the general population.

Further observations beyond the retrospective study

New mine management

Buttenshaw left MSC at the end of 2007. He was given a farewell ceremony by the communities at which there was mutual recognition of many lessons learned over the previous three years. He was replaced by Mike Bunch, a manager with a personality, philosophy, and communications style that quickly made a very positive impression on both employees at the mine and members of the greater community.

78 Retrospective from discovery to operating mine

Achieving full production at the mine proved to be technically challenging and the ramp-up process continued into 2008. In February, the tailing pipeline ruptured causing a large spill, which was quickly cleaned up. Residents were impressed by the speed of the response, the quality of the clean-up, and the close interaction with government regulators. Workers at the mine gained a sense of pride from the way this event was managed. Residents in the communities were similarly pleased at the way 'their mine' handled the situation.

During 2008, Sumitomo Corporation, a minority shareholder, initiated a restructuring of operations. Apex Silver was still the major shareholder but was facing financial extinction owing to cost overruns during construction and the costs of bank financing. In March 2009, Sumitomo assumed full (100 per cent) ownership of MSC.

Symbols of equality and respect

MSC adopted an equality policy that formalised some of the initiatives already in place. For example, now there was a single dining area for all workers and employees at the camp, whereas during construction there had been separate dining areas for managers. Also, everyone at the mine began wearing white safety helmets, contrary to the previous policy under which various categories of worker had coloured safety helmets with only managers wearing white. These were symbols with a major impact on individual attitudes in the work place and were also noted by family members and the greater community.

In May 2008, the President of Bolivia, Evo Morales, visited a pilot project for lithium recovery from the Salar de Uyuni. It was operated by COMIBOL and situated close to Rio Grande. The *Consejo Consultivo*, together with a delegation of MSC workers, travelled to Rio Grande and made a presentation to Morales. They stressed the importance of the mine to them, their satisfaction and commitment to working with and for MSC, and their desire not to see the company captured into the programme of nationalisation being promoted by the President (#17 on Figure 5.4).

In June 2009, President Evo Morales visited the MSC mine in person. The managers of the mine, all expatriates, briefly welcomed him. The main hosting responsibilities, however, were performed by local workers who guided their President around the mine site. Evo was as impressed by the pride the workers took in their mine as by the operation itself. As for the local community, pride in the mine and positive feeling towards MSC reached a new high.

Modernisation and the prophecy about abandoning the old ways

By mid-2008, some of the consequences of the presence of the mine were becoming visible. For example:

- Malnutrition had declined dramatically. Through company-sponsored programmes directed at employees and their families, people in general gained far more knowledge about good health and nutrition. There was an impressive improvement in the health of the population.
- From 1994 to 2008, education was upgraded from a one room classroom to a full complement of kindergarten to post-secondary education. This, of course, included numerous new buildings and classrooms. At first, there was a loss of almost all of the experienced school teachers because they went to work for much higher wages at the mine. As amenities in the towns improved, new teachers were attracted.
- There was an explosion of house construction and improvement in all the first-ring communities as young families built homes. This put additional strain on recently expanded and improved infrastructure.
- In 2008, people were still moving into the villages with the intention of seeking work at the mine, which placed additional demands on community resources and infrastructure.
- The number of vehicles increased dramatically (Figure 8.1). The favourites were pick-up trucks or SUVs. 'No Parking' signs began to appear in front of private driveway gates.
- The local inflation grew but exact figures are not available due to a lack of reliable baseline data.

FIGURE 8.1 On-street parking in San Cristobal.

80 Retrospective from discovery to operating mine

In summary, the towns closest to the mine began to have better problems. Instead of problems related to poverty, they had problems related to economic growth. As predicted by the prophecy, people became so rich they neglected to count their change in the marketplace. Nonetheless, some residents felt that there was another kind of loss as well; the loss of the old culture.

One version of the prophecy included the detail that people would live in housing with roofs that would shine in the sun. The selection of metal roofs by the resettlement committee (Chapter 6 'From Geological Discovery to Construction, 1994–2004') fulfilled this detail in the prophecy. More central to the prophecies was the idea that the people who received the gift of El Tío would abandon the old ways. By 2008, signs of this began to appear. Community authorities were concerned about the declining participation in community activities, particularly by younger people. They attributed the decline to a shortage of free time caused by so many people having full time employment.

Between 1994 and 2009, the first-ring communities had undergone a transformation that took hundreds of years in European society. However, the process was not smooth. In 2010 and 2011, there were two larger-scale conflicts that had elements from the distant past (see Chapters 1 and 2), the last four centuries (Chapter 3), the contemporary politics of the day (Chapter 4), and the specifics of the relationship between MSC and surrounding communities since 1994 (Chapters 6 to 8). In Chapter 9 we pick up the chronology again with a look at the years 2010 and 2011. We also expand the geographic scope to include the departmental and national capitals.

9

RE-NEGOTIATION OF ROLES AND RIGHTS

2010 and 2011

Adjustment to arrival of globalisation

The opening of the San Cristobal mine, the plans for a lithium mine nearby, and the relatively sudden rise in quinoa prices, brought economic improvement to the Bolivian Altiplano region. In a manner of speaking, the latest wave of economic globalisation finally touched this remote region, which had not experienced much economic change since the wave of globalisation that occurred with the arrival of the Spanish 500 years earlier. For many Spanish-speaking Latin Americans, the Spanish Conquest and its sequelae provided the mental template for what could be expected from globalisation (Montecinos, 2014). Altiplano residents were no exception.

MSC was a participant in a wave of globalisation around the turn of the 21st century that produced the greatest reduction in extreme poverty in human history (Bhalla, 2002; Lakner and Milanovic, 2013). Although the wave evolved from Western and Japanese economies, it led to the rise of new middle classes in the BRICS countries (i.e., Brazil, Russia, India, China, South Africa) and many other smaller countries (e.g., Botswana, Chile, Ghana, Indonesia, Malaysia, Mexico, Nigeria, Poland, South Korea, Taiwan, Thailand, Turkey). That same global economic integration has also now given us our first global recession, or something close to it. Nonetheless, some economists predict still further growth up to 2030 in the proportion of the global population classifiable as middle class, albeit more in China than in Western democracies (Freeland, 2015).

When organisations adapted to a steady-state subsistence economy meet organisations adapted to economic growth, misunderstanding is inevitable. Such misunderstanding worsened several simmering conflicts during the first five years after MSC began operation. It was a period when the election of the first indigenous President in South America, Evo Morales, spread a sense of finally shaking off the limitations of the colonised mindset that took root with the Spanish Conquest

82 Retrospective from discovery to operating mine

and subsequently continued for more than a century after national independence within a small urban elite. The competing perspectives that accompanied the move towards a 'decolonisation of the mind' quite predictably led to some civil unrest in the broader region around the mine.

Regional unrest: multiple issues

Inequality in incomes and water

Despite progress in equality at the mine itself, feelings of being left behind, disadvantaged, or discriminated against began to be felt in the communities in the greater area of influence of the mine, the so-called 'second-ring' of towns and villages. They began petitioning MSC to receive jobs and benefits. There was even a threat to blockade access to the mine. MSC and community leaders from San Cristobal moved to deal with this situation through the provision of information and negotiations to end the threat of blockades.

During 2009 and 2010, resentments against MSC related to water issues continued along the lines described in Chapter 8. The Moran report declared that MSC was responsible for a lowering of the water table in the south Altiplano desert. The agricultural producers in the region were suffering from a drought at the time. They often repeated the phrase, 'Water is life'. MSC's report (Minera San Cristobal, 2014) on the multi-party study led by Niltetsu found the drought attributable to climate change. However, although the report was concluded in 2012, it was not made public until 2014. Meanwhile, during the intervening two years, groups advancing indigenous rights 'like the *Comité Cívico Potosinista* (COMCIPO)' seized on the Moran report to justify inflammatory rhetoric to the effect that MSC was threatening lives. A few *campesinos* declared that the blasting in the open-pit was scaring away the clouds and causing the drought. Others with a more technical worldview believed the national government should share some of the blame for not having fulfilled promises related to water infrastructure projects. Versions of these critiques were incorporated into the demands of protestors during the 2010 mini-insurrection.

The resentments about water were heaped on top of complaints about the inequality that suddenly appeared when residents of the three closest communities started working at the mine. The residents of San Cristobal had negotiated the right of first refusal on jobs for which they were qualified or for which they could be trained. In practice, the residents of Culpina K and Vila Vila enjoyed the same privilege. The practice was formalised in 2011. A consequence of the practice was that very few mine workers came from second-ring communities.

The wealth of the workers from the three closest first-ring villages increased dramatically. According to one estimate, a family with two people working at the mine would have a combined household income of $4,000 per month. That is a reasonable household income in the United States, but in rural Bolivia it is fabulous. Families that only a decade earlier were suffering from malnutrition now suffered from a shortage of parking spaces.

By the end of 2008, the flow of wages and salaries from regular employment at the mine was having an impact well beyond San Cristobal and its sister communities. Almost a million dollars a month was pouring into the local economy in the form of purchases of food, clothes, shoes, building materials, household appliances and decorations, vehicles, and other goods and services. In addition, a similar amount was accumulating in the bank account held by the municipality of Colcha K, which encompassed San Cristobal and some 40 other small communities. Colcha K became one of the most cash-rich municipalities in Bolivia owing to its share of taxes and royalties paid by MSC. These were unprecedented flows of money in an area that previously was marked by poverty, often extreme rural poverty.

Most of the purchases by workers from San Cristobal and their families were being made in the town of Uyuni, which serves as the regional service and supply centre for the entire southern Altiplano. Merchants in Uyuni were happy to capitalise on the wealth arriving from San Cristobal and raised prices accordingly, which had unintended consequences. When people from elsewhere in the region travelled to Uyuni to buy essential goods, or went to local suppliers that had purchased items from wholesalers in Uyuni, they found prices increasing almost monthly. Rapid inflation of local prices forced many already poor people into a deeper induced poverty unable to afford even basic essentials.

Unsurprisingly, people living outside of the 'bubble' of wealth around San Cristobal were unhappy. A set of interviews completed in 2009 (see Chapter 11 for details) revealed these communities to be close to withholding the social licence. The signs of future social unrest were apparent. Most of the second-ring communities became responsive to the critiques advanced by indigenous rights and social justice organisations. Opposition grew against foreigners (e.g. Opinión.com.bo, 2011) and any water-users competing with agriculture. MSC was portrayed as fitting both categories. These complaints were assimilated into a discourse on inequality and discrimination which portrayed current events as a repetition of the past (see discussion in Chapter 11).

The relationship with the municipality of San Pedro de Quemes

The frustrations produced by the concentration of new wealth in the communities closest to the mine were particularly intense in a town called San Pedro de Quemes (see map in Figure 1.3). The region of Nor Lípez comprises two municipalities, Colcha K (population estimated at 15,000 in 2015) in the east and San Pedro de Quemes (population estimated at 1,200 in 2015) in the west. The town of San Pedro de Quemes is the municipal seat for the municipality of the same name. The municipality also contains several widely dispersed small communities, including the settlement of Avaroa, which is on the road and railroad that link San Cristobal with Chile. Because of these transportation routes, critical supplies for the mine move daily through the municipality of San Pedro de Quemes.

84 Retrospective from discovery to operating mine

Among the communities of the second-ring, San Pedro de Quemes (see map in Figure 1.3) was perhaps the best led and most outspoken in its demands to share in the wealth coming from the San Cristobal mine. During the latter part of 2008, the community twice blockaded the access road from the Chilean border at Avaroa, demanding employment at the mine and payment for the passage of vehicles travelling to and from the mine.

In April 2009, in response to an invitation to hold consultations on the issues, three company employees went to San Pedro de Quemes. Things did not go well, however. The employees from Minera San Cristobal were held hostage for three days. Although to outsiders this seems an odd way to begin what was, among many other things, an employment-seeking process, in the Altiplano it is a customary way to begin negotiations.

In the middle of the first night, the hostages managed to escape from the hut where they were being held. However, they soon realised that they would die within a day or two in the vast surrounding desert. Therefore, they returned undetected to their confinement. About half an hour after they returned, they were taken from their hut and forced to begin drafting an 'agreement'. The company employees had some influence because they were the only ones who were literate enough to actually write out the terms of the agreement. Negotiations lasted for two days with very little rest. Finally, an accord was signed and the hostages were released. However, because the accord did not contain any material commitments, dissatisfaction continued.

Early in 2010 leaders from San Pedro de Quemes issued renewed demands for employment at the mine and also contracts to transport goods and mineral concentrates. This was quickly followed by an expanded list of complaints and claims. In particular, San Pedro raised the issue of water use, complaining that the mine was taking too much and depleting a common resource. They demanded the mine pay a tax as financial compensation for using this water. Alongside of this were further material demands to expand services across Nor Lípez in the form of electricity, running water, and mobile phone access. The most complex and significant demand was for participation in the flow of taxes and royalties, which included a proposed formula for distribution in which 5 per cent of the funds directed to Colcha K would be diverted to San Pedro de Quemes. Finally, there were demands for social and economic support programmes similar to those enjoyed by the communities in the immediate impact area of the mine. FRUTCAS supported the demands for economic and social benefits but did not endorse the complaints around water.

Matters came to a head in April 2010. People from San Pedro de Quemes and other communities blockaded the railroad and highway at Avaroa on the border with Chile. Railcars loaded with mineral concentrate from the mine were overturned and their contents deliberately spilled onto the ground. The blockade of the highway also stopped the movement of fuel and other supplies from Chile to the mine. The small office maintained by MSC in Avaroa to handle import and export formalities was sacked and burned to the ground.

MSC and the San Cristobal communities appealed to Potosí's Nor Lípez Prefect as the higher level of government in the region to help negotiate a solution. In a few days, an agreement was reached and the ten-day blockade was lifted. MSC cleaned up the spilled concentrate and re-established the office in Avaroa. The company also restructured community relations initiatives and social investment programmes to include the many small communities of the 'second-ring'. At the same time, the *Consejo Consultivo* expanded its long term sustainable development planning to include San Pedro de Quemes and the other communities of the 'second-ring'. Over a period of three years, and with support from the Prefect, it was possible to significantly improve the physical and economic circumstances for the people involved. A formal survey completed in 2013 (see Chapter 11 for details) showed that the quality of the social licence granted by the communities of the 'second-ring' had risen to the level of full acceptance, indicating that the risk of renewed conflict was much reduced.

The 2010 mini-insurrection

The march on the City of Potosí in August 2010

The blockade at Avaroa in April 2010 had repercussions beyond the relationship between MSC and San Pedro de Quemes. The blockade was joined by groups from the provinces of Enrique Baldivieso and Daniel Campos. They included a cooperative engaged in smuggling, the political party that failed to win the last municipal election in the municipality of Colcha K, and the would-be revolutionaries of COMCIPO. Despite the diverse interests, an effective rallying cry was found in the traditional discourse that Potosí residents had been given a raw deal by outsiders. This centuries-old standard helped mobilise the general sense among second-ring residents of being left out of the prosperity they saw around San Cristobal.

In August of 2010 the regional discontent produced something of a 'mini-insurrection' across the Department of Potosí (#18 on Figure 5.4). The roads and airports connecting the department to the outside world were blocked by protesters. Gasoline and food shortages ensued. Tourists were stranded.[1] Some protesters began hunger strikes. The occupation of the power station that supplies MSC by hundreds of protesters caused a suspension of some operations at MSC. Other mines in Potosí also experienced production disruptions.

Organisations leading the protests demanded more economic development for the Department of Potosí and action on promises for infrastructure development. Demands included expansion of the airport for the City of Potosí, new roads, a smelter in the City of Potosí, and a cement factory.[2] A march on the City of Potosí, the capital of the Department of the same name, was met with a countermarch. One leader of the protesters received a cut on the head. After 12 days, the protest ended.

86 Retrospective from discovery to operating mine

Mine occupation of 2011

The mini-insurrection of 2010 in Potosí was at least partially motivated by a sense of being left behind economically. Historically, Potosí residents compared themselves with the rest of Bolivia, especially the big cities, when evaluating the extent to which they were receiving a fair share of the national economic wealth. However, with the abrupt increase in prosperity in the first-ring villages around the San Cristobal mine, the sense of being left behind was brought closer to home. It became more intolerable. Meanwhile, the residents of the first-ring communities were confronted with city people in their midst. Highly qualified employees were being flown in from cities like Cochabamba, Santa Cruz, and La Paz. Although first-ring residents were suddenly doing better than most of the rest of the residents of the department, they could not help but notice how these fly-in, fly-out employees appeared to be doing even better. The comparison with those 'outside' workers only served to highlight their feelings of not receiving their fair share, by any principle of distributive justice. In this way, both the 2010 mini-insurrection and the 2011 mine occupation were rooted in the historical grievances of Potosí residents. As this section shows, it is a discourse that can encompass many, diverse, specific exemplars.

Background conditions

In March of 2011, residents of the three first-ring communities occupied the mine and closed access to it (#19 on Figure 5.4). The triggering event was a road accident that caused the death of a community leader named Pablo Calcina from Culpina K. However, tensions had been building since the mine began operations. Essentially, the communities and the company had different ideas about what the rules of the relationship should be now that the mine was in operation. Pablo Calcina's death laid bare the unaddressed need to redefine the rules. Before examining the conflict and its consequences, it is necessary to provide a little more context.

The Job Fair organised by the company in August 2006, and the subsequent screening, training, and hiring was hugely successful in bringing local people into permanent employment at the mine. In January 2011, almost every family in San Cristobal and a majority in Culpina K and Vila Vila had at least one family member employed by MSC. Within the company, more than 50 per cent of the workers at the mine were from the three communities. The overlap between company and community was further visible through the presence of a company community relations office in each of the communities. Each community had its own liaison officer who was a member of the immediate community. Although the officers were employed directly by MSC, they were selected and approved through a vote in open assembly by the residents, his or her neighbours and friends.

The communities were generally happy with MSC and had granted and maintained a social licence to the mine for several years. Nevertheless, there were lingering complaints of non-compliance with the agreements signed for the resettlement of San Cristobal and land acquisition from Culpina K and Vila Vila. The provision of an adequate and secure supply of potable water was one such issue (see Chapter 8 for a more complete account); another was health services for the communities.

One of the provisions of the resettlement agreement with San Cristobal was that the company would provide a 'health establishment with different medical and surgical specialities for external and internal consultations, with delivery room, operating room, consulting rooms, rooms for patients staying in hospital, nurse's stations, pharmacy, kitchen, pantry, and other facilities'. In the minds of residents of San Cristobal, Culpina K, and Vila Vila this meant the construction and operation of a 'Second-Tier' or Regional Hospital. Bringing this into reality had proven difficult due to the multiple agencies involved. MSC had retained a consultant to advance the process by creating a 'Lípez Health Network' to coordinate the many small populations centres in the district, but progress remained slow. To honour the commitment to the communities, MSC had contracted *Grupo Empresarial de Salud San Bartolome S.R.L.* (GESSBA) to provide medical services based out of a clinic with limited resources situated in San Cristobal. The company also provided health insurance for all employees and their families that could be used at any health facility in Bolivia. These provisions were above the legal requirement in Bolivia but did not always satisfy the local people. They felt that the service provided by the GESSBA clinic in San Cristobal was inferior to that available inside the mine, which had a dedicated medical facility fully staffed and equipped to handle any industrial accident or incident. It was also well below the quality of medical attention available to the families of workers who lived in the cities of La Paz, Cochabamba, and Santa Cruz.

To the physical interrelationships should be added the sense of co-ownership, a much stronger sentiment than mere partnership in the mine. It was felt particularly strongly by residents of San Cristobal who had agreed to relocate their homes to make way for the mine. With the emotional belief that the mine was 'theirs' came a parallel sentiment of a 'right' that the mine be managed in such a way that it met the needs and expectations of the local residents. This attitude had created problems during construction when the communities had rallied to confront the company and demand the dismissal of managers who were viewed as discriminating against the local people or as having made decisions that prejudiced the position of the locals. Matters reached a head in March and April 2011 when a cascade of events over 16 days led to a fundamental restructuring of the relationships between MSC and the first-ring communities, and among the three communities themselves.

The 'detonator' of conflict

During the first week of March 2011, illness befell the son of the community relations officer in Culpina K, Pablo Calcina. His wife took their son to the GESSBA clinic in San Cristobal on successive days, where she was told not to worry about his condition, and no medication was offered. On the fourth visit, the attending

88 Retrospective from discovery to operating mine

doctor decided that the situation was now such that the boy should be transferred for treatment at the major medical facility in the City of Potosí, some five hours away by road. The GESSBA ambulance was made available for the journey. Since the city is some distance away, the family wished to accompany him, with Pablo insisting that he travel with his son. The ambulance thus carried a driver, the sick son, a nurse to look after the patient, Pablo, his wife, and their second son. However, there were not seat belts for everyone and Pablo took one of the seats without a belt.

The details of the accident are uncertain, although there is ample evidence that excessive speed was involved. Near Ramaditas, 30 kilometres north-east of the mine traveling towards Uyuni (see map in Figure 1.3) the vehicle left the road and turned over. Pablo was thrown out of the window and suffered severe head trauma and other injuries. Everyone else survived the crash safe and uninjured. However, the group were stranded without a radio to make emergency contact and outside cell phone coverage. Some 90 minutes later, a private car came on the scene and agreed to take Pablo, badly injured but still alive, directly to a clinic in Uyuni. His wife and two sons followed some minutes later in a second vehicle and arrived at the same clinic a little after Pablo. Apparently, there was a delay while confusion over health insurance was sorted out and only after this was it made known that Pablo had died on the way to the clinic. Nevertheless, the sequence of events at the clinic gave rise to the perception that Pablo had died while waiting for the insurance matters to be sorted out.

Pablo's son received treatment for his malady and survived.

News of Pablo's death was received with sadness and anger in Culpina K. He had been a much loved and respected leader in that community. The information reached San Cristobal and Vila Vila through the complex network of extended family relationships. A collective sensation of grief and anger grew quickly among the three communities.

The first manifestation of this anger came with a march to the mine by women from Culpina K and San Cristobal who saw the company as directly responsible for Pablo's death. They believed that the mine had failed to honour the reciprocity expected from the company; they felt betrayed. As one of the women who led the march explained, 'They gave us an unsafe vehicle that lacked seat belts, and the driver was not properly trained'. The women demanded better medical attention, branded the doctors involved as incompetent, and demanded their removal.

Because Pablo was a company employee, the union at the mine also took up the cause and pushed the matter a step further by asserting that his death could have be avoided if the transfer to the hospital had been by air rather than by road. The union petitioned the company for substantial improvements in local medical services and, like the women, demanded the removal of the two doctors who they considered to be incompetent and failing to apply company norms and policies. Because of the lack of a seat belt and the reports of speeding by the ambulance, they also demanded the removal of the individual responsible for industrial health and safety.

The cause initiated by the women was taken up by community leaders, who approached the issue as one in which they should have a direct role. As 'joint owners of the mine' they recalled the way in which matters had been addressed during the construction period – demand the removal of problem managers. A meeting and subsequent joint assembly of the three first-ring communities were called on March 14 and 15 at which a resolution was approved calling for the immediate dismissal of the two doctors and the manager of health and safety. The company response was to open negotiations with the community leaders.

The union took a more expanded approach and called an assembly of workers on March 18 that approved a letter to the company documenting the circumstances of Pablo's death, and other negative situations encountered at the GESSBA clinic. On the basis of this evidence the union called for the dismissal of the two doctors and the MSC manager for health and safety. It also called for the contract with GESSBA to be terminated, the immediate expansion of health insurance coverage, and construction of the long-awaited hospital. It also gave notice of a determination to 'fight to the ultimate' (a metaphor for strike action) if the demands were not met. The company response was to open negotiations with the union leadership.

Most parties consider the March 18 letter from the union to mark the beginning of the conflict, which remained latent for the next few days as discontent simmered within the communities. From the company perspective, the negotiations with communities and union leaders had gone well and there was belief that resolution could be obtained in a way that satisfied all parties. The company had signalled a willingness to discuss improvements to the medical support system, but refused to consider dismissing any individuals, which would contravene Bolivian labour law. However, the senior managers of MSC involved in these negotiations left the mine site before a final agreement could be reached.

Escalation to confrontation

Away from the discussions between community leaders and MSC managers, collective anger and resentment towards the company grew in all three communities. Recurrent sentiments that formed part of several different concerns were those of inequality and discrimination. They were part of complaints about both health care access and access to jobs and promotions within the company. Another frequent complaint was the failure of the company to honour its 'responsibility to look after people'. As this concern was shared and anger increased, people in San Cristobal recalled the company commitment to provide 'a hospital with corresponding ancillary spaces and facilities'. Not only had the company not built a hospital in the village, as the community wanted and expected, but the alternative provision of health care through the GESSBA clinic and insurance provided by the company had failed to protect Pablo.

As frustrations grew in San Cristobal, so did the list of unfulfilled commitments. It came to include the inadequacy of the supply of water to the village. To this was added a quest to see the removal of certain individuals in the Human Resources

90 Retrospective from discovery to operating mine

department who were accused by the residents of 'discrimination' and of giving the better jobs to 'outsiders'. Three families with outstanding claims for personal compensation for llama grazing lands within the area of expansion of the open-pit added their complaints to the list. Leadership of the protest moved to the men in San Cristobal.

Culpina K, however, also has its own issues beyond those directly related to the death of Pablo Calcina. The water supply to their community was even more inadequate than San Cristobal's and some had the persistent feeling that the agreement for Wila Khara tailing containment land was a poor deal. They wanted more from the company: ideally a development foundation and an agro-industrial company similar to that gained by San Cristobal under the resettlement agreement.

Vila Vila also had problems with its water supply but was more immediately concerned with the lack of cell phone coverage and the absence of a connection to the national electrical grid, long promised in their agreement with the company.

In San Cristobal, the male-dominated leadership quietly encouraged the collective anger generated by an unnecessary death and frustration over non-compliance with commitments made by the company. On or about March 22, leaders within San Cristobal observed that senior managers were temporarily not resident at the mine. This was seen as an ideal time to coordinate action with the other communities and put maximum pressure on the company. Meetings were convened in all three of the first-ring communities to plan an occupation of the mine. There were disagreements about how to do it because so many of the community residents themselves would suffer income loss if the mine were completely shut down. In the end, they decided to blockade the mine and allow residents to continue working for as long as possible. Action was declared in the form of limited strike action plus a blockade of the railroad and all road access, thus isolating the mine.

Chronology of the conflict

Key events during the days of open conflict between the company, the union, and the three communities are summarised in a calendar format below along with the lapsed number of days from the initial declaration of an intention to strike made by the union on March 18, 2011.

Day 6: Wednesday March 23

- The blockade and strike began. Community members occupied parts of the mine site. Mining operations in the open-pit were halted but the mill and concentrator plant continued operating. Material for the mill and plant was drawn down from the ore stockpile while mineral concentrates accumulated in shipping containers in the rail yard. The company contacted the Judicial Authority of the Administration of Mines and requested an '*Amparo Administrativo*' (in effect an Injunction) against all those parties involved in the blockade/strike.

Re-negotiation of roles and rights 91

Days 7–10: Thursday March 24–Sunday March 27

- On March 24 the company closed all operations as the ore stockpile had been exhausted and stood down all of the contractors. The communities issued a letter confirming their demands and intention to maintain the blockade/strike pending resolution provided by the company. Separately, they appealed to the Governor of Potosí for help in resolving the conflict.
- On March 25 the union issued a Declaration of Conflict (confirming strike action) and called on the company to meet the demands set out in the letter of March 18.
- Representatives of the Governor of the Department of Potosí made a fact-finding visit to San Cristobal and confirmed that the mine was blockaded, that the communities and the union had material issues, and that the primary objectives of the dissident population were (a) to secure a Regional Hospital for all the different communities and, (b) to gain priority for paving the highway from Uyuni, through the first-ring communities, up to the border with Chile.
- MSC's senior management assembled in La Paz to coordinate a response to the blockade and strike. They communicated by telephone with staff on site who maintained direct contact with the union and community leaders.
- There was a further exchange of letters and more meetings between company and community representatives, led by San Cristobal.
- Community leaders and negotiators were unable to separate community issues from labour and employment matters, which greatly complicated any attempts at negotiation. San Cristobal regarded the union as an unnecessary interloper and attempted to control all interactions with the company. By contrast, the union asserted that it had a clear responsibility mandated by law. The company agreed with the union.
- Language in communications from the union showed a progressive shift in emphasis. It became more adversarial in tone and broadened from representing workers alone to workers and communities and later workers and authorities, reflecting increased influence from the community leaders.
- MSC decided to push back firmly after having surrendered to demands in the past. MSC defended its decision-making prerogative and insisted that labour issues were separate from community issues.
- The parties called for help from the government, but the stalemate persisted through the remainder of the week, despite attempts by the Potosí government, regional representatives of the Ministry of Labour, and the *Federación Sindical de Trabajadores Mineros de Bolivia* (FSTMB – National Federated Union of Bolivian Mine Workers) to help resolve the conflict.

Day 11: Monday March 28

- The government of Potosí (Department of Social Development and Health) wrote to MSC requesting clarification of the causes of the conflict and an explanation of why the GESSBA clinic had been non-functional since the conflict began.

92 Retrospective from discovery to operating mine

- The company declared that it would not engage in any talks with the union until there was resolution on the non-employment related demands and concerns raised by the communities.
- MSC issued a public statement about the health benefits provided to employees, their families, and other residents of the three communities.

Days 12–13: Tuesday March 29–Wednesday March 30

- Internal differences surfaced in San Cristobal, with growing criticism of rent-seeking by some families (i.e., demands for personal, financial compensation). From the outset, MSC had refused to discuss personal grievances alongside community issues. These matters were taken off the table.
- There were rising concerns in all three communities that an extended shutdown would cost the workers significant lost income.
- As the strike reached day seven, a relatively long time for a mining dispute in Bolivia, with no apparent end in sight, the national government became concerned about the loss of approximately $2.5 million dollars per day in export revenues and $400,000 dollars per day in royalties and taxes. During a meeting with MSC senior management in La Paz, the Vice Minister of Mining signalled a willingness to mediate in the conflict.
- The government issued a press statement that it would not be negotiating with the union or the company because 'this is an internal company problem and the company has to solve it'.

Day 14: Thursday March 31

- In a move reminiscent of the action taken during construction of the mine, the communities and the union called for the intervention of Jonny Delgado and other trusted individuals with a historic association with the San Cristobal mine project to help mediate a solution to the conflict.

Day 15: Friday April 1

- The Ministry of Labour issued a letter calling on MSC, the union, community leaders, and representatives of FSTMB to meet in La Paz on April 2, 2017.
- The government and MSC made press statements that labour-related negotiations had not yet started.
- Union representatives and community leaders flew to La Paz to attend the meeting.

Day 16: Saturday April 2

- After what individuals involved in the negotiations described as a very long and difficult day, and with the Ministry of Labour and FTSMB acting as mediators, the company, union and representatives from San Cristobal, Culpina K, and Vila Vila reached an Accord of Understanding, which brought the active phase of the conflict to a close.

- The accord stated that the communities and the union would call off the blockade and strike; the company would drop the *Amparo Administrativo* (Injunction) against the union and community leaders; and, all parties would participate in a Dialogue Table with the intention of resolving the issues of labour relations and health.

Day 17: Sunday April 3

- Work resumed at the mine – all workers returned by 3.15 pm and full production was achieved the next day.

Resetting the relationship

With the strike settled, the blockade dismantled, and the mine back in full operation, the role of the Dialogue Table became one of defining the way forward for the actors involved in the conflict: the company, the communities, and the union.

Days 19–25: Tuesday April 5–Monday April 11

- The Dialogue Table was comprised of representatives of the three communities, the union, and the company. It met daily to work through a difficult process of bargaining and negotiations.

Day 26: Tuesday April 12

- An Act of Understanding and Pact of Harmony Health and Sustainable Productivity (AOU) was signed in the presence of the Ministry of Labour (as guarantor of the agreement) between MSC, the union, San Cristobal, Culpina K, and Vila Vila. The essential components of this agreement were;

  o To comply with the law and signed agreements; to use negotiation as the primary mechanism for resolving differences; and, to turn to pressure tactics such as strikes, etc. only after all other measures had been exhausted.
  o To create an Integrated Health System that included improvements in the delivery of health services to the communities.
  o To improve the San Cristobal Health Centre and put a renewed emphasis on the Lípez Health Network and the effort to create a Regional Hospital in San Cristobal.
  o In collaboration with the *Consejo Consultivo*, municipal authorities, and regional authorities, to put effort into a project to pave the highway between Rio Grande and the Chilean border.

94 Retrospective from discovery to operating mine

o   To clearly separate the union's responsibility for the interests and rights of its worker members from the responsibilities of the communities related to existing agreements with MSC, MSC's impacts on the communities, and themes related to sustainable development.

Day 28: Thursday April 14

- The AOU was approved by the union at an Extraordinary General Meeting and also by the communities in General Assemblies.

The consequences of conflict

Prior to the 2011 conflict, the company had always ceded to community demands (e.g. the firing of personnel disliked by the community during the construction phase). This time it stood firm. The demand for community control of Human Resources policies and certain specific Human Resource decisions was rejected. This was a turning point in the relationship because it created a refinement on the community side. By accepting the AOU, the communities acknowledged that the union, not the community leaders, had the legitimacy to negotiate over company employment policies. The union also gained national recognition for its role. The company successfully established recognition that there were limits to power-sharing with stakeholders.

Observers later noted that Culpina K and Vila Vila gained politically from the process. In the negotiations during the months that followed signing the AOU, they came away with their own development foundations, parallel to the San Cristobal Foundation, and also won inclusion in the group that had the right of first refusal on job openings. Because it started from a position of fewer benefits, Vila Vila gained the most by winning equality with San Cristobal and Culpina K. San Cristobal became less politically dominant among the three communities and the leaders who had led the strike and blockade lost credibility and prestige.

In terms of material benefits, the communities immediately received an improved emergency health support system, including ambulances and upgrading of the road to the closest hospital located in Uyuni. The conflict also energised the process of creating a Regional Hospital in San Cristobal. With all three levels of government (municipal, Departmental, and national) more fully aware of the issues the project moved from concept to reality relatively rapidly. Agreements for funding construction were signed with and between all three levels of government in which the municipality of Colcha K was able to utilise its share of funds from the royalty and tax stream derived from the San Cristobal mine. Similarly, an agreement with the Ministry of Health was required for staffing, etc. to operate the facility. MSC also played a role in helping to bring the various organisations together and, in particular, supporting the local municipal authorities. Within five years, a full service Regional Hospital was built in San Cristobal.

Members of the Community Relations Department were seen by MSC management as facilitating the conflict by writing letters in support of the demands made by the women and union immediately after the death of Pablo Calcina. This remained a problem within the company. Some mangers regarded community relations as systematically promoting the position of the communities.

Following the conflict, there was a slow process of recovery in all relationships. Interaction between the company and San Cristobal, Culpina K, and Vila Vila changed to a more formal, institutionalised format with clearly defined roles, responsibilities, and forms of interaction. With more defined objectives and responsibilities, the communities emerged as much stronger. Remarkably, confidence in the company increased within the three communities, as expressed in the level of social licence granted by them in a set of interviews conducted immediately before and after the occupation (see Chapter 11, section entitled '2011: The occupation'). Nevertheless, many members of the three communities mourned the days when the relationship with the company was direct and personal, with no third parties involved.

Criminal opportunism: smugglers agitate for advantages

Criminal activity includes elements of rent-seeking (discussed in Chapter 2) through the monopolisation of a given lucrative activity in a given geographic area. This is why underworld turf wars occasionally occur. Each organisation seeks to 'eliminate' its competition. Soon after the mine began operation, the number of trucking contractors needed by MSC stabilised. Some who were already familiar with criminal activity sought to gain a monopoly on the provision of transportation services to MSC.

Local smugglers saw the 2011 unrest around the mine as an opportunity to expand both their legal and illegal operations. MSC's concentrate goes to port via a rail line operated by a Chilean railway corporation. Rumours circulated about the smuggling of motor vehicles and drugs across the border, near the pass used by the rail line. A Nor Lípez trucking 'cooperative' that was smuggling goods across the border attempted to mount a political front with other trucking cooperatives to force MSC to abandon the railway and to use road transport instead. The plan would have caused severe damage to the existing road, spread dust along the road causing damage to crops, killed many more livestock, raised MSC's carbon footprint, and raised the risk of the company facing extortion attempts at the hands of the cooperatives. On the plus side, from the viewpoint of the protesting cooperatives, it would have created some very wealthy individuals in some communities. These trucking cooperatives voiced their demands during the 2011 occupation of the mine and became more insistent during 2012. This aspect of the regional discontent, however, dissipated when the leader of the most vocal 'cooperative' was convicted and imprisoned for smuggling.

96 Retrospective from discovery to operating mine

Discrimination as either inequity or inequality

The viewpoint from the first-ring communities

At the time of the mine occupation, access to health care was based on equity rather than equality. Those who lived closer to better health facilities (fly-in workers from the cities and workers inside the mine) received better care. The occupiers saw this as unfair because their cultural heritage told them that everyone should have equal access, not equitable access. Moreover, they had been promised a Regional Hospital. They viewed equitable but unequal access as discrimination. For details on the cultural context of the distinction, see the discussion of equity and equality in Chapter 2.

The occupiers also complained that doctors at the GESSBA clinic did not treat local people in a way they considered respectful. Therefore, they demanded that they be fired. Again, equality was the principle of fairness they thought had been violated.

Access to managerial jobs was based on qualifications and criteria used throughout the mining industry internationally. Few of the Nor Lípez employees had the qualifications for positions in upper management. As a consequence, the higher-level jobs were all occupied by 'outsiders'. This was viewed as unequal treatment, which therefore made it 'discriminatory'.

The company's responses varied on each matter. At the time of writing a Second-Tier hospital for San Cristobal is ready and awaiting a staffing agreement. It is the biggest and best in the region and has eliminated the need to ration health care access on an equity basis. In terms of access to jobs and promotions, there are now more opportunities for local people to access higher education. This creates more equal opportunities to qualify for positions allocated on the basis of equity (i.e., meritocratic criteria). However, young people who have returned from university with appropriate qualifications have not been hired. There have been few openings for them as of this writing. Indeed, in 2015 there were redundancies because a combination of lower concentrations of commercial minerals in the ore and lower prices for those minerals reduced the financial health of the mine.

In terms of access to jobs at the mine, San Cristobal had an agreement that gave its residents the right of first refusal for jobs for which they were qualified or trainable. During the negotiations to end the occupation of the mine, the right of first refusal was formally extended to Culpina K and Vila Vila. The communities saw that as fair because it accorded with the principle of equality.

A different principle of fairness, however, was applied to justify the original right of first refusal granted to San Cristobal residents. This was seen as fair because it was equitable. The San Cristobal residents had made a greater sacrifice by agreeing to the relocation and therefore deserved a greater share of the rewards. Here equality with surrounding communities would have been viewed as unfair.

The view from the second-ring communities

Throughout the first few years after operations began, there were complaints from the residents of second-ring communities about not getting equal access to jobs at the mine. Of course, the second-ring communities viewed the preference given to the first-ring residents as unfair because it violated the principle of equality. The growing prosperity of the first-ring communities could not be hidden, and it was having negative impacts on the second-ring. The unequal distribution of the benefits of this specific instance of 'globalisation' caused anger and resentment. It may be a stretch to compare the reaction of the second-ring communities to the reactions of Brexit and Trump voters to their experiences of globalisation. Nonetheless, there appears to be a common theme of anger at feeling 'left behind'.

To summarise, from the viewpoint of the first-ring communities, it was fair for them to be equal among themselves but unfair for the second-ring communities to also be equal with them. From the viewpoint of the second-ring communities, equality for all would be the ideal of fairness, regardless of sacrifices made by some and not others. In human affairs, every principle of justice reaches a point where its applicability is superseded by a different principle. Unconscious self-serving biases have been shown to play a role in determining when that point is reached (Babcock and Loewenstein, 1997).

Notes

1 www.bbc.com/news/world-latin-america-10949160.
2 A reprise of the protests in 2015 added a glass plant, a talc plant, a hydroelectric plant, and hospitals to the list. www.bbc.com/mundo/noticias/2015/07/150720_bolivia_protestas_la_paz_Potosí_ao.

PART 3

Stakeholder strategies from quantitative measures

10

SHIFT TO QUANTITATIVE RISK ASSESSMENT METHODS

The case study method used in Chapters 6 to 9 was well suited to the task of capturing the texture and detail of the amazing transformation that occurred in the communities around the MSC mine. In Chapters 10 to 12, we look at the period from 2009 to 2015 using a more quantitative method. The quantitative method is described in this chapter. It deals more with questions of influence, power, and social structure. It gives more insight into how MSC fits into the broader ecology of social, political, and economic dynamics of the Department and the country.

In many rural areas, the majority of stakeholders are at least initially united around a shared desire for social and economic development. However, there are often differing views about what development should look like or how to achieve it. Therefore, an efficient strategy for gaining a social licence is to increase the capacity of the stakeholder network to agree on shared goals and to collaborate towards achieving them in a way that will endure long after any resource project has finished and gone. Chapters 11 and 12 show how recommendations to MSC derived from the stakeholder interviews contributed to a noticeable increase in collaboration and measurable improvements in the region's level of social and economic development.

SLSN

Benefits of blending three types of information

The measures of the social licence that are described in the next section (page 104) become even more enlightening when combined with alternative views of what is going on with the stakeholders. In interviews with MSC's stakeholders, we took advantage of the synergies created by integrating information on (a) the verbal opinions expressed by each stakeholder, (b) the social licence level granted by each, and (c) the network position occupied by each stakeholder.

All three types of information were collected in interviews with stakeholder group spokespersons. First, they were invited to explain what was on their minds in their own words. Then, they rated their agreement with a set of statements that measured the level of social licence they granted. Next, they rated their relationships with other stakeholders using scales that indicate the level of collaborative capacity in the relationships. Finally, they were again invited to express their view in their own words. For more details on the content of the questionnaire, see Boutilier (2009, 2011) and the website www.socialicense.com.

In this section, we look at the nature of each type of information separately before showing how blending these information types together answers some very interesting questions that lead directly to a stakeholder relations strategy. The analyses make it possible:

- To identify natural clusters of stakeholders (e.g. by empirically observed connections) and summarise their concerns and perceptions.
- To discover the existing alliances and divisions among stakeholders.
- To determine how much influence each stakeholder has in the stakeholder network, and what it would take to win them as allies.
- To rank stakeholder concerns in terms of the socio-political risk they present for the project.
- To predict impending conflicts or alliances in the network.
- To show which issues are linked to each other in the minds of different clusters of stakeholders.
- To match clusters of stakeholders with clusters of issues to show who cares about what, and which potential alliances should be encouraged or discouraged.
- To determine the project's level of social licence to operate, both overall, and within any sub-groups.
- To assess the stakeholders' collective capacity to issue a durable, valid social licence to operate.
- To recommend programmes, policies, initiatives, and communications strategies that increase the company's level of social licence to operate while fostering self-sufficient progress of the community towards its chosen goals.

Quantification of the social licence

The story behind the measure

As described in Chapter 5, the term 'social licence to operate', in the sense that it is used here, was coined in 1997 by Jim Cooney, the Director, International and Public Affairs at the now defunct gold mining company, Placer Dome Inc.

Shift to quantitative risk assessment methods **103**

About two years later, Cooney participated in a Placer Dome project to prepare the company's mine on Misima Island, Papua New Guinea, for closure. Boutilier was contracted as a consultant to assess community needs, identify priorities, and track progress towards the ultimate goal of 'leaving behind a better future'. Boutilier and Cooney agreed that 'what gets measured gets done' but that in terms of social or societal goals the typical environmental-oriented approach of measuring concrete impacts (e.g. parts per million of contaminants) would miss the most important aspects. The goal became finding a way to measure changes in the social structure and resilience of the community. The ideal of community social capital seemed to hold promise in that direction.

In order to quantify the social structure, and the social capital embedded in it, Boutilier developed a method[1] that put the focus on the quality of relationships rather than concrete environmental and social impacts. Some of the measures are incorporated in today's quantitative measure of the social licence to operate. However, the conceptualisation of what was to be measured did not shift until ten years later when we developed our model of the levels of the social licence. In 2009, we had an opportunity to put the model to an empirical test. Thomson had been consulting on community relations with Sumitomo's MSC, reporting to Javier Diez de Medina, MSC's Manager of Social Responsibility and Environment at that time. Diez de Medina was a former leader of a development NGO who had heard Thomson talk about the Stakeholder 360® approach. All three of us were agreed that the best way to get a social licence is to foster the community's capacity to set its own goals and collaborate towards them. In 2009, Diez de Medina invited us to apply our ideas at MSC but insisted that we find some quantitative way of actually measuring progress.

Boutilier applied his experience in socio-metric scale development and came up with a set of 26 interview questions to be used in one-on-one interviews with the spokespersons for stakeholder groups. The questions consisted of agree/disagree statements to be rated on a 5-point scale. The original set of statements included some that were based on the four levels of the Thomson and Boutilier social licence model, some based on its three boundary criteria, and some on matters of justice and fairness. The latter were suggested by Dr. Leeora Black, managing director of the Australian Centre for Corporate Social Responsibility. She had found such statements useful in differentiating among levels of acceptance of mineral projects across Australia. Boutilier and Black used subsets of the statements in various studies with stakeholders beginning in 2009. Some statements were eliminated because they did not differentiate extreme supporters from extreme opponents. Eventually, a stable set of 15 statements was identified. Black (2013) included the statements in her short book entitled *The Social licenceLicence to Operate: Your Management Framework for Complex Times*. Using additional data from Africa, Latin America, and North America, Boutilier further reduced the list of statements to the 12 that are available at https://tinyurl.com/y7b9ty59 (or search at: www.socialicense.com).

104 Strategies from quantitative measures

Quantification of social licence levels

The English versions of the statements used to measure the social licence at MSC since 2009 are shown in Table 10.1. The statements are designed for use with representatives of community organisations in the general vicinity of an operating mine. They should be modified for use with different projects and stakeholder groups. For example, for an exploration project, the tenses of the verbs need to be changed and tone needs to be more oriented towards anticipated experiences. For stakeholders who do not have a direct relationship with the company or that play a regulatory or monitoring role (e.g., Ministry of Environment, news media), the statements can be modified to refer to the stakeholders' perceptions of the company's relationship with the citizenry or the relevant population.

Note that many of the statements refer to perceptions of the relationship with the operator. This was a deliberate strategy to make the measures comparable across time and cultures. Relationships have universal qualities, like trust, mutuality, and communication quality (e.g., listening, sharing information). Mining projects often have impacts that vary across projects. Therefore, measures that focus on impacts do not travel as well across time and cultures. In any case, impacts are only important to the extent that stakeholders deem them important. To that extent, the impacts affect the stakeholders' perceptions of the relationships. Therefore, by focusing on relationships, the measures automatically incorporate weightings of the importance of the impacts.

Averaging the ratings for the 15 statements produces the social licence score for the stakeholder. This is a real number in the range from 1 to 5. The Thomson and Boutilier model for the social licence uses a colour gradation for the background

TABLE 10.1 Fifteen agree/disagree statements used to measure the social licence at MSC

We are very satisfied with our relationship with Minera San Cristobal.

(Organisation/community) and Minera San Cristobal have a similar vision for the future development of this region.

We need the cooperation of Minera San Cristobal to reach our most important goals.

Minera San Cristobal listens to us.

Minera San Cristobal does what it says it will do in its relations with our (organisation/community).

Minera San Cristobal openly shared information that affects us.

We can gain from a relation with Minera San Cristobal.

In the long term, Minera San Cristobal makes a contribution to the well-being of the whole region.

Minera San Cristobal give more help to those who it affects more.

The presence of Minera San Cristobal is a benefit to us.

Minera San Cristobal takes our interests into account.

Minera San Cristobal shares decision making with us.

Minera San Cristobal is fair to everyone.

Minera San Cristobal respects our way of life.

Minera San Cristobal takes account of our interests.

Shift to quantitative risk assessment methods **105**

of the pyramid to signify the transition from one level of social licence to the next (see Figure 5.3). This gradation corresponds to the real number range from 1 to 5 when the average of the 15 ratings of the statements is calculated. However, for the purpose of creating a graph to show the level of social licence granted by different groups, it is both cumbersome and confusing to use fine gradations in colour. Instead, we created a system of distinct colours to represent each level of social licence. That necessitated dividing the range from 1 to 5 into brackets. Then the number of brackets had to be decided, a decision that would determine the breadth of each bracket.

The obvious choice was to use the same number of brackets used in the Thomson and Boutilier 2011 model. There were four brackets (i.e., withheld, acceptance, approval, and psychological identification). Thus, ideally, we would have four colours based on boundaries placed one quarter of the way along the range. That would equate the withdrawn social licences with all those scores of 2 or less. Acceptance would be 2 to 3. Approval would be 3 to 4. Psychological identification would be 4 to 5.

The problem with dividing the rating scale itself into brackets is that we know that people do not use the full range of any scale when rating their perceptions. They rarely use the extremes. Instead, we need to use, not the range of the rating scale presented in the questions, but rather the effective range used by stakeholders in their answers. That is the range we need to divide into brackets. To do that we turn to a technique called percentiles. The 50th percentile is that point where half the respondents got a score higher and half got a score lower. The 25th percentile is the point where 25 per cent of respondents got a score lower and 75 per cent got a score higher. If we want four brackets corresponding to the four levels in the Thomson and Boutilier model, then we perform a 'quartile split' (i.e., we define the bracket boundaries at those points that define each successive quarter of the scores, as opposed to scale points).

The quartile split solution works well but in the lower quartile it risks lumping together extreme opponents with people who are just moderately disgruntled. In trying to use social licence scores to develop stakeholder relations strategies, we often want to focus on the stakeholders who are the most unhappy and who granted the very lowest social licences. We want to know who they are and what their concerns are. For this, a quarter of the stakeholders is too big a group. A more select group is desirable. The simplest solution is to use smaller percentile ranges and then focus on the bottom percentile group.

For the MSC analyses, it was most convenient and useful to use brackets consisting of one-sixth of the scores. This is called a 'sextile split'. Table 10.2 shows the labels that were assigned to each sextile of scores along with their corresponding colour shades. Only the bottom sextile of scores was labelled 'withheld/withdrawn'. This tactic of using smaller percentile ranges helped avoid the danger of labelling unhappy but tolerant stakeholders as having withdrawn the social licence. Nonetheless, the choice of bracket criteria remains arbitrary. The ultimate criterion is how useful the brackets are for developing sound strategies.

106 Strategies from quantitative measures

TABLE 10.2 Labels assigned to sextiles of social licence scores

Sextile 1/6th	Verbal label
6	psychological identification
5	high approval
4	low approval
3	high acceptance/tolerance
2	low acceptance/tolerance
1	withheld/withdrawn

Validation of the social licence measure

Boutilier reasoned that the quantitative ratings of the social licence using the 15 agree/disagree statements would be at least partially validated if they were correlated with the sentiments expressed in the open-ended verbal comments indicating approval or disapproval. To that end, Boutilier performed an analysis that compared the frequencies of mentions of qualitative comment categories to the quantitative ratings of the social licence for the MSC mine across five years. This required developing and applying a standardised coding frame for the open-ended responses. The coding frame had two parts. The largest set of codes dealt with the content of the comment. For example, the global categories were things like water, pollution, comments on communication, and infrastructure. The second set of codes focused on the intent or 'voice' of the comment. Each comment was simultaneously coded as a criticism of MSC, a criticism of another party, praise for MSC, praise for another party, a factual observation, a suggestion for MSC, a general suggestion, a statement of need, and so forth.

The 'voice' codes indicating criticism of MSC and praise for MSC were combined in an odds ratio of the per capita mention frequency for each of those two categories in each of the five years. The odds ratio was expressed as the per capita frequency of praise comments over criticism comments. Higher numbers therefore indicate more acceptance or approval for the operation. To make the qualitative odds ratios graphable on the same scale as the quantitative social licence scores, both sets of five scores were converted to z scores, which express their distance from their own mean in standard deviation units. Figure 10.1 shows the results. The qualitative measure of approval correlated significantly with the quantitative measure of approval at $r = 0.92$ ($df = 4$, two-tailed $p < 0.02$). Note that although the ratio remained relatively flat in the year of the mine occupation (2011) the social licence score actually rose slightly. This suggests that the social licence score has more to do with the desire to continue the relationship, or not, than with feelings about any current efforts to reform or renew the relationship. This is consistent with the details of mine occupation (see Chapter 9) that suggest the communities wanted reforms, not a discontinuation.

Shift to quantitative risk assessment methods **107**

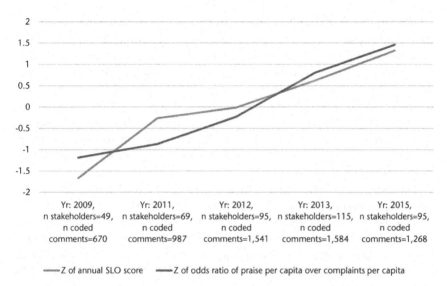

FIGURE 10.1 Five-year trends in standardised average rated social licence scores and odds ratios of compliments to complaints in open-ended verbal comments.

The findings shown in Figure 10.1 should be treated as encouraging early indicators. To improve confidence in the validity of the quantitative measures, future studies should look at more mines, in different cultures, with more refinements to the qualitative coding procedures. Chapter 12 deals with a different type of validation. It establishes the validity of the measure by showing that the strategies that the quantitative measures suggest produce the business results desired.

Quantification of concerns and priorities

Several approaches to developing a stakeholder relations strategy, or a stakeholder engagement plan as it is sometimes called, take account of the stakeholders' perceptions of impacts, priorities, expectations, and preferences. They also often include opinions on issues related to a project, for example, on environmental or economic matters. These things are essential for developing a stakeholder relations strategy but can yield much more insight when combined with data on the social licence and the stakeholders' social network.

There are hidden risks of coming to erroneous conclusions when asking stakeholders about impacts, issues, and priorities. The three main sources of error we have encountered are the: (a) stakeholders' inability to articulate what is really bothering them, (b) deliberate stakeholder obfuscation intended to hide involvement in illegal activities, and (c) the stakeholders' colonised collective mentality. We now look at each of these in detail.

108 Strategies from quantitative measures

The first source of error, lack of articulation, is dealt with in the part of the interview that measures the social licence. Basically, social norms prevent stakeholders from admitting to others, and even to themselves, that what is really bothering them is a lack of respect shown by the project proponents. Unable to articulate that underlying cause, they talk instead of proximate causes that are more socially acceptable, like fears of environmental damage (Franks *et al.*, 2014).

The second source of error, hiding illegal activity, is only detectable by investigative probing outside the stakeholder interview. We had an example of it in the 2012 interviews with the MSC stakeholder group that turned out to be a smuggling operation.

The third source of error, a colonised mentality, can be dealt with by posing the open-ended questions in a particular way. The aim is to deactivate what is often the default template, that of the rich world corporation owing a social and ethical debt of reparations for the devastation caused by colonialism.[2] That mindset is often a legacy of colonialism itself and is nourished across generations by local elites needing a safe scapegoat to blame for the dire consequences of their own exploitative institutions. In order to find ways of moving towards positive, collaborative relations, the questions need to avoid activating any such us-versus-them mindset. Instead, questions about impacts and issues should strive to activate a template of self-reliance and mutual respect, the hallmarks of a decolonised mindset.

Peter Senge and colleagues (Senge *et al.*, 1994) have devised a meeting facilitation process that has reliably achieved the deactivation of the colonised template and other templates that fail to put mutuality at the forefront. They have used it in cultural settings ranging from New York boardrooms to rural African villages. We modelled the open-ended questions posed to MSC's stakeholder upon that facilitation process.

We began with questions about stakeholders' concerns, their hopes and fears about the future. By then probing for follow-up comments we attempted to uncover the values exemplified by each hope and fear.[3] Next, the questioning moved to the advantages and disadvantages of the operation of the mine. Finally, the stakeholders were asked what should be done, without specifying who would or should do it. At the end of the interview, stakeholders were asked about the contributions their organisation or group was making to the advancement of development projects.

The verbal responses were read by trained coders who developed a list of categories that seemed to capture the most recurring ideas expressed by the set of stakeholders. The coders then classified each idea into a category. That allowed the counting of mentions of each category. The frequency of category mention was expressed as a rate per number of stakeholders. This was called the per capita mention rate. If a category was mentioned 20 times by the ten stakeholders interviewed in village X, the per capita rate of mention was 2 (i.e., 20/10). Some stakeholders might have not mentioned the category at all while others might have mentioned it multiple times. However, only one mention was counted in each response to each open-ended question. Stakeholders could only have multiple mentions of a category if they repeated the idea in response to several different open-ended questions.

After four years of developing sets of codes for stakeholders' verbal responses, a standard set of codes was developed based on all the years. The responses were then recoded using this single set of codes. The coding system consisted of the two parts described in the above section entitled 'Validation of the social licence measure'. The content-oriented part contained approximately 80 codes to describe the content of the comment (e.g., infrastructure, environment, and communications). The 'voice'-oriented part contained 11 codes to describe the intent or 'voice' of the comment (e.g., blame, praise, statement of fact, request, suggestion, etc.). It is the ratio of these voice codes, namely praise for MSC and criticism of MSC that is graphed in Figure 10.1.

The standard coding frame allowed us to compare trends in the per capita mention rate of issues across the years. It also allowed a multi-year comparison of the voice of the comments. As shown in Figure 10.1, the ratio of blame to praise for MSC correlated highly with the level of social licence granted per year by all stakeholders.

Quantification of stakeholder influence

Extracting a stakeholder network from everything in the world

The third kind of data that contributes synergistically to a stakeholder relations strategy is network data. By itself, network data answers the question, 'What relationships exist among the stakeholders?' Combined with social licence scores and coded verbal comments it identifies groups of supporters or opponents and their concerns, which is key to deciding how to improve the level of social licence granted to a project.

The analysis of stakeholder networks is an application of social network analysis (Wasserman and Faust, 1994), which is a branch of sociology that has been taken up by all the social sciences and their applied fields (Borgatti et al., 2009). One early application of social network analysis in business, which used data from interviews with members of networks, focused on the ties inside organisations. Rob Cross and his colleagues used task and friendship ties inside organisations to develop strategies for things like organisational value change, downsizing without capacity loss, and team collaboration (Cross and Prusak, 2002; Cross et al., 2005). Social network analysis was also applied to inter-company networks in the study of things like inter-locking directorates (Boyd, 1990; Carroll and Sapinski, 2010), collaboration and knowledge-sharing networks (Powell et al., 1996; Stuart, 1998), supply chain relations (Dyer and Nobeoka, 2000), and numerous other topics.

At San Cristobal, we applied social network analysis to networks outside the company, with a focus on community and government organisations that could

110 Strategies from quantitative measures

affect the continuance of the project or that would be strongly affected by it. Those with enough influence and knowledge to convert their opinions into impacts on the company generally tend to be opinion leaders (Katz and Lazarsfeld, 1964). In networks where a high proportion of the members know each other personally (e.g., specialised professions, rural communities), the opinion leaders tend to end up as leaders of groups (e.g., clans, tribes) and organisations (e.g., professional associations, local government leaders). The converse is also true. Those who become group leaders tend to gain much more influence over the opinions of others.

By narrowing the field of network participants to leaders of stakeholder groups or organisations with significant stakes we avoided the problem of counting everyone in the world as a stakeholder of MSC. It is technically true that the operation of the San Cristobal mine has an impact on everyone in the world through its carbon footprint and its impact on the prices of silver, lead, and zinc. However, these impacts are generally so small that most people would not notice their absence were MSC to disappear.

Even with this simplification, we still faced the challenge of defining the exact boundaries of the stakeholder network at a level of detail sufficiently specific to say who is in and who is out. The general strategy was to err on the side of over-inclusiveness. We interviewed everyone who looked like they might be beyond the boundary so that we could later count them out if they had negligible connections to the network. We started with a list of stakeholder organisations suggested by MSC community liaison staff and added any others discovered through searching through media files on the mine. During the interviews, we also asked interviewees who else they thought should be interviewed. We made a point of getting such recommendations from those whose positions or jobs put them in touch with all elements and strata of their communities (e.g., school headmasters, religious leaders, popular retailers, local politicians, health care providers). When a group or organisation was recommended by three interviewees, we tried to interview them too. However, usually they were already on the list.

After the interviews, it was relatively easy to identify the core of the MSC stakeholder network and any significant outlying clusters. To draw a boundary delimiting the periphery, we identified interviewees who had no connection with anyone else, according to both their own interview data and the connections data provided by everyone else. We considered them outside the network and dropped them from the list of interviewees for the next set of interviews 15 months later. However, we kept their responses in the data for the current set of interviews. This probably caused us to err on the over-inclusive side, but the disadvantages of over-inclusiveness are smaller than the disadvantages of under-inclusiveness. Over-inclusiveness is just a waste of time. Under-inclusiveness creates the risk of missing an unanticipated negative impact from a looming controversy.

To obtain the network data, we dedicated the last part of the interview to asking about the quality of relationships with other stakeholders of MSC. Not all

Shift to quantitative risk assessment methods **111**

stakeholders appeared on the network graphs in all years. Some disappeared while others came into existence. Also, the methods for eliciting network contact information evolved from 2009 to 2013. The method used in 2013 has been used every year thereafter.

Changes in methods by year

In 2009, the interviews were confined to the villages closest to the mine and a few stakeholders representing Altiplano organisations. The organisations were listed by name and the interviewees were asked if their organisation had a relationship with each one.

The same method was used in 2011 but many more were listed. To manage the recall task, the list was divided into sections for each of the closest villages and for the rest of the Altiplano. There was also a section for additional nominees. This method appeared to have increased the reporting of relationships.

In 2012, the number of categories of stakeholders was expanded but no specific organisations were listed by name under any of the categories. The resulting network was less dense with relationships than the 2011 network, even though it included more stakeholders because interviews were conducted in both the Departmental and national capitals for the first time.

From 2013 to 2015 the same geographic range of stakeholders was covered but neither categories nor names were presented to the interviewees. Interviewees were left to report whatever relationships were 'top of mind'. This method produced networks that were sparse but that contained only the relationships that were so important that they came immediately to mind.

Generally, the changes in methods followed the principle of erring on the side of gathering too much information initially before narrowing down the focus. We applied the principle both to the range of stakeholders interviewed and the number of relationships elicited from each stakeholder. The changes in the methods affected both. In the case of the number of stakeholders interviewed, the expansion of the number of stakeholders up to 2012 was driven by the growing realisation that the whole set of stakeholders who could affect the project needed to include those in the capital cities. The 2012 method was arguably over-inclusive across that broader geographic range than the 2013 and 2015 methods. In terms of eliciting more relationship reports from each stakeholder, the 2011 method was probably the most over-inclusive because it prompted interviewees with both categories of stakeholders and names of stakeholders. The later 'top-of-mind' methods permitted more influence from memory filtering on the part of the interviewee. That is a good thing because it reveals the interviewees current prioritisation of relationships.

In the next chapter (Chapter 11), we look at the results uncovered by these methods and measures. In Chapter 12, we examine the strategies that emerged by combining the stakeholder census information with the knowledge of company personnel who deal daily with stakeholder issues.

Notes

1 See www.stakeholder360.com.
2 Alternatively, it may be phrased as neo-colonialism, or neo-liberalism, or some other 'ism' that did not originate at the local level. They are all shorthand ways of referring to a disruption to the previous local social order.
3 The probing technique used is known as 'laddering'. For a description of its application in this context, see Boutilier (2009; pp. 175–177).

11

CO-EVOLUTION OF RISK HOTSPOTS WITH BOLIVIAN POLITICS AND ECONOMY

2009–2015

2009: storm clouds on the horizon

In November of 2009, the interviews with stakeholders found MSC to have a social licence score of 3.0 out of a maximum of 5. This corresponds to the high acceptance category by international standards (see the Chapter 10 section entitled 'Quantification of social licence levels' and more detailed description available at https://tinyurl.com/y7b9ty59).

Figure 11.1 shows the stakeholder network for 2009. The level of social licence granted by each stakeholder is indicated by the shade of the node (rounded squares) for the stakeholder. The discussion for Figure 10.1 explains how an essentially continuous measure of relationship was turned into more strategically convenient categories using the sextile split technique. The darker shades indicate a high level of social licence. The white nodes indicate stakeholders who were not interviewed, and therefore could not have given a social licence score, but who were mentioned as relationship partners by at least one who was interviewed.

All the lines indicate relationships that were rated above 4 on a 5-point scale. That means they were strong enough to support inter-organisational collaboration. Weaker relationships were reported in the data but they are not shown on Figure 11.1 in order to emphasise the relationships that support immediate collaboration.

The vertical position of the node indicates the influence level of the corresponding stakeholder. Higher nodes are likely to be more influential because they are more well connected to well-connected others, as quantified by each node's score on eigenvector centrality (see Bonacich, 2007, for a comparison of centrality measures).

114 Strategies from quantitative measures

When a group of nodes are highly connected among themselves, they form a 'cluster'. The more ties they have among themselves, the more 'dense' is the cluster. Two clusters that are unconnected form two 'components' of the network. The space between unconnected nodes or clusters is called a 'structural hole'. Structural holes can vary in degree from the complete absence of ties to the complete disappearance of any distinction between the *a priori* clusters. A node that connects two otherwise unconnected nodes or clusters is said to be a 'bridger'. It 'bridges' the structural hole. Structural holes can also be bridged by a tie between two nodes that themselves are each well connected to their respective clusters.

Nodes with ties that bridge structural holes between clusters tend to have higher scores on betweenness centrality. Betweenness centrality is higher when the node is on a higher percentage of the shortest pathways among all pairs of nodes in the network. For example, word-of-mouth messages would more often have to pass through the nodes with higher betweenness centrality, assuming the messages travel the shortest possible pathways. In Figure 11.1, the larger nodes have higher betweenness centrality. The labels for the nodes are composed of abbreviations that give information about the organisation's geographic ring and socio-economic sector (see Table 11.1).

The left side of Figure 11.1 is populated mostly by the first-ring community organisations (with 'r1' in the label). They are mostly from the mining communities. Towards the top, there are a few second-ring ('r2') government organisations ('gv'). The government organisations are municipal and tend to have many ties distributed among the communities in their municipality.

The right side of the graph, is populated more by second-ring and third-ring organisations. They represent organisations of agricultural producers and indigenous regional organisations with offices located more than 50 kilometres from the mine. Notice that they have only one tie with a first-ring organisation (i.e., r1cpind23). This indicates a structural hole between the miners and the agriculturalists.

TABLE 11.1 Legend for node names in network graphs

Geographic ring	Socio-economic sector	Socio-economic adjective
XXccccc	ccXXccc	cccXXX
r1 = ring 1	cp = community, 'pueblo'	ind = indigenous (or grassroots, local)
r1 = ring 2	dv = development	cty = community (incl. education and social)
r3 = ring 3	ec = economic cps = cooperatives, producers, or union ('sindicato')	
	gv = government	prb = private business
		snr = senior (i.e., government above village level)

Co-evolution of risk hotspots

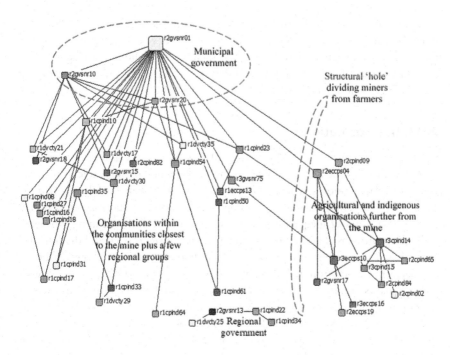

FIGURE 11.1 MSC's stakeholder network in 2009 based on ties of strength 4 out of 5.

The middle and bottom left of Figure 11.1 is populated mostly by representatives of organisations from the four villages closes to mine (i.e., 'ring 1' or 'r1'). The social licences ranged the full gamut from withheld to psychological identification. In the local villages the main issues were dust pollution and water shortages.

In 2010, MSC built a dome to contain the dust from the stockpile. At a cost of over $10 million, it was the largest dome in the Southern Hemisphere and was completely effective in containing the dust. The company also implemented a campaign to inform stakeholders that the water used by the mine was not contaminated but was nonetheless unsuitable for drinking or crop irrigation because of its high salt content. Several groups of stakeholders visited the mine. Some watched the general manager drink the water to prove that it was not contaminated.

The top of Figure 11.1 is occupied by three regional government representatives. Their well connectedness means they were probably aware of the diversity of opinion in the network. That may be why their social licences were in the acceptance level, indicating some ambivalence.

Generally, those at the bottom right of Figure 11.1 either withheld the social licence or granted it at a very low level. Their main issue was the income inequality that was created by the high wages received by the miners. To restore justice, which they equated with income equality, they wanted either the closure of the mine or economic development to raise the incomes of agricultural

116 Strategies from quantitative measures

producers and others who did not have jobs at the mine. In 2010, MSC supported expansion of the mandate of the economic development dialogue led by the *Consejo Consultivo* to address regional income inequality. At the same time, the San Cristobal Foundation, funded by MSC, refocused its granting activity on agricultural development projects.

2011: the occupation

In the next tracking wave, in May 2011, MSC's average social licence score rose to 3.3 out of 5, which corresponds to high acceptance or high tolerance using the sextile classification system in Table10.2. So many stakeholders had joined the dialogue on regional economic development that it was the most mentioned theme. The issues of inequality in access to health care and to mining jobs were also very controversial at the time, so much so that villagers occupied the mine for more than a week right in the middle of the interviewing period (see Chapter 9 for details). In addition to addressing these concerns, MSC continued with the regional economic development focus and assisted local communities with a petition to obtain a hospital for the town of San Cristobal.

Figure 11.2 shows the 2011 stakeholder network. The other network graphs in this series show relationships (i.e., lines) of strength 4 out of 5 on the measure of collaborative capacity in the relationship. Figure 11.2 is different because it shows only the relationships that were rated at 5 out of 5. The graph was restricted to

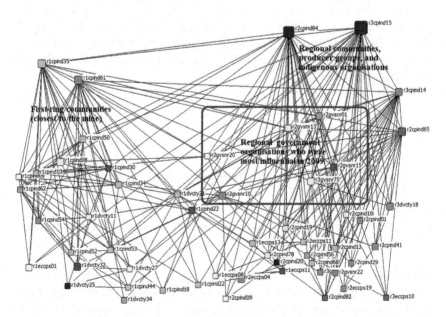

FIGURE 11.2 MSC's stakeholder network in 2011 based on ties of strength 5 out of 5.

this high criterion in an attempt to eliminate less strong relationships and, thereby, make it more visually interpretable. At the tie of strength level 4 out of 5, there were so many lines that they obscured each other.

The proliferation of strong ties is probably attributable to both methodological and substantive factors. The method used in 2011 was the most directive in terms of helping interviewees remember all the relationships their organisations might have with other organisations. Substantively, the period was characterised by a high level of mobilisation among the stakeholders. Less than a year earlier, there was a small insurrection in the Department of Potosí, supported by some of the agricultural producer organisations that appear at the bottom right of both the 2009 and 2011 graphs. Moreover, at the time of the interviewing, the first-ring communities around the mine organised to occupy the mine. The research literature on socio-political mobilisation (Flora *et al.*, 2006; Tindall and Robinson, 2006) suggests that these events probably increased the density of the stakeholder network as well as the strength of the ties within it.

Several additional noteworthy shifts can be noted from 2009 to 2011. The regional government organisations that were most influential in 2009 (see blue rectangle in Figure 11.2) were only of moderate influence in 2011, but they maintained their central position in terms of communicating between the first-ring stakeholders and the second- and third-ring stakeholders.

The most influential organisations in 2011 appear at the top right of Figure 11.2. They were agricultural and indigenous organisations that granted low tolerance social licences in 2009. This represents a dramatic shift in both social licence granted and influence exerted. The shift was accompanied by many more acceptance and approval level social licences among those influenced by these two. This illustrates a good strategy for raising the social licence of a project. First, attempt to raise the level of social licence granted by cluster leaders; then, try to make those new supporters more influential in the broader network.

The first-ring communities appear on the left side of Figure 11.2. In 2009, several withheld social licences but none withheld the social licence in 2011. Indeed, there are only two at the low acceptance level. The rest mostly range from high acceptance to high approval. This might seem odd, given that these same organisations were occupying the mine at the time. However, the apparent contradiction disappears when the details of the occupation are examined. The occupation was not about the presence or continuance of the project. Rather it was a power struggle for control of certain decisions (e.g. in human resources). Chapter 9 presents more details on the occupation.

2012: horizons expanded to the capital cities

In July and August of 2012, MSC's average social licence score did not rise significantly from the year before (2011: 3.3, 2012: 3.4). Regional economic development continued to be the main concern of stakeholders. Capital city stakeholders (i.e.,

La Paz and Potosí City) were interviewed for the first time in this wave. They perceived a lack of communication from MSC. MSC continued with the regional economic development initiative, with more emphasis in the municipal level. At the same time, new liaison processes were set up for the capital cities.

The left side of Figure 11.3 shows discernible clusters for the four communities of the first-ring, although these were interspersed with a few regional organisations. The cluster at the top left was the closest village, San Cristobal. The one to its right in the middle of the graph was the furthest of the four, Rio Grande. The two dense clusters at the bottom left were the other two nearby villages. Generally, the levels of the social licences granted in all these communities rose from their 2011 levels.

The right side of Figure 11.3 is more complicated and accounts for more of the withheld social licences in 2012. The top right stakeholder (r2eccps11) granted a low acceptance social licence and was well connected among second- and third-ring stakeholders. This was a transportation contractor of MSC who had strong ties with other transportation contractors. Most of them were cooperatives, at least in name, although the difference between a cooperative and a private enterprise can be blurry in Bolivia. Often coop leaders concentrate power at the top of the organisation. It is also common for coop 'members' to sub-contract the actual work to low-paid non-members. Some of the transportation contractors on the right side of Figure 11.3 had also participated in the 2010 mini-insurrection and continued to demand that MSC divert concentrate transportation from rail to road. These interviews were done before one of the transportation cooperative leaders was jailed for smuggling.

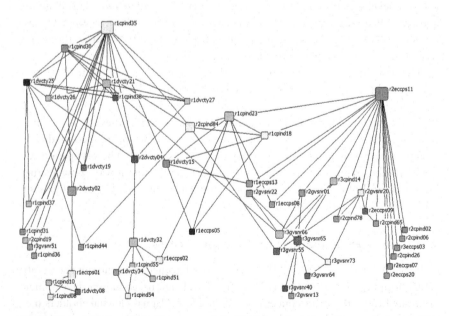

FIGURE 11.3 MSC's stakeholder network in 2012 based on ties of strength 4 out of 5.

Co-evolution of risk hotspots **119**

The loose cluster at the bottom right with the stakeholder labelled 'r3gvsnr65' at the centre was composed of government representatives in both Potosí and La Paz. They were mostly political supporters of the nationalisation of resource industries. Three of them withheld the social licence. Their relative interconnectedness among themselves was identified as a factor raising the risk of nationalisation for MSC. However, the severity of the risk was counterbalanced by the fact that their local community contacts granted moderate social licences. Also, these government stakeholders had no direct ties with the other identified risk cluster, the disaffected transportation contractors.

2013: the free market shows that it can benefit *campesinos* too

In November 2013, MSC's average social licence score rose from 3.4 to 3.5, which corresponds to the approval level. Quinoa prices had risen sharply, to the benefit of regional producers. One of the company's strongest critics from the previous year, a transportation contractor, was discovered to be a smuggler attempting to pressure the company into giving him cover for an expansion of his illegal operations. His drag on the social licence scores was not present in 2013 because he was in jail.

The main preoccupation among the rest of the stakeholders was the need for more training in business management and technical fields. This wave provided the first evidence that the regional economic development focus launched in 2010 was bearing fruit. More stakeholders were interested in embracing free markets.

Figure 11.4 shows that the most influential stakeholder in 2013 was the same municipal leader who was most influential in 2009 (r2gvsnr01). The social licence he granted rose from high tolerance/acceptance in 2009 to low approval/support in 2013.

Of all the relationships maintained by the five who withheld the social licence in Figure 11.4, only one was a tie with someone who granted a low acceptance social licence. The rest of their ties were with those who granted social licences of high acceptance or higher. This indicates that they did not have anyone with whom to collaborate in any efforts to withdraw the social licence from MSC.

The four clusters on the bottom left of Figure 11.4, headed respectively by r1cpind10, r1cpind35, r1dvcty17, and r1cpind63 were the four communities closest to the mine. Three of the four had direct ties to the municipal government leader, r2gvsnr01. The fourth community, San Cristobal, did not have such a link, perhaps because of a growing political rivalry. San Cristobal, headed by r1cpind35 in Figure 11.4, was growing in political influence throughout the municipality and broader region.

The government representative at the top right (r3gvsnr64) was a politician who withheld the social licence and who, by virtue of his position, had relationships with several well-connected stakeholders. However, he was alone among those in the top half of the chart in not being a member of any triangle of relationships. Therefore, despite being well connected, the structure of his personal network did not contain the nucleus of a socio-political front or movement.

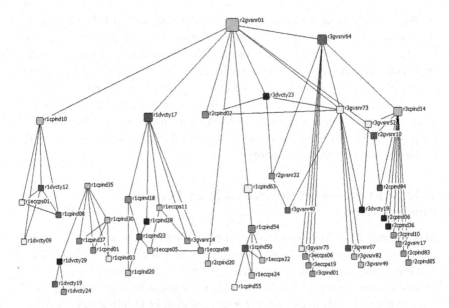

FIGURE 11.4 MSC's stakeholder network in 2013 based on ties of strength 4 out of 5.

The cluster on the right side headed by r3cpind14 was composed of many of the same groups and communities that granted very low or withheld social licence levels in 2009. In 2013, they were probably the strongest support base for MSC. They had changed from being the main opponents to being the main supporters. Their conversion had a great deal to do with increasing incomes made possible by several regional economic development initiatives combined with the rising price of quinoa. Several of the producer groups had begun exporting to the international market. In 2009 they complained about income inequality and in 2013 they could see the income gap closing at a satisfactory rate.

2015: the political emergence of San Cristobal town

MSC's overall social licence rose again from 3.5 in 2013 to 3.7 in 2015. The most influential stakeholder in 2015 (r1cpind35) had been the most influential in only the San Cristobal community in 2013. By January and February of 2015, he was poised to win the Colcha K municipal election a few weeks after the interviewing. He did indeed win and replaced the incumbent (r2gvsnr01) who had been the most influential stakeholder in the whole network in 2013. This reconnected the community of San Cristobal (leftmost cluster in Figure 11.5) to the network. The social licence among the most strongly connected stakeholders in San Cristobal also rose considerably from the 2013 level.

The head of the cluster on the extreme right of Figure 11.5, r1cpind05, was a group involved in some of the wide-ranging negotiations between the community

Co-evolution of risk hotspots   121

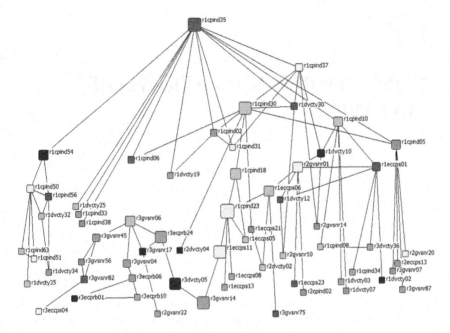

FIGURE 11.5   MSC's stakeholder network in 2015 based on ties of strength 4 out of 5.

and the company that took place from 2013 to 2015. This cluster represented some hardliners who were not satisfied with the outcome.

The loose cluster forming the rest of the right side of Figure 11.5 was composed of the other three first-ring communities and several regional government authorities. Their social licence levels were generally in the acceptance to approval levels. None of the stakeholders who were included in the Figure 11.5 graph withheld the social licence.

The nearly disconnected cluster at the bottom left headed by r3gvsnr06 was comprised mainly of government departments, state corporations, and industry associations. Geographically they were located in Potosí and La Paz. The cluster included three triangles. None of the triangles were cohesive units of social licence withholders, but several of the important stakeholders in the cluster could not be interviewed. The interviewing took place while many were involved in an election campaign. We did know that some of them withheld the social licence in previous years (e.g. r3gvsnr14) but we did not know if their opinions had changed. That cluster was identified as needing further monitoring.

The network graphs showing social licence levels, combined with per capita rates of issue mentions, proved to be very valuable in identifying potential sociopolitical risks and strategies for reducing them. Equally important, they highlighted otherwise hidden opportunities for creating new alliances for raising the level of social licence. In the next chapter, we look in more detail at the strategies that were developed each year.

12

FROM FINDINGS TO STRATEGIES THAT WORK

The initiatives with MSC's stakeholders usually took two or three years to show results. We begin this chapter with a list of the main strategic recommendations made based on each round of interviewing each year. The subsequent sections tell the multi-year stories of specific initiatives related to each recommendation.

Issues and recommendations by year

2009

The biggest concern of stakeholders in 2009 was dust from the stockpile at the mine. This was not the basis of recommendation because construction of a dome to control the dust had already begun. It cost more than $10 million to build and, when it was finished, it was the largest dome in the Southern Hemisphere.

The gap between the wealth of the mine workers and everyone else was identified as the greatest risk in 2009, and reducing it was a top priority. Therefore, a recommendation in 2009 was to foster more collaboration among four groups that had some combination of budgets and plans for regional economic development. They were the municipality of Colcha K, the *Consejo Consultivo*, FRUTCAS, and the *Mancomunidad de Lípez*.

The MSC mine is in the municipality of Colcha K. Some of the royalties MSC pays return to the municipal government. In 2009 the municipality had not spent any of the receipts. As a result, the municipal treasury had amassed approximately $7 million while residents complained about not seeing any local benefits of the presence of the mine.

The municipal consultative council (*Consejo Consultivo*) was comprised of representatives from the communities of the municipality and advised the municipal administration. The council had developed a regional infrastructure plan.

From findings to strategies that work **123**

FRUTCAS was one of the leading *campesino* organisations. They maintained significant influence with the national government and had a plan for regional development.

The *Mancomunidad de Lípez* is a voluntary cooperative of community administrations and smaller municipalities. It pools some administrative functions. The *Mancomunidad* also had a regional development plan with a budget.

None of these organisations were capable of fomenting regional economic development alone. Unfortunately, they were not talking to each other about what they might be able to do jointly.

2011

The main recommendations for 2011 centred on overcoming perceptions of discrimination and unfairness. Improved access to health care, jobs, technical education, and water were all recommended as part of the process of making the company's meritocratic operating principles appear less unjust in a culture that valued equality over equity. The recommendations included collaborations to improve access to health care, access to higher levels of technical training, a review of hiring and promotion criteria to give adequate credit for work experience, and continued collaboration to find ways for both mining and agriculture to prosper. Water issues were the focus of the latter.

2012

In 2012, the quantity and quality of communication from MSC and the quality of relationships with MSC joined economic development as top issues. Many of these complaints about the relationship quality turned out to be pressures for more favouritism in awarding contracts. The transportation cooperatives were particularly vocal and applied pressure through their advocacy for withdrawal of MSC's social licence. At the same time, the 2012 interviews were the first to include the capital cities and therefore uncovered more issues related to nationalisation. The recommendations placed both the local and the national pressures in the context of the curse of natural resources and its attendant rise in rent-seeking entrepreneurship (see Chapter 2 for a full discussion). The 2012 study recommended rejecting rent-seeking pressures in favour of working with others, especially the municipality, to foster market-based economic opportunities for entrepreneurs (e.g. help with ISO certifications). To support that, it also recommended implementing a communications plan that emphasised wealth creation over wealth redistribution.

2013

In 2013, attitudes had shifted considerably regarding the legitimacy of the free market and international trade. This helped MSC's social licence. Water was now seen in roughly equally measure as both a production input and a symbol of 'life' itself.

124 Strategies from quantitative measures

The demand for technical and administrative training and skills surged. Further efforts to create multi-sectoral collaboration towards meeting these needs was recommended, but to be applied after the impending elections.

2015

In 2015 stakeholders talked more about sustaining their gains after mine closure. It was recommended that the mine closure discussion be encouraged in order to take attention away from proposals that would create dependency and to draw more attention to development proposals of a self-sufficient nature. The issue of mineral processing in Bolivia and a national industrialisation policy emerged. It was recommended that MSC work with like-minded bodies to proactively develop a feasible policy position on this question.

Dust reduction initiatives

As mentioned, MSC built a $10 million dome over its ore stockpile to prevent dust from being blown across the mine site, over llama grazing areas and cultivated land, and towards the town of San Cristobal. However, complaints continued in subsequent years about dust raised by traffic on the roads, which covered crops and sometimes entered houses. The complaints mostly came from communities west of the mine, mostly in the second-ring. The traffic in that direction is mostly tourist SUVs and buses. This led to calls for MSC to take on the responsibilities of the national government and pave the roads. The company has resisted this call. For the roads to and from the mine, however, MSC used water to suppress dust. However, in the semi-desert of the Altiplano, this method is also controversial. Eventually MSC engineers developed a safe, low-cost compound to put on the roads that sealed the surface for up to six months. Dust complaints have disappeared.

Water initiatives

Education about non-pollution

In 2010 and 2011 tours of the mine were organised to educate stakeholders about MSC's water use. The main objective was to dispel the false belief that MSC was polluting water supplies. A secondary objective was to emphasise that the water MSC uses is too salty to be used for either agriculture or human consumption. The mine is less than 50 kilometres from the largest salt flat on earth, the Salar de Uyuni, which covers an area about the size of Lebanon. Finally, the initiative increased awareness of the role of global climate change in altering rainfall patterns.

Increased agricultural production and closing the income gap

Through the San Cristobal Foundation, quinoa production in the first-ring villages expanded rapidly from 2012 onward, especially in Culpina K. The key was the introduction of micro-irrigation technology which made better use of existing water resources. Meanwhile, the local price of a bag of quinoa went from half a bag of rice to three full bags of rice, a 600 per cent increase. This, along with the successful efforts of agricultural and indigenous groups to promote exports to international markets, resulted in a reduction of the income gap between mining families and agricultural families.

Human water consumption and community infrastructure

Water for human consumption was the second most mentioned issue in 2009, after dust. In subsequent years MSC began making deliveries of potable water to the first-ring communities. The mention of water quality and potable water declined sharply in 2011 and 2012 (see Figure 12.1) but it spiked again in 2013 for three reasons. First, it was a dry year. Second, the increased acreage dedicated to quinoa cultivation placed more demands on the water supply. Third, noting the increased demand from agriculturalists, the government officials in favour of nationalisation began promoting MSC's water use as a barrier to sustainable development and therefore a justification for at least higher taxes, if not outright nationalisation. In a desert, water is frequently the flashpoint for political differences.

The per capita rate of household water consumption in San Cristobal exceeds that of La Paz, even though San Cristobal is in a desert and La Paz is surrounded by glaciers. By 2015, disagreements emerged about what is written in the overarching 'mother' agreement (*'convenio madre'*) regarding MSC's responsibilities to supply first-ring villages with household water. We examined the agreement ourselves and had to agree with the company that their responsibilities extended to only the original families, who now comprise a smaller per cent of the whole population.

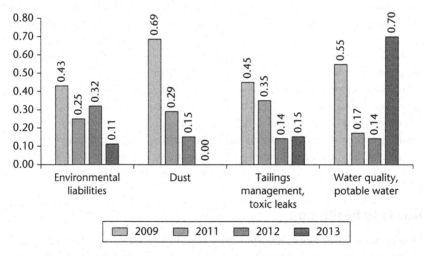

FIGURE 12.1 Per capita frequencies of environmental and water issues from 2009 to 2013.

126 Strategies from quantitative measures

Those in the community who also agree with this interpretation feel it is the responsibility of the municipality to help with the infrastructure needs of growing communities. They became frustrated with the lack of action from the municipality and nominated their own candidate for municipal president (i.e., similar to a mayor) in the 2015 elections. He won.

True-CSR (corporate social responsibility) versus pseudo-CSR

The three-way political dynamic among the company, the municipality, and the community is one we have seen played out numerous times on different continents and under different political systems. The responsible government, be it municipal, state, or national, sees the presence of a mine as a windfall for residents. They have jobs and therefore are not as needy as others in the jurisdiction. The government therefore ignores the needs of the mining community. The community has low expectations of government anyway and therefore turns to the company to fill the gap left by government. We have seen companies react in two basic ways.

One reaction, which we shall dub the 'pseudo-CSR/dependence' path, is to start taking on government responsibilities, usually in infrastructure but sometimes in health and education as well. This reaction often prompts outsiders to move to the mining community in order to benefit from the superior amenities. In extreme cases, the communities have more than tripled in population. This increases the cost to the company but also increases the pressure on the company to continue or expand the services.

The other reaction, which might be best labelled the 'true-CSR/independence' path, involves strengthening the social capital within the community network so that it can exert more effective political pressure on the government, rather than on the company. The more local the government: the more effective this approach. Many mayors quickly realise that the mining community has political clout and can become a credible political actor if not placated. In the San Cristobal case, the community's increased disaffection with the municipal government was reflected in the 2013 network graph showing no strong tie between the community and the municipal president (see Figure 11.4). The 2015 network graph (Figure 11.5) shows what happens to mayors who call the bluff of mining communities that have developed dense internal ties and a determination to get what they deserve from the municipality. Figure 11.5 was based on data from several weeks before the municipal election but nonetheless reflects the outcome. The company, of course, has a large role to play in fostering that community cohesiveness on the political front. Indeed, this is core to the concept of community development.

Access to health care

One of the areas in which discrimination was alleged during the 2011 occupation of the mine was access to health care and related services. The 2011 stakeholder strategy report recommended action on this issue.

The 2011 discussions around health care access were triggered by a road accident in which a Culpina K leader was killed while riding in an ambulance with his sick son on the road to a full service hospital in Potosí. The road is dangerous, and the travel time is several hours. At the time, the health needs of the community were being attended to by a clinic with very limited capacity to deal with complex medical conditions or trauma. On the other hand, the mine maintained a high quality medical facility to attend to any 'on the job' condition or industrial emergency. Moreover, the company had made a written commitment to install a regional hospital in San Cristobal as one of the conditions in the resettlement agreement. The communities applied equality principles and therefore found the differences discriminatory.

Various proposals were put forward, including flying sick or injured community members to hospital. As the discussion progressed, it became clear that proposals of that sort would only change the boundary of discriminatory access without solving the root problem. Furthermore, the second-ring communities experienced poor access to medical support even more severely. It was agreed that the distance to the hospital was everyone's problem. Thus, action was accelerated to fulfil MSC's original promise to see that San Cristobal had a regional hospital. San Cristobal now has that hospital.

Communications planning

The 2012 recommendations outlined a communications plan aimed at altering the grassroots discourse around the mine's role in Bolivian society from one of owing a debt of wealth redistribution to one of contributing to wealth creation and helping others to make their contribution as well. The election of a former MSC employee to the position of municipal president in 2015 contributed to meeting that local objective. Meanwhile, MSC has tried to maintain a low media profile nationally. The 2015 study included interviews with newspaper representatives for the first time. As of 2015, no initiatives had been launched at the level of the national discourse on resource nationalism. However, in 2016, journalists were invited to tour the mine. The main message was that MSC operates at higher standards of worker safety, community benefit, and environmental stewardship than the state-controlled mines.

The limits of stakeholder strategies

MSC's experience with developing stakeholder strategies from open-ended comments, measures of the social licence, and stakeholder network ties illustrates how socio-political risk can be managed in a quantifiable, verifiable way. Intuition might be quicker, but the process described here is more transparent and accessible to everyone, even those without political instincts.

The success of this approach to strategy development can be pushed too far. Sometimes Human Resource departments want to turn social licence scores

128 Strategies from quantitative measures

into key performance indicators (KPI). That means the social licence measures would be used in annual evaluations of the performance of community relations personnel. We think this should be approached with great caution because it can often take three years for a strategy to be reflected in higher social licence scores. For example, when dealing with a local tyrant who has great sway over stakeholder opinion but ultimately puts his own interests above those of the stakeholders, a sound stakeholder strategy would result in a lower social licence score in the first year. The tyrant would turn everyone against the project because the strategy would threaten his privileged position. If KPI were assessed annually, by the second year the human resources department might falsely conclude that the strategy implementer was performing poorly.

Stakeholder strategies are intended to move the project from a lower to a higher level of acceptance and approval. However, the path is often not a straight line. Raising the social licence level is more like sailing a yacht. You can take a straight-line course when the wind is behind you and you have a spinnaker. More often, however, you'll need to take a zig-zag tacking course for at least part of the journey. Sometimes your best strategy is to go backward for a stretch in order to catch more favourable winds in another place. And then there are those times when you can only tie up in port and wait for the weather to improve. Sometimes you do not get to the destination on time. Nonetheless, changing the schedule is better than sinking the boat. The political winds and currents around a project are ever-shifting and only partially predictable. Strategy processes are useful tools, like compasses and charts. They reduce the risk, but they can never take the surprises out of stakeholder politics.

PART 4

Distinctive features and conclusions

13

WOMEN AND THE SAN CRISTOBAL MINE

Women and mining

Mining is an industry which has always been male-dominated. Wherever it operates, a strongly masculine aura and male-oriented culture manifests in various ways, both overt and in more subtle forms. From the first contact between the exploration team that discovered and evaluated the mineralisation at San Cristobal through to the present day, material contact between the communities and MSC has been almost exclusively between men: male community leaders and male company managers. It was well into the construction phase, ten years after initial discovery, that MSC hired a woman to engage with the communities, which opened the way for women to communicate directly with the company rather than mediated by transmission through the men. The arrival of the mine produced significant consequences for women, both positive and negative, that are distinct from those experienced by men.

Historical overview

Prior to discovery of the giant ore deposit in 1995, the three communities closest to the site (San Cristobal, Culpina K, and Vila Vila) were isolated, depopulated, and living a very traditional *campesino* (rural worker) lifestyle. Economic activity depended heavily on quinoa production and remittance monies from family members who had migrated out to find work in cities within Bolivia and in mines in Chile and Argentina. Llama husbandry, typically the responsibility of the women, provided a further occasional source of income and food supply. Seasonal production of vegetables provided the principle source of food security. Annual incomes were low and gender roles well defined.

132 Distinctive features and conclusions

The initial response of the community to the exploration team charged with evaluating the mineralisation at San Cristobal was one of caution: previous experience with mining companies had not been positive. As the parties got to know each other, the relationship strengthened, and the men started to become animated by the possibility of work at a mine operated by people they found credible. The women were a little less enthusiastic, concerned as to the nature of changes that would come with a new mine and more receptive to the negative images of social and environmental harm supplied by FRUTCAS and the Church. Nevertheless, the younger women came to see the prospect of a mine as a positive, an opportunity for their men and their children. The necessity of relocating the community to make way for the mine caused further concerns, particularly for the older women who did not want to leave the home they knew and loved. They led the minority that voted against relocation.

The majority vote for resettlement, a *de facto* endorsement for development of the mine, led to a planning process in which the women were under-represented. The result was dissatisfaction with the design and construction of houses in New San Cristobal. After the long wait for a decision, the announcement in 2004 that the company would go ahead with construction sparked a new interest in all members of the communities in the prospect of gainful employment. There was considerable optimism among both men and women for the final arrival of the much-anticipated full employment. For a brief period, there were no negatives.

During construction of the San Cristobal mine and the initial year of operations, MSC had no formal policy with respect to gender or non-discrimination in employment. The principal driver for decisions on employment came from the need to comply with the commitments set out in the agreements with the communities and a general desire to maximise local employment as a means of avoiding negative reactions from the local population. The relevant wording in the San Cristobal agreement reads:

> The Company will give priority for contract of workers of active age to members of the population of San Cristóbal as named by the community authorities for the development of the mining project during the phases of exploration, construction and exploitation and to effect this the Company will give them practical courses of training to effectively use their abilities and will to work.

Washington Group did have an unwritten policy of encouraging women into the labour force because of positive experiences elsewhere that had shown women to be more cautious, responsible, and reliable operators of trucks and heavy equipment. It is perhaps noteworthy that such approaches would be considered illegal under current Bolivian law and regulations, introduced since the mine came into production, which prohibit discrimination or 'favouritism' towards any group or class of people.

The construction period provided abundant opportunities for temporary employment and all local residents who wished to work were able to do so. In addition, many people from outside the district, almost all male, were brought in to meet the needs for skilled workers, trades, and general labour. A camp was established to house this labour force, which peaked at more than 3,000 occupants in 2006. Many local women found employment at the camp and the associated catering facility.

Washington Group began pre-stripping of the ore-body in 2006 and in the process assembled the first permanent workforce. An equal opportunity approach was taken by Washington Group that included an attempt to hire women as truck drivers and heavy equipment operators. The customary ban on women working in the mine, firmly linked to underground mining, was weakened in the face of the very different conditions presented by an open-pit operation. Nevertheless, there was strong resistance from men in the community who resented the idea of women taking what were considered then (and to this day) to be the most prestigious jobs in the mine. Despite the opposition and associated harassment, two women were trained to drive the 200-tonne haul trucks. They were still working in this capacity in 2016.

Construction proved to be a highly stressful time for the local population, including the women. Those working for the various contractors and sub-contractors complained of being discriminated against and verbally abused. There is no documented record of any physical abuse of women, such as rape or assault, nor any anecdotal account of such extreme situations. In-migration to San Cristobal, Culpina K, and Vila Vila was dominated by returning family and extended family members, who understood community norms of behaviour. Away from the workplace, contact between local women and men from outside the communities was limited with the men living in the camp several kilometres away. Prostitution, a frequent aspect of construction projects, was largely contained, involving a few individuals from outside the district (and none from the communities). On the other hand, it was the local women who mourned the loss of landscape that came with excavating the open-pit and led the cause for recovering the culturally significant stones and other artefacts.

As construction advanced into 2006, concern in the local population moved to the question of who would gain permanent employment in the mine. In August of 2006, MSC held a Job Fair for the residents of the local communities which profiled permanent positions that would be available once production commenced (Valverde and Martínez, 2008). People were invited to sign-up for the jobs that were of interest to them. All individuals, male and female, were tested for aptitude and literacy skills and if accepted were offered placement into training programmes prior to permanent employment. Individuals lacking literacy skills were given remedial training and, on passing the literacy test, offered permanent employment. It is noteworthy that a significant number of women seeking permanent employment expressed interest in working in the mineral processing plant.

134 Distinctive features and conclusions

As training and hiring moved ahead, community leaders communicated their concerns to the Community Relations team regarding female 'heads of single parent families', whom they felt should be assured of the best paying permanent employment they could obtain in order to avoid being marginalised into poverty when temporary employment ended. In response, the Community Relations team undertook a survey that identified 30 such women. Of these, five had secure incomes (teachers, commercial activities, etc.) and four did not wish to work at the mine. The remaining 21 women were offered employment in various areas following an aptitude and literacy evaluation. Seven of these women, aged from 20 to 62, were trained to work in the plant (Minera San Cristobal, 2007).

Following termination of the contract with the Washington Group in 2010, Sumitomo restructured the workforce resulting in an additional three women being hired to drive the largest haul trucks.

With continuous full time employment, the women in the communities found themselves faced with a number of gender specific challenges. It was the women who continued to be responsible for managing the home, family, livestock, and sustaining the cultivation of vegetables for domestic consumption. Worse for some, the arrival of regular income – new wealth – resulted in marital stress of various forms. There was increased alcohol consumption, incidents of family violence (including the death of one woman), and men deserting their families in favour of younger women.

Women in the mine

The prevailing cultural norm in Bolivia is that women do not work inside a mine. They should not be involved in the extraction of ore from the ground due to the common belief that their presence will cause the valuable minerals to disappear (Godoy, 1990). The claim that, by their very presence, women can collapse the wealth of a mine seems to have been brought to Bolivia by the Spanish and propagated by the priests that accompanied the colonists. This fear is, in turn, derived from the First Inquisition and the quest to eradicate the old, woman-centred beliefs of northern and central Europe by demonising them as the realm of heretical witches.

Although convention prevents women from entering a mine in Bolivia, they can work at and around a mine, and have often done so in significant numbers (Godoy, 1990). Typically, they work as *paileros* processing the ore delivered to them by the men, carefully separating the valuable minerals from gangue. It was perhaps with this in mind that, at a meeting with senior management from MSC in August 2004, the male-dominated leadership of San Cristobal declared work in the mine to be the exclusive domain of the men. They were, however, quite comfortable with women working in more conventional roles such as catering, housekeeping, and administration.

The situation in 2016

As explained in the preceding paragraphs, the situation for women has changed substantially since 2004. Today, women are employed across all areas. They work in the open-pit, the ore processing plant, the administration, and the camp and catering service that is under contract to Newrest Catering Bolivia S.A. At the end of 2016, women represented 13.3 per cent of the total workforce (all roles) employed directly by MSC, most of them in conventional positions such as secretarial, administration, Human Resources, and Community Relations. One woman held a management position as Superintendent of a unit in the mine. Furthermore, 80 per cent of the women working at MSC were from the local communities of San Cristobal, Culpina K, Vila Vila, and Ramaditas. The remaining 20 per cent came from outside the region, mostly from the cities of La Paz, Cochabamba, Potosí, and Santa Cruz. They commute to the mine site on a rotational basis.

Women made up 20 per cent of the workforce in the plant and 5 per cent of the workforce in the open-pit mine and related activities. The advance from 'no women' to a significant number of women in unconventional roles in the mine and plant is worthy of attention. In 2015, MSC identified a total of 67 women as being in unconventional occupations, including (but not limited to), chemical engineers, systems analysts, mechanics, electricians, plumbers, heavy equipment operators (including heavy equipment dispatch), control supervisors and operators in the plant, and security guards.

The figure of 20 per cent in the plant is a major step towards the 30 per cent considered to represent a key threshold for gender inclusion in the international mining industry. On closer analysis, it is significant that in the concentrator section of the plant, 29 per cent of the workers are women. Of these, two of the eight persons in the control room are women, as are three of the four persons responsible for managing flotation circuit reagents. Informally, male workers talk of the plant being 'run by women' and 'their stronghold'. The number of women working in the open-pit, although relatively low, is significant since these individuals occupy some of the most sought after, prestigious, and highest paid positions at MSC.

MSC reports that, from the start of production through to 2016, there had been only 'two or three' formal complaints from women of harassment in the workplace; all of which were resolved satisfactorily.

Perspectives on women in the mine workplace

A study was completed in 2013 (Hohn *et al.*, 2013) that aimed to gain a more complete understanding of the transition from *campesino* life to mining community and how this had affected the women working at the mine. It was followed up with further interviews in 2015. The findings describe the challenges and opportunities that have come with work at the mine.

Perspective of the women

To varying degrees, the women say that they enjoy their work very much and take great pride in their roles at MSC. Most of them feel there are excellent opportunities for potential advancement. However, some note that upon inquiry regarding

136 Distinctive features and conclusions

professional development, they were somehow discouraged or held back from advancement by their direct supervisor or manager. Two women had advanced as far as they believed possible. They would like the opportunity for continued professional development but noted that there is no clear path in place for any further advancement. An opinion was expressed that, even though there were opportunities for women, there are still more opportunities for men.

For women with families, whether a single parent or married with children, there was unanimous articulation of the immense difficulty of balancing a family life and work at MSC. In addition to sacrificing time with their children, more than one participant cited strain with their spouse because of their work schedule.

The majority feel that women in the workplace are treated equally and with respect. Among the women in unconventional roles, only a small minority feel they have to work harder than men to receive respect in the workplace. Most women indicate that they are exposed to some level of machismo ranging from more subtle behaviours to, in some cases, overt and reportable harassment. Those women who had been with MSC for six or more years, noted that the overall situation has improved significantly.

A clear majority report no issues or tension with their immediate families (parents, siblings) regarding their employment or roles at MSC. Many reported that their families were proud of their daughters' or sisters' accomplishments and ability to support themselves.

Among women commuting from La Paz, some indicate that their social network has essentially evaporated: they no longer have any friends outside MSC. Because their time at home is precious, family is prioritised. The result is that, for these women, the original social network of childhood friends and university peers has been entirely lost and replaced with mine site co-workers.

When asked how they would advise a younger generation of women as to whether they should work at the mine, most women thought the opportunity to work at MSC was well worth pursuing. However, many qualified their response by stating that it is very complicated to balance work with family life – and, if they were asked, they would only recommend working at MSC to a single woman. One respondent would advise young women to finish school before applying because the opportunities would be that much greater.

Almost all of the women indicate that their job at MSC has made their lives better, regardless of some of the workplace struggles (machismo, work-family balance). They have improved their own lifestyle, can provide things for their children that they never thought they could, and are appreciative of this opportunity.

Perspectives from the local communities

Community leaders talk of the movement of women into employment at the mine as having occurred almost without negative comment within the community. There is strong support for women working in general, pride in their achievements, and approval regarding their economic success. Envy from other women appears to be the principal negative element. The following material concerns, observations, and perspectives were noted:

> The proactive recruitment of single women head of households has been successful in ensuring that these families are not marginalised into poverty. However, since the opening of the mine, a new group of women have become head of single parent families (both as a result of divorce and unplanned pregnancies) and need to find work (preferably at the mine) or risk falling into poverty

There is concern that where both parents of a family are working at the mine, children may not receive adequate care and attention. Community leaders are particularly pleased with the day-care centre in San Cristobal for very young children (six months to three years eleven months of age) of MSC employees. It is felt the centre is a success and serves a genuine need, particularly for single mothers. However, at the time of writing, there is no similar facility for women in Culpina K or Vila Vila.

Concern is expressed regarding significant stress in work-life balance for women working at the mine and having to continue to manage a household, children, and, in many cases, animals and seasonal aspects of food production (planting and harvesting). On the other hand, support for working mothers has emerged in the form of an informal service industry that provides care for children and aged parents, as well as janitorial and culinary skills, which employs both younger and older women in the communities

In general, the transition from the pre-mine situation, where women had well-defined roles dominated by managing domestic affairs, to employment at the mine, has taken place with very little comment and minimal disruption to community level activities. Within the local communities, women's networks and support groups remain strong and important for the women themselves. Membership of women's groups such as the *Club de Madres* (Mothers Club) has remained relatively stable, although participation has become episodic for the working women.

By and large, community leaders feel that employment at the mine is a positive activity for women, notably for those who are unmarried or who head single parent families. For the latter group, employment is essential. Without stable employment, their families would experience significant financial stress due to local inflation driven by the wealth flowing from the mine. In this respect, the traditional community value of equality is manifested once again.

There are, however, serious negatives that present themselves. Throughout the local communities, women have found themselves handling new family dynamics that have come with the money gained from regular employment. Entirely new responsibilities have emerged such as the management of second and third houses and businesses purchased as family investments in Uyuni and Potosí. There has also been growth in the use of drugs, particularly among youth, that has become a concern largely shouldered by the women in the communities. The mine has brought

138 Distinctive features and conclusions

changes that continue to ripple through the local communities, some of which are almost invisible, and often affect women disproportionately.

Company initiatives to support women in the workplace

While there are no formal policies or procedures in place with respect to gender and hiring at the San Cristobal mine (such protocols are illegal under Bolivian law), MSC takes great care to ensure that there is gender equality (opportunities for employment) and pay equity (that women are paid the same as men for the same jobs). In practice, MSC is very pleased with its female workers, who are perceived as dedicated, productive, responsible, and loyal to each other and the company.

In recognition that working at the mine site generally, and extended rotation specifically, is difficult for women with families, MSC has implemented a range of initiatives to help women with work-family balance and to keep in better contact with their families including: (a) increased telephone and internet capacity and access; (b) changes in shift-work and rotations schedules to better balance work and family life; and, (c) the opening of the day-care facility in San Cristobal.

Company initiatives to support women in the community

In the early years of operation, MSC used a variety of approaches to try and help the women adjust to the presence of the mine. Initially, the focus was on programmes intended to build capacity that were designed and delivered by the company. For example, programmes in money management, health and diet, and in creating small businesses. Subsequently, emphasis shifted to broader social initiatives generated from within the communities and coordinated with the *Consejo Consultivo*, which reflect the vision and priorities of the women themselves. These have tended to emphasise aspects of health, education, support for youth, and other family-related concerns that are seldom high on the agenda promoted by the men.

A further perspective

Talking to workers at the mine, management, and residents in the host communities of San Cristobal, Culpina K, and Vila Vila yields considerable anecdotal evidence that the visit to the mine by Evo Morales, the President of Bolivia, in August 2009, had a significant impact on the dynamics between male and female employees.

Morales was overwhelmed by the physical scale of the operation and impressed by the 200-tonne trucks that moved ore and waste rock to the plant and dump piles respectively. He was invited to ride in one of the huge haul trucks by a woman from the local community and taken completely by surprise by the way she followed him up the ladder into the drive cabin, started the machine, and then drove him away on a tour of the open-pit. Also taken aback were the journalists travelling with Morales and documenting the visit. On the President's return to the base of operations, the journalists were more interested in interviewing the diminutive woman who had handled the enormous truck with such confidence, than asking Morales for his impressions of the mine.

It was perhaps at that point that the male workers realised that the women were much more than annoyances and members of the opposite sex to be harassed and teased. By all accounts, they realised that their women were pioneers within Bolivia and worthy of value rather than disrespect.

Concluding thoughts

Company-community agreements included clauses for the prioritisation of local employment, which opened the opportunity for women to apply for work. Somewhat later, a number of economically vulnerable women (all single parents) were identified by the community as a priority for permanent employment opportunities. In practice, women have not been deterred from applying for unconventional positions or advancing towards them. Importantly, there has been acceptance by the local community and male counterparts as they prove themselves in unconventional roles.

The singularly high proportion of women in the concentrator section of the plant is not easily explained. While they seemed to have unconsciously adopted the traditional role for women in Bolivian mining, of separating the valuable minerals from worthless materials, it may more realistically reflect comfort with the idea of working indoors and was certainly the best paying opportunity at the time of initial hiring in 2006. At that point in the history of the San Cristobal mine, all jobs on the mining side operated by Washington Group had been filled. The open-pit was still seen the domain of the men. The few women working there had to deal with significant harassment.

Despite the economic successes, the arrival of the mine has brought changes in the social dynamics of the communities, including at the level of individual families, which are specific to the role of women. The result has been increased stress for many of the women, who find themselves assuming new or expanded responsibilities and rendering them disproportionately more negatively affected by the mine than the men.

Today, the women working for MSC are defining themselves; as opposed to having their gender roles and gender identity defined by history (and their men). The workplace is not completely devoid of 'machismo'; women continue to work through the issues, but they note that the situation has improved significantly over time.

14

THE TROUBLE WITH LLAMAS

Apparently, back in 1998 and 1999, no one was thinking about the llamas; far less planning a future for them. One of the most remarkable features of the resettlement and land acquisition agreements with San Cristobal, Culpina K, and Vila Vila is the absence of any mention of llamas grazing in the areas to be vacated. The EIA and Social and Environmental Action Plan (EAP) prepared by Apex Silver are similarly silent on the fate of llamas displaced by construction of the mine and tailings facility. However, it is interesting to see that compensation for land acquired for the mine and tailings facility was calculated using llama units (the area of land needed to support one llama being equal in value to that of a llama). There is reference in the EIA to the numbers of llamas grazing at Wila Khara on the land subsequently used for the tailings facility, but no similar accounting of llamas in the area of the future open-pit and plant site. The EAP includes a generic programme of assistance in llama husbandry. Nowhere is there any mention of relocating llama herds.

People involved in the negotiations recall that the emphasis throughout was on land and compensation in terms of land units. When it came to relocation, all of the discussion was around moving the people of San Cristobal, the church, and the cemetery. The subject of llamas came up in the context of the San Cristobal Foundation. In the agreement to establish the Foundation and associated agro-industrial company there is specific mention of future commercialisation of llamas for their meat and wool. It seems that there was a collective assumption that the llamas would just move. There was certainly no suggestion that they would be culled or otherwise disappear. This was to prove a serious oversight and a source of one of the most complex and fractious aspects of the San Cristobal project.

About llamas

Llamas have been part of the cultural and economic life of people in the high Andes for more than two thousand years. The animals that can be seen around

The trouble with llamas **141**

San Cristobal and other communities on the Altiplano are semi-domesticated and range free across the landscape. They know and are known by their owners and the shepherds who spend some time with them throughout the year. Historically, llamas were used as pack animals with San Cristobal a centre for the llama trains that carried goods between the silver mines of Bolivia and the Pacific Coast. Many of the residents were *llameros*, managing the pack trains, breeding llamas, and looking after the animals. The use of llamas for transport declined rapidly at the beginning of the last century and the relationship between people and llamas became more typical of that found across the Andes. Llamas became a source of food security: you could always sell a llama or kill one and eat it. By extension, they symbolised wealth. They also continued to have great cultural and religious significance. To this day, the sacrifice of a llama is central to a number of the festivals and ceremonies held throughout the year by the Quechua- and Aymara-speaking peoples of Bolivia and Peru.

When it comes to llama husbandry, and the relocation of llamas, there are some singular characteristics to be kept in mind. Without being too technical, these are:

- Llamas are social animals. Throughout the Altiplano of Bolivia, they live in groups named '*tropas*' or herds led by a dominant individual (male or female depending on the composition and age range of the herd).
- Llamas are communal animals. Individuals are born into the herd and the females normally remain in this group for life. They graze and sleep together and, more significantly, travel to water sources and drink together. Interestingly, members of the herd all defecate in the same place, creating piles of faecal matter that are a convenient source of fertiliser for the food crops grown by the local people.
- Llamas are territorial animals. Each herd has its own area of land within which it ranges searching for food. Territories often overlap, but the herds normally avoid each other. Similarly, given the very few sources of fresh water, herds often share the same places to drink, but take great care to avoid being there at the same time as another group. Finally, the herd has its own specific place that female llamas return to each year in April to give birth. The limits of the territory, the location of good pasture, the water sources, and the birthing areas are passed down from generation to generation. Consequently, the families that own the llamas know exactly where to find their animals. They know the owners of other animals found in the same area. They also always know the condition of their own and their neighbour's llamas.

Around San Cristobal and Culpina K, llama herds vary in size from a dozen animals to more than a hundred (maximum of more than 400). The herd may have a single owner or have multiple owners, typically members of an extended family. Every llama carries a mark in the form of coloured wool strands in each ear that indicate ownership.

Armed with this information, it should already be apparent that relocating llamas is never going to be simple or straightforward.

142 Distinctive features and conclusions

Relocating the llama herds

When it came to moving the llama herds, the communities of San Cristobal and Culpina K were working blind. There was no relevant Bolivian experience to draw on, at least no recent experience, and no clear guidance available to the communities or the company. The best available local knowledge suggested that it should be possible to persuade herds to move to new areas if there were adequate sources of water immediately available. Hence, throughout the process there was an emphasis on locating and improving sources of permanent sweet, fresh water and building gravity-fed water troughs so that the animals had easy access to drink.

In the months immediately after the move to New San Cristobal, there were initial attempts to relocate llama herds in the belief that mine construction was imminent. These proved frustrating and largely unsuccessful. The relocation created high stress in all animals. The herds constantly tried to return to the home territory. There were numerous cases of spontaneous abortion among pregnant females. An unacceptable number of animals died of starvation in the following dry season. With the 2001 announcement of an indefinite delay in mine construction all attempts at llama relocation were quietly abandoned. Similarly, ideas of commercialising the llama for meat and fibre were also put aside pending construction of an all-weather access road that would allow the transport of product to the national market.

During the years of waiting for the mine, MSC provided a programme for communities intended to increase llama production through improvements to pasture areas. The improvements consisted of planting grasses and constructing drinking water troughs. The activities were concentrated in locations considered most suitable for the future relocation of lama herds.

The decision to go ahead with mine construction was finally made in early 2004 and was relayed to the people of San Cristobal, Culpina K, and Vila Vila. The initial response of the local population was to focus on the prospect of employment. Relatively little consideration was given to the llama herds. Nevertheless, the announcement of construction marked the start of a struggle to align two powerful realities: the rhythms and cycles of nature that controlled the llama herds and the linear engineering timetables that controlled mine construction and its costs. The experience has been described by a former General Manager as 'a cascade of crises, challenges, lessons learned and repeated revisions to the grand plan.' The elements of this struggle may be best revealed through the notes made at the time by one of the authors (Thomson) during regular visits to the site. These are presented below in italics, together with further commentary on the process of llama relocation. Emphasis in bold is by the author.

To give some idea of the number of animals and herds involved, prior to the relocations, some 1,700 animals owned by 29 families in 21 herds occupied territories in and around the area of the mine open-pit and plant site. Approximately 1,400 animals owned by 9 families grouped in 5 herds lived in the area of Wila Khara that subsequently became the tailings disposal facility. In addition, llama

The trouble with llamas **143**

grazing areas were impacted by construction of the water-well field, tailings pipeline, and railroad. Financing for mine construction provided by the commercial banks required MSC to comply with the provisions of the Equator Principles and hence the Performance Standards of the International Finance Corporation branch of the World Bank. Under the Performance Standards, any infringement of, or construction on, llama grazing areas (and other impacts on agricultural production) triggered the requirement for compliance with the relevant standard for Involuntary Resettlement,[1] which necessitated a plan of action to manage, mitigate, or provide compensation for the impact.

The situation in August 2004 was summarised as follows:

> *Under the mistaken belief that llama relocation had been underway since 2000 the initial questions to be asked on site were, "How well have the llama herds settled into the new areas? Was the form and timing of compensation appropriate and commensurate with the level of disruption?" Actual answer: In reality, **the llama have not moved! And there is no coherent plan** to manage llama relocation!*

An immediate requirement was the formulation of an action plan for llama relocation, which was developed over the following three months.

By March, 2005, the access road running west to the border with Chile had become operational. The road east to Uyuni lacked a bridge over the Rio Grande, which was scheduled to be in place by May. A steady stream of heavy haul trucks was bringing construction materials to site from Chile. Construction had begun on the camp that would house workers. The engineers were alarmed at the number of llamas roaming the site.

> *Specifically, there is now the urgent necessity to relocate llama herds that have been allowed to continue grazing in the construction areas.*
>
> *A **program to assist the relocation of llama herds is currently planned for the 2005–6** budget year and includes improving/increasing water sources and improving pastures. However, this is starting very late and there are reasonable doubts of the likelihood of real success because of the known difficulties in relocating llama, the time necessary to effect any improvement in pastures, and the adverse relationship between the cycle of growing seasons and the development timetable.*

In November, 2005, the General Manager and other members of the construction team were almost speechless with frustration at the continued presence of llamas. The animals were moved out of the construction area on an almost daily basis, but then returned immediately. They appeared to be indifferent to the presence of heavy equipment and constant traffic movements.

> *The relocation of llama herds that have traditionally grazed in the area of the open pit and construction zone is now actively in progress. Relocating llama is not easy and*

144 Distinctive features and conclusions

there have been significant losses in the herds relocated earlier in the resettlement process. Discussions are in progress with the company to develop a process that minimizes the stress of relocation and may reduce losses.

*A plan is being developed in consultation with the community for the relocation of llama and sheep herds[2] displaced from grazing lands **on and around Wila Khara**. It is hoped that the 18 to 24 months available before large scale use of the tailings area will be sufficient to enable relocation of llama with minimal losses.*

The April, 2006 report noted that stripping of the open-pit had driven most of the llamas out of this area of construction, but elsewhere there were ongoing efforts to keep them away with varying levels of success. It was now a regular sight to see llamas roaming through the camp area and leaping over fences to graze on the small patches of grass planted as landscaping around the dormitories and canteen.

*The relocation of llama herds that have traditionally grazed in the area of the open pit and construction zone continues to be a challenge. **At this time of year, the llama return to traditional birthing and feeding areas** near water and **a large number are to be seen in and around the Toldos sector of the construction site**.*

The start of railroad construction in the Kaysur sector of the line is being delayed for 60 days to allow llama calving and seasonal grazing activities to conclude in the area of the fresh water springs.

Observations in October, 2006, included a note that, following the Job Fair held in August, the attention of most of the local population was diverted by the processes of interviewing, training, and hiring. Llama relocation slowed down temporarily.

On the other hand, management at MSC had come to realise that it would be necessary to fence the Wila Khara tailings storage facility in order to keep the llamas out and safe. This was a significant unplanned and unbudgeted expense. Construction of a chain link fence around the facility was launched as a matter of urgency and was completed in the first quarter of 2007.

The February, 2007 report noted that, early in 2007 two llama specialist technicians were hired as *promotores* with a specific mandate to assist in managing llama relocation. The *promotores* identified the most suitable areas to move the animals into and how to improve the quality of those pastures. Simultaneously, MSC hired shepherds to watch the relocated llama herds and prevent them migrating back to former home territories.

MSC moved to comply with the Equator Principles' requirements by initiating negotiations with each owner family with a view to signing formal agreements that set out the forms of support provided by the company to mitigate and manage the impacts on the llamas.

In June, 2007, construction of the mine was rapidly approaching completion and production start-up was days away, but many llama herds had yet to be successfully relocated.

*Eighteen llama herds are being relocated progressively around the open pit, plant site and tailings facility as water sources are built to improve the usefulness of new grazing areas. This process is happening **in an atmosphere of crisis and time pressure** as development of the open-pit advances rapidly and the psychological impacts of seeing the full scope of the mine, with the attendant requirement for the herds to be removed, is absorbed by the owners of the llama. In addition, although the llama specialists are identifying grazing lands with the potential to accommodate the herds, there are already other herds using those areas. The result is additional pressure on existing resources and, as a consequence, the relocation has a ripple effect that impacts to some degree many families in the community, with attendant social stress.*

__The company is working on a revised plan and schedule for development of the open pit__ based on the assumption that llama herd relocation will be essentially complete by October of this year.

Families with llama herds in process of relocation away from eastern parts of the zone of operations of the open pit sector of the mine expressed alarm that MSC planned to bury two water sources beneath waste rock dumps. MSC, has, however, reviewed the situation and will make changes to the operational plans to avoid destroying these water sources in the short term, and will communicate this to the relevant families and the community in general. A long-term solution will be sought following further technical evaluation and community consultation. As a consequence, there is a delay in finalizing agreements with the families.

Families with llama herds in the zone west of the camp and commissary complained of gross contamination of the watercourse downstream of the camp in an area where the resettlement of llama herds is placing heavy demand on existing resources. MSC management has committed to an immediate clean up.

The December, 2007 report noted that, MSC had launched a multi-year Llama Improvement Programme implemented by specialist technicians attached to the Community Relations and Sustainable Development department of the mine. This was part of a larger, integrated effort to support sustainable development in the host communities in collaboration with the *Consejo Consultivo*. The programme had two aspects, a basic llama assistance package that included pasture improvement, parasite control, a breeding programme to improve quality of the herds, and an enhanced programme directed at the relocated llama herds. The enhanced relocation programme had the added elements of hiring shepherds to manage the animals as they adapt to a new territory and the purchase of forage to supplement the food available from local pastures.

__The only outstanding active resettlement issue relates to displacement of llama herds__ from the area of mining operations. This matter has been pending since 1999 and, as such, represents the final element to the process of resettling the community of San Cristóbal.

Infrastructure has been constructed to provide water sources for llama herds displaced from the construction zone and pasture improvements are in hand. However, details of

146 Distinctive features and conclusions

the form of assistance to owners to help with the relocation and adaptation of the llama to new grazing locations have to be resolved with each owner family.

MSC has made adjustments to the mine plan *with the result that llama belonging to four families, previously identified as affected, will not now be affected and thus may stay where they are.*

Two families previously thought to be unaffected are now claiming to be affected by dust from the mine blowing onto llama grazing areas. This situation is under study and a plan will be prepared before the end of December 2007.

Five families who lost all grazing land to make way for the open pit have emerged as not only the most important group from the perspective of level of degree of affectation, but also the most complex in terms of negotiating an agreement.

Dust is an ongoing problem of concern to both the company and its neighbours. There are concerns that dust from the ore stockpile may affect the health of workers in the plant, while the community is concerned that dust is contaminating forage in llama grazing areas.[3]

The full reality of relocating the llama herds was apparent in April 2008, as demonstrated by the following observations.

Llama relocation *from the mine construction site and Wila Khara* ***has emerged as being much more complex than originally perceived*** *and has created significant social issues. The situation may be summarized as follows:*

- *The displaced llama herds are being relocated into areas with existing llama populations resulting in crowding and overgrazing;*
- *Llama herds have been growing because of changes in use (not being culled for food or sold for subsistence needs, now that there is wage income at the mine) and improved health as a result of the assistance programs provided by MSC, leading to greater crowding and overgrazing;*
- *Crowding leads to further displacement into adjacent areas, also with existing llama populations, creating a ripple effect;*

The cumulative effects have created tensions between neighbours and communities;
MSC now sees the llama relocation as requiring a more geographically extensive area of intervention with programs of assistance and at least three years of implementation to manage the various direct, indirect and induced effects.

To this should be added perceptions of potential harm to people, livestock and farm land from dust and groundwater contamination from the Wila Khara tailings facility. Each of these developments was managed on an individual, ad-hoc basis and the lack of co-ordination has become particularly evident in the social consequences of successive llama herd displacements created by construction of the mine and its associated facilities.

The trouble with llamas **147**

In June, 2008, a gate in the fence around the tailing facility was left open allowing a group of llamas to enter. Two animals died after drinking water from the tailings pond.

Evidence of limited, but significant, progress was apparent in November 2008.

> *Agreements have yet to be concluded with three of the fourteen families confirmed as directly affected by llama herd relocation at the mine site. MSC has made repeated attempts to reach an agreement without success and offers to go to mediation have been rejected by the families.[4] It should be noted that the llama herds are not at risk since they have been brought into the overall llama relocation program.*
>
> *The anxiety around llama relocation noted in April is now in the past (there have been no complaints from owners for several months) and the company has moved to implement Phase 2 of the process. This focuses on helping the llama adapt to the new locations, managing the herds to reduce overgrazing and initiating trials to select plants that would be successful in providing improved pastures for the animals. Early indications are positive and there is optimism that losses due to the stress of relocation will be minimal, however other challenges have emerged. There is growing evidence that over the next few years the llama herds will be characterized by larger, healthier animals and that reproduction rates will go up. This raises the potential for increased overgrazing. As a consequence, there is need to develop agreed strategies among the owners to manage herd numbers as well as pastures. MSC has initiated training and education programs with the owners with the objective of improving skills and provoking collective herd management strategies.*

In November, 2009, the mine was operating at full production, but llama relocation remained unfinished business.

> **The relocation of llama herds** *displaced from the area of the mine and Wila Khara tailings facility* **remains an active issue.** *The drought affecting the region, now into a third year of reduced rain, has complicated efforts to facilitate the adaptation of the herds to new grazing areas* **and it is not clear if the process is succeeding or not.**

On the ground, the situation at Wila Khara was deeply distressing to the owners of the llamas. Despite the continuous presence of shepherds, the animals persisted in trying to enter their historic territories. Herds would pace for hours along the fence searching for a point of entry to reach the high-quality pasture on the other side they could see and smell. Individual animals were seen charging the fence trying to force a way through, others tried to scramble under or dig beneath the fence.

> *For the herds displaced from Wila Khara, the focus on supporting individual families was found to be unsuccessful. A collective approach involving all affected families and rooted in the community structure of Culpina K has been adopted with apparent success to date.*

148 Distinctive features and conclusions

> *The relocation of animals displaced from the mine site has not progressed well* due to a lack of cooperation from the owners of some of the herds. As a consequence, MSC has modified its approach to reduce the risk of inter-personal confrontation, moving to apply peer pressure within the San Cristóbal community through formation of a Comité Mixto to manage the relocation process. To date this appears to be functioning.
>
> *It is now evident that llama relocation will be a lengthy process.* Current opinion from the professionals supervising the process on the ground is that it is probable that three more years of support will be necessary and perhaps a 'generational shift' in the llama population before the herds fully adapt to the new pasture locations. It is evident that the relocation of llama herds will drag on for some time and require significant support from the company to assure a successful outcome.
>
> The Llama Improvement Program sponsored by MSC and the enhanced programs for the displaced llama populations is seeing early success in improved animal health, fertility and weight gain. At the same time, regular income and continuous employment at the mine or ancillary service and supply positions has resulted in the elimination of llama slaughter for food and frequency of involvement in herd management by the owners. To this is added the fact that some of the llama herds have been resettled into areas where other herds were already established. The combined effects of these factors create a future scenario of expanding llama populations on a reduced area of suitable grazing lands. Under these circumstances some form of collective management by the owners is required to avoid a crisis brought on by overgrazing. An agreement is needed within and between communities on the size of llama herds so that an optimum number of healthy animals can be sustained. *Developing a long-range strategy for llama herd management will probably require a difficult and protracted process of negotiation with and between owners.*

By 2012, there was reluctant realisation that the only way to secure the open-pit and the safety of llama was to fence the entire area. Fencing began during that year in priority sectors where there were the most frequent llama encroachments and was complete in 2015.

The quinoa factor

Among the clauses in the land acquisition agreement signed between Culpina K and the company for the use of Wila Khara as the tailings disposal facility is a section titled 'For agriculture'. In this, the company became obligated to provide a 103 horsepower New Holland brand tractor plus various parts and accessories: a plough, a seeder, a water tank,; and a pump, all for communal use. The community had a vision of increasing the production of quinoa on communal lands as a commercial activity, starting with a tractor to plough and seed more ground than had been possible by hand.

On moving from San Cristobal to the site of Culpina K, the founding families had identified a location that was not only close to the emerging road system, but also proximate to good soils suitable for agricultural use. Notably, the lands immediately east and south of the community are ideally suited for quinoa. From the earliest days, the community had produced a surplus of quinoa, which was sold to their neighbours or to travelling buyers who transported the product to the larger population centres of Oruro, Potosí, and La Paz. Despite the high quality of the quinoa grown in Culpina K, growers were vulnerable to the questionable practices of the travelling buyers and ended up receiving very low financial returns. With the promise of an all-weather road linking the San Cristobal mine with Uyuni and the national road network, came the potential for direct access to the larger market. Culpina K saw a future in the commercial production of quinoa.

The five-year delay in building the mine was a source of some frustration for the quinoa growers because they remained isolated from the larger market and overly dependent on the travelling buyers. On the other hand, as part of the programme of assistance put in place by the company, Culpina K received training and capacity-building in quinoa production, harvesting, storage, and preparation for sale. Both yield and quality improved to the satisfaction of the growers and the area under cultivation increased. This expansion was to the east of the village towards San Cristobal, into the area identified in the mine plan (but unknown to the local population) as the site of a water-well field. In 2005, the unauthorised construction of a road through these fields of quinoa sparked the first major conflict between the local population and the mine.

With the opening of the all-weather access road to Uyuni, quinoa from Culpina K was for the first time transported and sold direct to the major marketing and packaging companies in La Paz. It even found its way into international markets. The quality of the product, which included the premium grade red and black quinoa, was rewarded financially. Culpina K was establishing itself as an agricultural centre rather than a mining community, despite the fact that a majority of the men now worked at the San Cristobal mine. The *Consejo Consultivo* identified Culpina K as a future regional centre for quinoa production and incorporated this objective into its short- and long-term planning for the district.

Through the latter years of the last decade, quinoa experienced a rapid growth in popularity in Europe and North America as a healthy, nutritious food. Demand increased accordingly, as did prices paid to producers. Culpina K, in common with many other communities in Bolivia and Peru, expanded production, moving into areas that had not been previously cultivated. As a result of the 2011 conflict with San Cristobal, Culpina K gained its own Foundation and with it the financial and organisational ability to further expand quinoa production. In 2014, the Culpina K Foundation, with assistance from MSC, secured international aid funding for a large, modern storage and sorting facility. By that time, families from both San Cristobal and Vila Vila had also started growing quinoa commercially and the total area under cultivation across the district had expanded exponentially.

It is an unfortunate reality that the expansion of cultivated land for commercial quinoa production was on soils that also previously supported some of the best llama grazing pastures. The inevitable result was the forced displacement of the

150 Distinctive features and conclusions

llamas from their established territories into the territories of other herds. In a number of places these herds displaced by quinoa found themselves not only competing with established herds but also with herds relocated from the mine site and Wila Khara. An immediate consequence was overgrazing and a need to support the herds with additional forage brought in from elsewhere. In turn, conflict broke out between families within the communities over grazing 'rights', responsibility for the forced displacement created by the quinoa growers, and the question of 'who was gaining and who was losing?'

The situation in 2015

As of the end of 2015, llama relocation remained one of the unresolved issues created by the arrival of the mine. Llamas still wander through the area around the processing plant and rail yard and among the buildings of the mine camp. Shepherds are needed to watch the relocated animals to prevent them wandering back towards or into their traditional range. Overgrazing is a problem where the relocated herds and established llama populations now have to share the same territories. To this is added the displacement of llamas owing to the expansion of quinoa cultivation. Together, they have created an unforeseen and unintended level of stress within and between the communities of San Cristobal and Culpina K.

It is now recognised that relocating llama herds is difficult, but not impossible. However, it takes time. From early optimism that herds could be relocated in a matter of months, informed opinion has become that it takes years, perhaps ten years or more, to successfully establish a herd in a new location. Within the communities, there is ambivalence as to how to respond to this reality. There is the question of trade-offs; people are better off because of the mine. The llamas may also eventually be better off. Perhaps their suffering is the price paid for the people to have better lives.

Llamas remain important to the people. Llama ownership is a matter of pride and families continue to celebrate the ceremonies that mark the llama year. For example, llama-owning families gather to eat, drink, dance, and sing during an annual event to '*enflorar*' one-year-old animals. At the start of the ceremony, brightly coloured strands of wool are inserted into the ears of the young llama, which identify which herd and owner the animal belongs to. After being marked, the young male llama are dressed in a '*chaco*', which mimics the harness used historically by a pack animal and preserves the tradition of initiating the animals into the world of working llamas (Consejo Consultivo, 2008). Through each year, carefully selected llamas are sacrificed at the festivals and rituals held in the communities as an offering to *Pachamama*, the earth goddess. In San Cristobal, the idea of commercialising the llama for meat has resurfaced with the *Consejo Consultivo* recognising the town as a future centre of llama production. The *Consejo Consultivo* has also recognised Vila Vila as a centre for the production of animal feed, forage for llamas.

The mine has changed other dynamics around llama husbandry and quinoa production. With steady employment and regular pay cheques, workers are able to pay shepherds to look after their animals rather than make this a family responsibility. Planting, harvesting, and more particularly sorting, grading, and storage of quinoa is now carried out by paid workers. In both respects, one of the predictions made by *El Tío* long ago is coming true: 'the new wealth would mean that people would no longer need to work the land or care for animals'.

Notes

1 In the case of the San Cristobal project, MSC was required to comply with World Bank Operational Directive 4.30 (OD 4.30) Involuntary Resettlement.
2 Lacking any strong sense of territoriality, the sheep were relocated with relative ease under the guidance of their owners acting as shepherds.
3 The dust problem was, finally resolved in 2011 by building a dome over the stock pile.
4 This dispute was to drag on for several years and to this day is a source of friction between the company, the families involved, and the community of San Cristobal.

15
CONCLUDING OBSERVATIONS

In this chapter, we make some concluding observations on the two intertwined themes of the book: (a) how resource development transformed communities, and (b) how what the industry learned in the process can transform resource development.

The first section of this chapter reflects on the changes as experienced by the communities most affected by MSC, and a few of the more obvious wider impacts. We look at what residents of San Cristobal themselves had to say about the transformation they experienced. In the second section of this chapter, we look at broader applications of the social licence concept to whole industries, whole economic sectors, and to government.

Story woven from many threads

We had very practical motives for studying the evolving relationships between MSC and its stakeholders, and among MSC's stakeholders themselves. The fundamental goal was to foster collaborative relations that would benefit both the company and its stakeholders. From this goal came the need to understand diverse perspectives and their comparative influence in the stakeholder network. In turn, that entailed understanding diverse views of legitimacy and fairness and the process of building trust. Moreover, to make all this fuzzy social stuff compatible with business management processes, it had to be quantifiable.

In their own words

The Nor Lípez province of the Bolivian Altiplano has changed dramatically since Larry Buchanan discovered the deposit at San Cristobal. Perhaps the most widespread change is the growth in income from quinoa cultivation. In the first-ring of communities around the San Cristobal mine, community members went from shortages of basic medicines for their children to shortages of parking space for their full-size pickup trucks. Signs saying '*No Estacionamiento*' (No Parking, Figure 15.1) have popped up in the central part of town. Perhaps the best way to understand the transformation is to ask the community members themselves how they perceive it.

In 2015, we interviewed community members specifically about how they experienced the transformation that accompanied the arrival of the mine. Here are translated notes on their replies.

> There has been a loss of the 'organic' transmission of traditions. The young people and returning families participate, but it is more of a show than an expression of personal feelings. Values have been weakened; people live in a bit of a vacuum. They have lost their roots without gaining a new identity as Europeans. They exist in a 'mix' and look for status to define identity – for

FIGURE 15.1 'No parking' sign in San Cristobal, 2011.

154 Distinctive features and conclusions

example they do not eat quinoa or llama meat. However, they have over-come major obstacles to get where they are now – they have dealt with the stigma of '*indígena*'.

A generational shift is very obvious with the young people growing up with different values. They are not as interested in our traditional rituals: before everyone participated. Now it is just the most interested.

We were very close in the old town; we shared and supported each other. We followed the old traditions and everyone had a role. Today we are a strong community, including the people who moved in to find work, but money and the internal economy of services has replaced the old ways (of reciprocity). People pay others to do their *faenas* (translator note: 'community duties') for them.

Our young people have better education, so the future is better for them. Some have already become professionals with university qualifications. They want to work at the mine, but there are no openings for them. The company says they must have experience.

Garbage is a problem we never had before – now the mess seems to be everywhere

We are in transition, losing our traditions. San Cristobal is doing best at keeping the traditions alive.

We have better medical care, the school is better, everyone has work, but we have crime and family problems that never existed before.

The last comment is significant. Social problems (e.g., family violence, family break-up, drugs, alcohol, petty crime, vandalism, teen pregnancies, etc.) are significant but very little talked about. Many in the community see them as internal issues related to failures of self-control and breakdown of traditional values and governance practices that have come with the arrival of large regular incomes. There is reluctance to 'blame' the company for any of them.

From the above comments, it seems that the prophecy about turning away from the old beliefs about *El Tío* and the old traditions is being fulfilled. Of course, the same has been happening in rural villages all over the world for many centuries, prophesied or not.

Traditions are only part of the broader story of social transformation. Although Bolivia retains its long-standing distinction of being the poorest country in South America, the municipal government of Colcha K, in which the mine is located, has become one of the best financed in Bolivia. Most of the money in municipal coffers comes from royalties paid by MSC, but increasingly quinoa production and tourism are broadening and stabilising the economic base of the region. About five years after MSC reached full production for the first time, many of the communities in Colcha K moved beyond the quest to satisfy basic infrastructure needs such as potable water and sanitation systems. They began seeking better schools, health services, street lighting, public parks, and sports facilities.

Indeed, the mine has impacted people and changed lives across a broad area of Nor Lípez. As noted by one community member:

> At the beginning, the peripheral communities like San Pedro de Quemes blamed San Cristobal for accepting the mine and creating some very real social problems. Now they applaud San Cristobal and the mine for being the source of wealth flowing through the region.

The regional hospital in San Cristobal will save thousands of lives. It will produce noticeable improvements in the statistics on life expectancy compared with the past and with other remote rural regions of Bolivia. Statistics might seem dry and boring to outside observers, but to the residents themselves, they are the accretion of life and death dramas. When they lived in the old village of San Cristobal, Larry Buchanan and Karen Gans carried on a learning-oriented conversation between themselves about the relative costs and benefits of giving up the old lifestyle in exchange for the new one. The decisive factor was confronting their own ignorance about the harsh impacts of traditional poverty on health and life expectancy.

What is too often left out of discussions of the loss of traditions is that the traditional lifestyle is a poverty lifestyle and that poverty kills. It kills innocent children overnight. It kills young mothers in childbirth. It kills suddenly, indiscriminately, without warning. As Buchanan and Gans noted, the villagers were not able to brush aside or romanticise the poverty of the traditional lifestyle. Although some wax nostalgic today, at the time they saw a chance to improve their lives collectively and they took it.

Going back is not an option, although there are concerns at the level of dependency on the mine, particularly in San Cristobal. Moreover, the emergence of economic inequality is something that did not exist in the old town, mainly because everyone was equally desperately poor. The words of a community member, nonetheless, make it clear that inequality is a new kind of problem:

> People's vision is driven by money, from work at the mine. Too many simply take advantage of the mine, have every family member employed, and then form companies to provide services. Some families have become very rich while others have not. The difference between the rich and the rest is getting bigger and will soon start to create problems.

In 2015, fear that the mine might have to shut down production because of the global decline in metal prices was widespread in the communities. It provoked thought about what will happen when the mine is finally exhausted and closed permanently. Questions of sustainability resonate among families and give a new urgency to the economic diversification championed by the *Consejo Consultivo*. As noted by a community member:

156 Distinctive features and conclusions

Culpina has become a quinoa centre: San Cristobal would like to be a centre for meat – and in reality, is already a centre for health (hospital) and education (school and technical institute). Tourism is important for some families.

However, for the foreseeable future, the mine and the communities will be interdependent and rely on each other in many ways. The quality of this relationship was, is, and will be, a strong determinant to the success of all parties. Perhaps it is appropriate to leave the last word on the subject to a community leader who had seen the whole history evolve:

> Our relationship is like a marriage. We got together and created a 'baby': the mine. That was the best. We have had our ups and downs, but basically, we need each other and most of the time we get along well. I believe we respect each other and are committed to finding ways to make things work.

The challenges keep mutating

The last year for which we reported data and events was 2015. However, that does not mean that they all lived happily ever after. As of this writing, in early 2018, new challenges have arisen. They may prove to be as serious as any previously encountered.

The most pressing problem arises from the way in which the original residents who agreed to the mine invested in their children's education. Many of those children eventually went off to various cities to attend universities. Some even studied abroad in Chile, Argentina, and the United States. Their parents told them that if they returned with the proper qualifications, they would get good upper management jobs at the mine.

For the past five years, they have been returning with their qualifications as engineers, lawyers, architects, and so forth. Unfortunately, none of the incumbent employees have vacated their positions. Now there is a pool of highly educated but underemployed professionals in the first-ring communities. Every year their numbers increase, as does their frustration at not having the form of employment they had expected would be available.

To make matters even more tense, these young professionals were given training and practice to prepare them to take over the leadership of their communities. This is happening at a time when medium-term planning, both in the community and in the company, increasingly includes planning for the closure of the mine. The young professionals are not interested in going back to herding llamas. Many talk of the need to promote even more industrial or commercial development in the region.

It is too early to predict how this challenge will play out. The opportunities are as impressive as the risks. It seems safe to predict, however, that the first-ring communities will undergo another qualitative transformation, one way or the other.

What is the entity that needs a social licence?

Company department, company, industry, economic sector

The problems faced by MSC drew attention to some of the broader dimensions of the concept of the social licence to operate. Conceived as stakeholder acceptance, the social licence concept overlaps in interesting ways with political science concepts like institutional legitimacy and the social contract. In this final section, we allude to these broader debates.

At one extreme, it appears that the entity granted a social licence can be as small as a department within a company. In the March 2011 occupation of MSC's mine, the data from both before and after the occupation indicated that MSC's social licence had actually risen slightly compared with 15 months earlier, although it fell among those directly involved in the occupation. However, on average even the occupiers stopped short of withdrawing MSC's social licence. Interviews with protesters and company personnel indicated that the villagers' principle concerns were with the policies and actions of the Human Resources department and the medical unit of the company. Before the occupation, the community members reportedly had a vigorous debate about alternatives to shutting down the whole mine. Because most of them depended on the operation of the mine for incomes, they would have preferred to shut down only the Human Resources and medical departments. Indeed, they did keep the mill section operating for about a week during occupation. In the end, they decided that the shutdown of the whole operation was a blunt instrument, but the only effective instrument at their disposal. These observations suggest that it was only two departments that lost their social licences, even though the withdrawal could not be implemented with enough precision to avoid affecting them all.

Other cases make clear that a specific company can lose its social licence and be replaced by another that has a high social licence. In Bolivia, COMIBOL, the state-owned company, has a social licence to continue mining projects, both exploration and operations, that were previously owned by private companies. Those private companies first lost their social licences, typically owing to conflicts with local communities, and then, with political interventions that followed, they lost their legal licences. While they had no social licence, but retained their legal licences, it was only the threat of state intervention that permitted them to continue operating.

Whole industries can suffer a decline in their social licence, or a rise. The tobacco industry in Western countries has suffered a steep decline in its social licence. In international public opinion surveys by GlobeScan from 2001 to 2013 (GlobeScan, 2013), the tobacco industry consistently scored lowest on perceived CSR performance. The mining industry scored second or third lowest. Moreover, there are several cases in South America where municipalities and states or provinces have banned mining after the public withdrew their acceptance of it.

158 Distinctive features and conclusions

For example, in the Argentinian Province of Chubut, the stakeholder coalition that withdrew the social licence of the proposed Esquel mine extended its opposition to the whole mining sector. The provincial government wanted the mining revenues but yielded to the demonstrable political power of the anti-mining stakeholders and banned open-pit mining and cyanide use throughout the province.

At an even broader scale, whole sectors sometimes lose their social licence and then face restrictions on their legal access to markets or other vital resources. Domestic protectionism is an example of withdrawn social licences that lead to legal restrictions on operations. For example, many countries impose foreign ownership restrictions in the food or energy sectors. There have been occasional attempts in modern times to eliminate the whole corporate sector, and even the whole private sector. Perhaps the largest-scale and most thorough attempt was Mao Zedong's Great Leap Forward (1958 to 1962) (Chan, 2001). Even private gardens were forbidden beyond what was deemed necessary for family consumption. Rather than tolerate steel-making companies, backyard furnaces were launched in an attempt to meet the identified need for steel. The ensuing famine and economic contraction was then blamed on bourgeois attitudes, which the Cultural Revolution (1966 to 1976) tried to stamp out. Echoing the same discourse, Nicolas Maduro, Hugo Chávez's successor to the Presidency of Venezuela, blamed the country's 54 per cent inflation rate (in 2013) on the 'parasitic bourgeoisie' and deployed the army to force retailers to slash prices (Nunes, 2013). To the extent that these government actions were responses to popular perceptions, they can be viewed as a whole sector having its social licence restricted or withdrawn.

When applied at the level of whole industries and economic sectors, the concept of the social licence appears to overlap with the concept of the social contract. It suggests the view that the social contract is an accord among the most powerful actors and coalitions in the national political network regarding which rights and responsibilities will be accorded to, or withdrawn from, themselves and other actors and coalitions.

Legal licences need a social licence

Finally, it should be noted that even government legitimacy depends on popular acceptance, which is another name for a social licence (Morrison, 2014). Government laws and policies must have a social licence. A recent case in Canada underlines the point that government policies and regulations also need a social licence. Canada's National Energy Board held hearings on a permit application for a bitumen pipeline from the oil sands of Alberta to the Pacific Coast. The narrowness of the mandate for the hearings, and changes that the government made to the rules for submissions, touched off a national controversy in which the regulatory process itself was accused of not having a social licence (O'Neil, 2014; Simpson, 2014).

Summary

As the stories and findings in this book have shown, at the frontiers of globalisation it is more than a specific mining project that has to be accepted by the community. The arrival of a representative of Western capitalism, or Chinese capitalism for that matter, brings new opportunities and challenges, new institutions and discourses, new conflicts and collaborations. It is all too easy to focus on only the negative, or the positive. There are always some whose lives improve and some whose lives get worse. A balanced view of the transformation requires acknowledging both in their actual proportions.

The history of the mine at San Cristobal is woven from many threads. They stretch back to events and processes in motion before the election of Evo Morales, before the opening of the mine, before the discovery of the mineral deposit, before the Bolivian National Revolution of 1952, before Bolivian independence, and even before the Spanish Conquest. They include the different institutional structures that created different channels of historical development for the culture that created the international corporation on the one hand and the culture that created the distinctive Altiplano society of Potosí on the other hand. Some threads even stretch back into the prehistory of human evolution in small tribal groups more than a hundred millennia ago.

Above all, this is a story about maintaining a relationship. A relationship is a balancing act between self-interest and mutual interest, between the short-term and the long-term, between clear boundaries and the vulnerability that comes with trust. Because relationships are ever-changing, maintaining a balance can never be reduced to a political process, a set of legal rights, or a code of ethics, although these are helpful guides. Keeping a relationship balanced sometimes requires making an objection and going through a period of conflict until a better equilibrium is found, at least temporarily. A relationship that survives all of this rebalancing is based on mutual communication and respect. It is a relationship in which both parties strive in their own way to move the relationship to the level of mutual support and approval. In inter-personal relationships, that is called commitment.

REFERENCES

Babcock, L. and Loewenstein, G. 1997. Explaining bargaining impasse: The role of self-serving biases. *Journal of Economic Perspectives*, 11(1): 109–126.

Baptista Gumucio, M. 2015. *San Cristobal: Una Mina Sin Par en la Historia de Bolivia*. La Paz, Bolivia: Mariano Baptista Gumucio.

Barba, A. 1640/1817. *Arte de los Metales*. Madrid, Spain. Available online at: https://archive.org/details/artedelosmetales00barb.

Basabe, N. and Ros, M. 2005. Cultural dimensions and social behavior correlates: Individualism-collectivism and power distance. *Revue Internationale de Psychologie Sociale*, 18(1): 189–225.

Bhalla, S. 2002. *Imagine There is no Country: Poverty, Inequality and Growth in the Era of Globalization*. Washington, DC: Institute for International Economics.

Bjorvatn, K. and Naghavi, A. 2011. Rent-seeking and regime stability in rentier states. *European Journal of Political Economy*, 27(4): 740–748.

Black, L. 2013. *The Social License to Operate: Your Management Framework for Complex Times*. London: Do Sustainability.

Bonacich, P. 2007. Some unique properties of eigenvector centrality. *Social Networks*, 29, 555–564.

Borgatti, S. P., Mehra, A., Brass, D. J., and Labianca, G. 2009. Network analysis in the social sciences. *Science*, 323(5916): 892–895.

Boutilier, R. G. 2009. *Stakeholder Politics: Social Capital, Sustainable Development, and the Corporation*. Sheffield, UK: Greenleaf.

Boutilier, R. G. 2011. *A Stakeholder Approach to Issues Management*. New York: Business Expert Press.

Boyd, B. 1990. Corporate linkages and organizational environment: A test of the resource dependence model. *Strategic Management Journal*, 11(6): 419–430.

Brautigam, D. A. and Knack, S. 2004. Foreign aid, institutions, and governance in Sub-Saharan Africa. *Economic Development and Cultural Change*, 52(2): 255–285.

Brinton, C. 1965. *The Anatomy of Revolution*. New York: Vintage Books.

Buchanan, L. and Gans, K. 2008. *The Gift of El Tio*. McLean, VA: Fuze Publishing LLC.

References 161

Carroll, W. K. and Sapinski, J. P. 2010. The global corporate elite and the transnational policy-planning network, 1996–2006. *International Sociology*, 25(4): 501–538.

Chan, A. 2001. *Mao's Crusade: Politics and Policy Implementation in China's Great Leap Forward*. Oxford and New York: Oxford University Press.

Consejo Consultivo. 2008. *Cuentos, Mitos, Tradiciones y Leyendas del Gran Lípez*. La Paz, Bolivia: Consejo Consultivo.

Cross, R. and Prusak, L. 2002. The people who make organizations go – or stop. *Harvard Business Review*, June: 105–112.

Cross, R., Liedtka, J., and Weiss, L. 2005. A practical guide to social networks. *Harvard Business Review*, March, 124–132.

Crouch Zelman, E. 2015. *Our Beleaguered Species: Beyond Tribalism*. USA, Createspace Independent Pub.

Cunningham J. W. 1818. *A World without Souls*. London: J. Hatchard.

Dunbar, R. I. M. 2011. Social brain: Mind, language and society in evolutionary perspective. *Annual Review of Anthropology*, 32: 163–181.

Dyer, J. H. and Nobeoka, K. 2000. Creating and managing a high performance knowledge-sharing network: The Toyota case. *Strategic Management Journal*, 21(3): 345–367.

Ellis, E. 2013. Babies choose sides before they can speak, UBC study concludes (with video). *Vancouver Sun*, March 13.

Farthing, L. C. and Kohl, B. H., 2014. *Evo's Bolivia: Continuity and Change*. Austin, TX: University of Texas Press.

Flora, J. L., Flora, C. B., Campana, F., Garcia Bravo, M., and Fernandez-Baca, E. 2006. Social capital and advocacy coalitions: Examples of environmental issues from Ecuador. In R. E. Rhoades (Ed.), *Development with Identity: Community, Culture and Sustainability in the Andes*: 287–297. Cambridge, MA: CABI Publishing.

Fogel, R. W. and North, D. C. 1993. Economic Performance through Time. Retrieved October 10, 2015, from www.nobelprize.org/nobel_prizes/economic-sciences/lau reates/1993/north-lecture.html.

Franks, D. M., Davis, R., Bebbington, A., Ali, S. H., Kemp, D., and Scurrah, M. 2014. Conflict translates environmental and social risk into business costs. *Proceedings of the National Academy of Sciences*, www.pnas.org/cgi/doi/10.1073/pnas.1405135111: 1–6.

Freeland, C. 2015. The disintegration of the world. *The Atlantic Business*, May: 15.

Freeman, R. E. 1984. *Strategic Management: A Stakeholder Approach*. Boston: Pitman.

Gardikiotis, A. 2011. Minority influence. *Social and Personality Psychology Compass*, 5(9): 679–693.

GlobeScan. 2013. *GlobeScan 2013 Radar: Business in Society*. Toronto: GlobeScan.

Godoy, R. A. 1990. *Mining and Agriculture in Highland Bolivia: Ecology, History and Commerce among the Jukumanis*. Tucson, Arizona: University of Arizona Press.

Greene, J. D. 2013. *Moral Tribes: Emotion, Reason, and the Gap between Us and Them*. New York: Penguin.

Hall, C. M. and Power, H. 2016. Social license to operate and adaptive co-marketing: Exchange, social capital and community-based social marketing. *Preprints*, 2016110149. doi: 10.20944/preprints201611.0149.v1.

Hernández, B. M. and Fernández Moscoso, M. 2014. Investigación 1: ¿Es posible construir beneficios mutuos entre comunidades y empresas mineras?: El caso San Cristobal. In B. M. Hernández, M. Fernández Moscoso, M. Yapu, D. Romero Romay, P. Rocha Portugal, G. Damonte, M. Glave, J. C. Sanabria Arias, E. Coyoy, and E. Urrutia (Eds.), *América Latina hacia la Inclusión Social: Avances, aprendizajes y desafíos*. Guatemala: ASIES.

162 References

Hohn, M., Thomson, I., and Dalence, P. 2013. Gender modernity in mining: A case study from Bolivia. *SRMining 2013 Proceedings*, GECAMIN, Santiago, Chile.

Humphreys, M., Sachs, J. D., and Stiglitz, J. E. 2007. Introduction: What is the problem with natural resource wealth? In M. Humphreys, J. D. Sachs, and J. E. Stiglitz (Eds.), *Escaping the Resource Curse. Initiative for Policy Dialogue*: 1–20. New York: Columbia University Press.

Jacobson, H., Murillo, C., Ruiz, L., Tapia, O., Zapata, H., Delgadillo, E., and Velasco, C. 1969. *Mineral Deposits of the San Cristobal District, Villa Martin Province, Potosí, Bolivia. Bulletin 1273*. Washington, DC: United States Geological Survey.

Joyce, S. 1997. *San Cristobal, Evaluation of the Current Socioeconomic Situation*. Confidential report for Apex Silver.

Joyce, S. and Thomson, I. 1999. Earning a social license. *Mining Journal*, 332(8535) (June): 441–443.

CristobalKatz, E. and Lazarsfeld, P. F. 1964. *Personal Influence: The Part Played by People in the Flow of Mass Communications*. New York: Free Press.

Knack, S. 2001. Aid dependence and the quality of governance: A cross-country empirical analysis. *Southern Economic Journal*, 68(2): 310–329.

Knight Piesold. 2000. *Minera San Cristobal S.A. San Cristobal Project, Environmental Impact Assessment*. Denver: Knight Piesold.

Knight Piesold. 2001. *Apex Silver Mines Corporation, Proyecto San Cristobal, Plan de Gestión Social, Planes y Programas*. Retrieved from Denver: Knight Piesold.

Kolstad, I. 2009. The resource curse: Which institutions matter? *Applied Economics Letters*, 16(4): 439–442.

Lakner, C. and Milanovic, B. 2013. *Global Income Distribution: From the Fall of the Berlin Wall to the Great Recession. Policy Research Working Paper 6719*. Washington, DC: World Bank.

Loayza, F., Franco, I., Quezada, F., and Alvarado, M. 2001. Turning gold into human capital. In G. McMahon and F. Remy (Eds.), *Large Mines and the Community: Socioeconomic and Environmental Effects in Latin America, Canada and Spain*. Ottawa, Canada: International Development Research Centre.

López, E. 2009. La industria minera: una industria sedienta. Caso Minera San Cristobal. In *Comisión para la Gestión Integral del Agua en Bolivia, Justicia Ambiental y Sustentabilidad Hídrica*: 67–90. Cochabamba, Bolivia: CGIAB.

López, C. A. and Ferrufino, R. 2009. Estado de situación de dos sectores productivos fundamentales: hidrocarburos y minería. *Análisis de Coyuntura*, 9, May. La Paz, Bolivia: Fundación Milenio.

CristobalMadrid Lara, E. R., Cuenca Sempértegui, A., Lafuente Tito, S., López Canelas, E., and Rodríguez Alanez, J. L. 2012. Coro Coro and Challapata: Defending collective rights and mother earth against development mining fetishism. *Environmental Justice*, 5(2): 65–69. doi:10.1089/env.2011.0027.

Mehlum, H., Moene, K., and Torvik, R. 2006. Institutions and the resource curse. *The Economic Journal*, 116(508): 1–20.

Minera San Cristobal. 2007. *Familias Vulnerables. November, 2006*. La Paz, Bolivia: Minera San Cristobal, (internal document).

Minera San Cristobal. 2014. *Folleto de Agua*. Minera San Cristobal, La Paz, Bolivia.

Moffat, K. and Zhang, A. 2014. The paths to social license to operate: An integrative model explaining community acceptance of mining. *Resources Policy*, 39(0): 61–70.

Moffat, K., Zhang, A., and Boughen, N. 2014. *Australian Attitudes toward Mining: Citizen Survey – 2014 Results*. Brisbane: CSIRO.

Molina, J. M. 2007. *Aqua y Recurso Hídrico en el Sur de Potosí*. La Paz, Bolivia: Foro Boliviano sobre Medio Ambiente y Desarrollo (FOBOMADE).

Montecinos, V. 2014. Spanish-speaking Latin America: Politicized economic thought. In V. Barnet (Ed.), *Routledge Handbook of the History of Global Economic Thought*: 158–166. London and New York: Routledge.

Moore, W. H. 1996. The social license to operate. *PIMA Magazine*, October, Paper Industry Management Association, Norcross, Georgia, USA, 22–23.

Morales, J. A. and Sachs, J. 1988. *Bolivia's Economic Crisis*. *Working Paper 2620*. Cambridge, MA: National Bureau of Economic Research, Harvard University.

Moran, R. E. 2009. *Mining Water: The San Cristobal Mine, Bolivia*. *Title in Spanish: Minando Agua*. Uyuni, Bolivia: Federación Regional Única de los Trabajadores Campesinos del Altiplano Sud (FRUTCAS) and Comisión para la Gestión Integral del Agua en Bolivia (CGIAB).

Morrison, J. 2014. *The Social License: How to Keep Your Organization Legitimate*. London: Palgrave Macmillan.

Moscovici, S. 1980. Toward a theory of conversion behavior. In L. Berkowitz (Ed.), *Advances in Experimental Social Psychology*: 209–239. New York: Academic Press.

North, D. C. 1990. *Institutions, Institutional Change and Economic Performance*. Cambridge, UK: Cambridge University Press.

Nunes, R. 2013. Venezuela's president blames soaring inflation on 'parasitic bourgeoisie,' deploys army to force stores to slash prices. *The National Post*, November 13. Retrieved from http://news.nationalpost.com.

O'Neil, P. 2014. Group sues over Harper limits on pipeline hearings. *Vancouver Sun*, August 13. Retrieved from www.carriersekani.ca/news/group-sues-over-harper-limits-on-pipeline-hearings/.

Powell, W. W., Koput, K. W., and Smith-Doerr, L. 1996. Interorganizational collaboration and the locus of innovation: Networks of learning in biotechnology. *Administrative Science Quarterly*, 41(1): 116–145.

Quisbert Salinas, F. 2001. *Los Lípez: Sangre y Oro*. Cochabamba, Bolivia: CEDENA.

Senge, P., Kleiner, A., Roberts, C., Ross, R. B., and Smith, B. J. 1994. *The Fifth Discipline Fieldbook: Strategies and Tools for Building a Learning Organization*. New York: Currency/Doubleday.

Simpson, J. 2014. Define 'onsultation' and 'social license'. *The Globe and Mail*, October 22. Retrieved from www.theglobeandmail.com/globe-debate/define-consultation-and-social-licence/article21199386/.

Stuart, T. E. 1998. Network positions and propensities to collaborate: An investigation of strategic alliance formation in a high-technology industry. *Administrative Science Quarterly*, 43(3): 668–698.

The Diggings. 2017. *Mesa De Plata Mine: Silver Deposit in Potosí, Bolivia*. https://thediggings.com/mines/usgs10089904 (accessed April 17, 2017).

Thomson, I. and Boutilier, R. G. 2011. Social license to operate. In P. Darling (Ed.), *SME Mining Engineering Handbook*: 1779–1796. Littleton, CO: Society for Mining, Metallurgy and Exploration.

Thomson, I. and Joyce, S. 2008. The social license to operate: what it is and why it seems so hard to obtain. Prospectors and Developers Association of Canada Convention. March 3, 2008. Toronto, PDAC.

Tindall, D. B. and Robinson, J. 2006. Network diversity and social movement identification, Paper presented at International Sunbelt Social Network Conference (Sunbelt XXVI), April 24–30, Vancouver, British Columbia, Canada.

164 References

Valverde, A.H. and Martínez, J. 2008, *Sistematización, Análisis, y Perspectivas de la Experiencia San Cristobal (1996–2008)*. La Paz, Bolivia: Minera San Cristobal (internal document).

Wasserman, S. and Faust, K. 1994. *Social Network Analysis: Methods and Applications*. Cambridge, UK: Cambridge University Press.

Weber, M. 1983. *Max Weber on Capitalism, Bureaucracy and Religion: A Selection of Texts*. London: Allen and Unwin.

World People's Conference on Climate Change and the Rights of Mother Earth. 2010. *Peoples Agreement*. Retrieved November 29, 2017, from https://pwccc.wordpress.com/2010/04/24/peoples-agreement/.

Zhang, A., Moffat, K., Lacey, J., Wang, J., González, R., Uribe, K., Cui, L., and Dai, Y. 2015. Understanding the social licence to operate of mining at the national scale: A comparative study of Australia, China and Chile. *Journal of Cleaner Production*, 108(Part A): 1063–1072.

INDEX

1952 revolution 23, 159
1994 to 2004 preconstruction period xix, xxi, 10, 48–9, 51–8, 60, 80, 132–4
1994 to 2008 San Cristobal case study methods 48–50, 69, 101
1994 to 2011 period xix, xxi, 10, 48–50, 51–8, 60, 69, 80, 101, 125, 132–9
1995 mineral deposit discovery xxi, 7, 11, 23–4, 28, 31, 41, 51–2, 74, 132, 152–3, 155
2000 water controversy 33–4
2004 to 2006 construction period xix, xxi, 49, 58, 59–67, 132–4, 139, 142–8
2007 to 2009 transition to operating mine period xix, xxi, 3, 48–50, 68–80, 144–8
2009 dust concerns xxii, 69, 115–16, 122–3, 125
2009 to 2015 quantitative study methods period xix, xx, xxi, xxii, 101–12, 113–21, 122–8, 153–4
2009 water controversy xix, 70–7, 82–3, 115–16
2010 and 2011 conflicts/unrest xix, xxi, 16, 19–20, 23, 41, 80, 81–97, 116–17, 123–7, 157–8
2010 mini-insurrection 85–6, 117, 118
2011 occupation of the mine xxi, 86–97, 106, 116–17, 157
2012 nationalisation risks xxii, 12, 17, 119, 123–4
2015 situation, llamas 150–1, 154
2016 situation, women 134–5
2018 challenges 156–7

abbreviations' list xxvi, xxvii
Abengoa Spain 33
acceptance, social licence to operate (SLO) 42–8, 50, 51, 58, 60–1, 66–7, 85, 105–7, 113–14, 116–17, 118–19, 121, 128
Accord of Understanding 93
accountabilities 13–16
Achopalla stone 64–5
acknowledgements xxiv, xxv
Act of Understanding (AOU) 93–4
adobe 54–6, 58
Africa 81, 103
agreements 54–5, 60–2, 65, 68–9, 72–4, 82–7, 93–4, 96, 125–7, 132–3, 140, 144–50
agriculture xviii, xx, xxii, 4–10, 14–15, 23–7, 30–2, 55–8, 62, 83, 90, 114–17, 123–6, 131–5, 140–54; quinoa xviii, 4, 58, 81, 120, 124–5, 131–2, 148–50, 152–4, *see also* llamas
Aguas del Tunari consortium 33–4
air drainage methods, carbon dioxide hazards 8
alcoholism 134
Altiplano region xx, xxiii, 4–8, 14–15, 25–31, 61, 65, 70–1, 77, 81–2, 111, 124, 141, 152–3, 159
Amayapampa conflict 32
ambulances 94
Andean Development Corporation 58
Andean Silver Corporation (ASC) 51–2
Andes 21, 24–5, 27, 29–31, 36, 53, 70, 141

166 Index

Animas silver mine 8, 61
Antofagasta port 6, 7, 8, 10
Apex Silver Mines Limited 11, 51–2, 56–7, 59–60, 63, 78, 140
approval level, social licence to operate (SLO) 46–50, 52, 58, 59, 69, 78, 86–7, 105–7, 117, 119–21, 128
aquifers 71–2, 75–7
Argentina 6, 9, 27, 131, 156, 158
Arica 6
articulation problems, stakeholders 107–8
artificial intelligence xiv
artists 58
ASC Bolivia LDC 51, 52–3
Australia 19, 26, 60, 103
author biographies i, ii, xiv, xv
Avaroa 9–10, 57, 83–5
Ayllus traditions 5–6, 9–10, 22–3
Aymara language 5, 16, 22–3, 26–8, 29–30, 141

banks 17, 48–50, 61, 66, 78, 83, 143
Bánzer, General Hugo 25–6, 33–4
Baptista Gumucio, Mariano 3, 23
Barba, Alonso 5
bartering 9
Battle Mountain Gold 26, 29
Bechtel 33
in the beginning, historical context xviii, xix, xx, 3–11, 131–4, 139, 155, 159
'betweenness centrality' concepts 45–6, 114–16
biases xvi–xvii, 20, 97
Black, Dr Leeora 42–3, 103
Bolivia, 1952 revolution 23, 159; background i, xvii, xx, 3, 13–20, 21–8, 29–37, 74–7, 131, 154; Chilean antagonism 34; economic crises xx, 23–5, 29, 33–4, 154; geography 4–6, 24–6, 70–1, 75–7, 83–4, 154–5; independence classist state 17, 21–2, 81–2, 159; inflation 24–5, 79, 83–4, 137, 158; traditional dress 30
Bolivian politics, 2011 occupation of the mine 92–7, 116–17, 157; Capitalisation reform 27; co-evolution of risk hotspots with Bolivian politics/economy xix, xxii, 113–21; Constitution 36–7, 55–6; decentralisation 26–8; economic crises xx, 23–5, 29, 33–4; historical context xvii, xix, xx, xxi, 17–18, 21–8, 29–37; indigenous rights 26–7, 29–32, 36–7, 81–3; International Labour Organisation (ILO) 29–30; neo-liberal reforms xx, 23–8, 29–31, 33–7, 63, 112, 119–20,

123–4; Popular Participation Act 26–7; resentment discourses xx, 21–8, 29–31, 82–3, 89–90, *see also* Morales, Evo
Botswana 19
Boutilier, R.G. 47, 102–3, 104–6, 112
Brazil 27, 81
Brexit 97
BRICS countries 81
'bridger' concepts 114–16
Brinton's theory 28
Bruce, Scotty 26
Buchanan, Larry xviii, xx, 3, 10, 11, 28, 31, 51–2, 74, 152–3, 155
bullying allegations, communities and resource companies xvii
Bunch, Mike 77–8
bureaucracies, fairness/justice principles 14–15
Butch Cassidy and the Sundance Kid 28
Buttenshaw, Graham 59–60, 66–7, 68, 77

Cabrera, Myriam 46
Calama 10
Calcina, Pablo 86, 87–90, 127
camp management 59–60
Canada 11, 19, 26, 27, 31, 32, 37, 60, 158
cannibalism xviii, 7
Capacirca 32
Capitalisation reform, historical context 27
capitalism 13–14, 16–20, 24–5, 76, 159
carbon dioxide hazards 5, 8
carbon footprint 110
Cárdenas, Victor Hugo 26
cartels 18
Catering International and Services (CIS) 59–60, 62
catering services 59–60, 62, 68, 135
Cayman Islands 51
cement factories 85
cemetery relocations 55, 140
Cerro Rico silver mountain 21–3, 37, *see also* Potosí silver mine
CGIAB 75–7
Challapata conflict 31
Chapare 24–5
Chávez, Hugo 158
chickens 23
Chile 6–10, 19, 34–5, 62, 66–8, 70, 77, 83–4, 91–3, 95, 131, 156
Chilean railway corporation 95
China 36, 81, 158, 159
Christianity xxi, 4, 6–7, 8, 16–18, 29–31, 35, 41, 52, 55, 132, 134
'Christmas Massacre' unrest in 1996 32
Chuquicamata copper mine 6, 10–11

Index **167**

Chuquina 26, 29

churches xxi, 8, 16–18, 29–31, 35, 52, 55, 132, 134, 140

clean-ups, pipeline rupture in 2008 78

cleaner/safer practices, Minera San Cristobal (MSC) 23

Clevenger, Jeff 59

clientelism 12–13, 16–18; definition 18; prevention methods 19, *see also* institutional theory

climate change xvii, 75, 76–7, 82–3, 110, 124

closures, silver mines xx, 9–11, 24–5, 27–8, 29–32, 124, 155, 156

clusters 102, 110, 114–21

co-evolution of risk hotspots with Bolivian politics/economy xix, xxii, 113–21

coca 24–5, 34

cocaine 24–5, 34, 95, 137–8

Cochabamba 25, 27, 33–4, 75, 86–7, 135

Coeur Mining 37

Colcha K 6, 8, 26, 72, 74, 83, 85, 94, 122–3, 154

collaboration benefits 67, 101, 103, 109, 113–14, 116–19, 122–8, 145–8, 152–9

'colonisation of the mind' 82, 107, 108–9, 112

colour gradations, social licence to operate (SLO) 104–5, 113–17

Colque, Alberto 53

COMCIPO 82–3, 85

COMIBOL state-owned mining company 11, 17, 24, 27–8, 30, 37, 78, 157

commitment concepts 159

committees, relocation/resettlement considerations 53–6

'commodities super cycle' period 36–7

communal feasts/celebrations 9–10

communications planning, strategies that work 127

communities i, xvi–xvii, xviii, xix, xx, 3–20, 21–8, 31–7, 41–50, 51–8, 59–67, 102–12, 114–28, 131–9, 140–51; bullying allegations xvii, 60, 61–5; *Consejo Consultivo* leadership group 67, 69, 78, 85, 93–4, 116, 122–3, 138, 145–6, 149–50, 155–6; Don't lie. Don't steal. Don't be lazy code-of-behaviour 15; empowerment processes 53–6, 67, 104; first-ring communities 9–10, 23, 68–9, 79–80, 82–3, 85–97, 114–21, 122–4, 127, 152–9; historical background xxii, 3–11, 131–4; maps of the mines 6–8, 9–10, 56–7; marriage analogy 156; overview of the book xvi–xxiii, 3; power concepts xvii, 18–19,

42–6, 65, 67, 117, 158; relocation/resettlement considerations xviii, xxi, 11, 26, 29, 52–6, 60, 69, 72–5, 86–7, 90, 96, 125–7, 132–3, 140–8; second-ring communities xxi, 82–3, 84–5, 97, 114–19; third-ring communities 114–16, 117; tribalism preferences 13–16, 110, 159; women in the workplace perspectives 136–8, *see also* cultural issues; San Cristobal community; social licence to operate; unrest

Community Relations Department, problems for MSC 95, 134, 145

compensation for land xxii, 18–20, 56, 90, 140, 143

COMSUR 26–7, 32–3, 37

conclusions xx, xxii, xxiii, 80, 152–9

confrontational negotiation traditions, cultural issues 63–4, 84

Confucian China 14

Consejo Consultivo leadership group 67, 69, 78, 85, 93–4, 116, 122–3, 138, 145–6, 149–50, 155–6

Constitution 36–7, 55–6

construction period, 2004 to 2006 construction period xix, xxi, 49, 58, 59–67, 132–4, 139, 142–8

contracts, Minera San Cristobal (MSC) 59–60, 157–8

Cooney, Jim 42, 102–3

cooperatives, historical context 24–6, 29–32, 37, 74, 85, 118, 123–4

copper mines 10–11

Cordillera 70

corporate social responsibility (CSR) 103, 126, 157–8, *see also* responsibilities

Corregidor elections 8

corrosion issues, water sources 71

corruption 18

credibility perceptions 46–50, 56–8, 66–7, 69, *see also* legitimacy perceptions; social licence to operate

criminals 85, 95, 107, 108, 118–19, 154

Cross, Rob 109

CSUTCB union 30–1, *see also* IPSP group

Culpina K community 9–10, 56–9, 61–9, 72–7, 82–3, 86–90, 93–6, 124–7, 131–2, 135–7, 140–2, 147–50

cultural issues i, xvii, xviii, xix, xx, xxi, xxii, 3–7, 9–20, 21–5, 30–7, 53–4, 63–4, 80, 107–9, 134–9, 140–1, 150, 153–9; *Ayllus* traditions 5–6, 9–10, 22–3; challenges xvii, xviii, xix, xx, xxi, xxii, 12, 20, 53–4, 80, 153–7; 'colonisation of the mind' 82, 107,

168 Index

108–9, 112; confrontational negotiation traditions 63–4, 84; *El Tío* xviii, 6–7, 10–11, 80, 151, 154; llamas 140–1, 150; sacred stones xxi, 64–5; supernatural/superstition beliefs xvii, xviii, xix, xx, 3–7, 10, 25, 30–1, 64–5, 76–80, 134–5, 141, 150, 154; traditional dress 30; women 131, 134–9
Cultural Revolution, China 158
Cunningham, John William 41
'curse of natural resources' xx, 12–13, 17–18, 123–4; definition 17–18; prevention methods 18, *see also* nationalisation; rent-seeking
cyanide-leaching methods 31, 158

dams 33
Daniel Campos 85
day-care centre facilities, women 137–8
de Castro, Margarita 46, 49
decentralisation, historical context 26–8
Declaration of Conflict 91
'decolonisation of the mind' moves 82, 108–9
'degree centrality' concepts 45–6, 114–16
Delgado, Jonny 26, 51–2, 54, 57, 59, 63, 92
dependency theory 12, 21, 126
destiny 11
Dialogue Table 93
Diez de Medina, Javier 49, 66–7, 103
discrimination 35–6, 60, 61–5, 78, 82–3, 86–7, 89–90, 96–7, 115–16, 122–6, 127, 132–9; first-ring community inequity/inequality viewpoints 96, 97, 115–16, 122–4, 127; inequity/inequality aspects 96–7, 115–16, 120, 122–6, 127, 136; second-ring community inequity/inequality viewpoints 97, 117
divorce rates 137
Don Mario mine 37, *see also* Orvana Minerals
donkeys 7
Don't lie. Don't steal. Don't be lazy code-of-behaviour 15
Dreamers group 67
drilling programmes 51–2, 74
droughts 75, 82–3, 147
drugs 24–5, 34, 95, 137–8, 154
Dunbar's number 13–16, 20
dust concerns xxii, 63, 69, 115–16, 122–3, 124–6, 146
dust dome 115–16, 122–3, 124–6
Dutch East India Company 16

eastern Bolivia, geography 25–7, 29–30, 70
economic benefits i, xvi, xviii, xx, xxi, 5–7, 21–3, 27–8, 36–7, 62, 65, 78–80, 81–97, 115–25, 127, 137–8, 148, 151, 152–9, *see also* income; wages
economic crises xx, 23–5, 29, 33–4, 81, 158
economic diversification 154–6, *see also* llamas; quinoa; tourism
Ecuador 42
education 9, 16, 26–7, 28, 73–4, 79, 124–6, 138, 154–5, 156
'eigenvector centrality' concepts 45, 113–16
El Alto 27, 35
El Tío xviii, 6–7, 10–11, 80, 151, 154; definition xviii, 6–7; description 6–7; the gift xviii, 6–7, 11, 80, 151; mid-1980s prophecy version 10–11
elites 12–13, 16–18, 21–3, 33–4, 44, 62, 65, 82–3
empowerment processes 53–6, 67, 104
England 16–18, 19, 26, 33, 97; Brexit 97; entrepreneurial encouragement 19; Glorious Revolution of 1688 16–17; Industrial Revolution 19; innovations 19, 26; institutional theory 16–18; Spanish contrasts 16–18
the Enlightenment 13–14, 16–18
Enrique Baldivieso 10–11, 72, 85
Enron 27
entrepreneurs 13, 18–20, 25–6, 123–4
Environmental Action Plan (EAP) 140
environmental activists 30–1, 61
Environmental and Economic Development Commission 77
Environmental Impact Assessments (EIAs) 56–7, 71, 72–3, 75–6, 140
environmental issues xvii, xxii, 19–20, 23, 29–36, 42–52, 56–7, 61–4, 69, 71–7, 107–9, 115–16, 124–7, 132, 140–51, 154–5, 158; Equator Principles 48, 143, 144, *see also* llamas; pollution
environmental permits, San Cristobal mine 56–7
equality principles xx, xxi, 12–16, 20, 25, 54–5, 61–3, 78–80, 82–7, 89–90, 96–7, 122–4, 127, 133–6, 138–9; abuses 14–15, 61–3, 65; definition 13–14, 15–16, 96; discrimination inequity/inequality viewpoints 96–7, 115–16, 120, 122–6, 127, 136; free riders 14–15; overview xx, xxi, 14, 15; symbols of equality 78–80, *see also* fairness
Equator Principles 48, 143, 144

Index **169**

equity principles xx, xxii, 13–16, 96–7, 115–16, 120, 122–6, 127, 136, 138–9; abuses 14–15; definition 13, 14, 15, 96; discrimination inequity/inequality viewpoints 96–7, 115–16, 120, 122–6, 127, 136; overview xx, xxii, 14–15, *see also* fairness; resource companies
error types, interview data 107–9
Esquel mine 158
evaporation rates, water issues 70–2
evolutionary theory xx, 12, 13–16
exports 23, 27, 34–5, 68, 120, 125

fairness xix, xx, 12–20, 43–4, 54–5, 63–4, 86–7, 96–7, 103–16, 123–4, 138–9, 152–9; contrasting principles 13–15, 96; free riders 14–15; historical roots of divergent views xix, xx, 12–20; small/large society comparisons 13–15, 20; wages 15–16, 20, 96–7, 123–5, *see also* equality principles; equity principles; evolutionary theory; institutional theory; justice; social licence to operate
family investments 137–8
favouritism 12–13, 15, 20, 123–4, 132
feasibility studies 52, 56, 124
fencing decisions, llamas 148
Fernandez, Carlos 57, 58, 59–60
fertilisers 141
financial crises 23–5
First Inquisition witchcraft beliefs, women 134
first-ring communities 9–10, 23, 68–9, 79–80, 82–3, 85–97, 114–21, 122–4, 127, 152–9; definition 9–10, 23, 68–9; discrimination inequity/inequality viewpoints 96, 97, 115–16, 120, 122–4, 127, *see also* Culpina K community; Rio Grande community; San Cristobal community; Vila Vila community
flotation mills 68
focal organisation impacts, social licence to operate (SLO) 44–5
foreign investment, historical context 24–7, 29–33, 36–7, 158
Foundation, San Cristobal community 55–6, 58, 94, 116, 140, 149
four-level model concepts, social licence to operate (SLO) 46–8
free market attitudes from 2013 119–20, 123–4, *see also* neo-liberal reforms
free, prior, and informed consent rights (FPIC) 30–1
free riders, fairness 14–15

freehold purchases from the Spanish, San Cristobal community 5, 30
FRUTCAS rural worker (*campesino*) collective 30–1, 52, 61, 75, 76–7, 82, 84, 122–3, 132
FSTMB 91, 92–3

Gans, Karen xviii, xx, 3, 10, 11, 23, 52, 155
garbage problems 154
geography, Bolivia 4–6, 24–6, 70–1, 75–6, 83–4, 154; San Cristobal community 4–6, 70–1, 154–5
GESSBA medical services 87–9, 91–2, 96
The Gift of El Tío: A Memoir (Buchanan and Gans) xviii, xx, 3, 6–7, 11, 80, 151
Glencore 37
globalisation xvii, 81–2, 97, 159
GlobeScan surveys 157–8
Glorious Revolution of 1688, England 16–17
Godoy, R.A. 134
gold 23, 26, 29, 31–2
Goni *see* Sánchez de Lozada, Gonzalo
Google Ngram 41
Greene, J.D. 13
grievance mechanisms 65
Guinea 18

health care xxi, 27, 72, 79, 87–90, 91–4, 96, 116–17, 123, 126–7, 138, 154–7; agreements 93–4, 96, 127; ambulances 94; improvements 94, 116–17, 126–7, 138, 154–5; overview xxi; Pablo Calcina's death 86, 87–90, 127; unrest 87–9, 91–2, 93–4, 96, 116–17, 126–7, 157
health insurance 87–9
heap leach gold mines 26, 31
Hedionda silver mine 5, 8
helmets 78
Hernández, Muriel 53–4
historical context xvii, xviii, xix, xx, xxi, 1–37, 131–4, 139, 140–1, 155, 159; in the beginning xviii, xix, xx, 3–11, 131–4, 139, 155, 159; Bolivian politics xvii, xix, xx, xxi, 17–18, 21–8, 29–37; overview xix, xx, xxi
historical documents, 1994 to 2008 San Cristobal case study methods 48–50
historical roots of divergent views, fairness xix, xx, 12–20
Hohn, M. 135
horses 7
hostages 84
hotels 58

170 Index

house designs, relocation/resettlement considerations 54–5, 72, 79, 80

human resource policies/procedures 15, 61, 63–4, 89–90, 94, 117, 127–8, 135, 157–8, *see also* jobs

human rights' abuses xvii, 29

hunger strikes 85

hydrocarbon resources 34–7

Ilo 34

in-migration pressures 69, 72–4, 79, 125–6, 133–4

Incan empire 16, 23

income xxi, 15–16, 20, 62, 65, 78–86, 96–7, 115–16, 120–6, 131–4, 148, 151, 152–9; inequalities 82–3, 85–6, 96–7, 115–16, 120, 122–3, 124–6, 155–6; statistics 82–3, *see also* wages

India 81

indigenous rights, historical context 26–7, 29–32, 36–7, 76–7, 81–3

Industrial Revolution, England 19

inflation 24–5, 79, 83–4, 137, 158

influence concepts, stakeholders 44–6, 65, 109–11, 113–21

information types, quantitative socio-political risk assessment techniques 101–2

infrastructure investments 36–7, 57–8, 74, 79, 85, 93–4, 109, 117–20, 122–3, 125–6

innovations 13, 17–20, 23, 25–6, 71–2, 74, 78–80, 124–6

institutional theory xx, 12–13, 15, 16–20, 21–8, 69, 123–4, 157–8, 159; 'curse of natural resources' xx, 12–13, 17–18, 123–4; definition 12–13, 16–17; English/Spanish contrasts 16–18; Glorious Revolution of 1688, England 16–17; overview xx, 12–13; path dependence 21, *see also* clientelism; rent-seeking

International Labour Organisation (ILO), Convention 169 29–30

International Waters 33

internet access 138

interview data xxii, 48–50, 66, 83–4, 85, 101–2, 103–9, 110–11, 113–21, 122–8, 135–9, 153–9; 1994 to 2008 San Cristobal case study methods 48–50; error types 107–9; inclusiveness considerations 110–11, 113–17; question types 103–10, *see also* quantitative socio-political risk assessment techniques; stakeholders

Inti Raymi gold mine 26, 29, 30–1, 52, 62

IPSP group 30–1, *see also* CSUTCB union; MAS–Movement towards Socialism

Iquique port 6, 8

ISO certification 19–20, 123

issue framing concepts 46

Japan xvi, 37, 66, 68, 77

Japan Oil and Gas Corporation 77

Jaukihua Aquifer 71–2, 75–7

Job Fair in 2006 65–6, 86, 133–4, 144–5

jobs xxi, xxii, 5, 8, 15–18, 23–30, 32, 52, 55–69, 78–86, 96–7, 115–16, 123, 131–9, 142–50, 152–9; discrimination 60, 61–5, 78, 82–3, 86–7, 89–90, 96–7, 115–16, 132–9; economic crises 23–5; helmets 78; International Labour Organisation (ILO) 29–30; over-qualified applicants 156; overview xxi, xxii; San Pedro de Quemes 83–5, 155; selection processes 65–6, 82–3, 86, 96–7, 123, 132–9, 144; shift work 68, 138; single parent families 67, 134, 137, 139, 154; statistics 135–6; symbols of equality/respect 78–80; training 55, 58, 66–7, 82–3, 86, 96, 119–20, 123–4, 132–4, 144, 149, 156; types 58, 131–9; waiting periods 56–8, 59–60, 64–5, 142; working conditions 78–80, *see also* wages; women

joint ventures 37, 96

Joyce, Susan 42, 46–7, 49

Judicial Authority of the Administration of Mines 90–1

justice 12–20, 97, 103–12, 115–16, 123–4, 159; contrasting principles 13–15, 97; small/large society comparisons 13–15, 20, *see also* fairness

Kaplan, Thomas 51, 59

Kaysur spring 72

key performance indicators (KPIs) 128

Knight Piesold 73

knowledge-sharing networks 109–10

La Paz 6, 25–7, 33, 34–5, 73, 86–7, 91–3, 118, 119, 121, 135, 136, 149

Laguna Colorado 77

languages 5–6

Lazo, Ascencio 53

lead 27, 32–3, 51, 52, 68, 71, 110

leased mining rights 37

legal historical context xx, xxii

legal licences 42, 46, 157–9

Index **171**

legitimacy perceptions 46–50, 56,
57–8, 60–1, 62–7, 69, 152–3; losses
62–5; recovery factors 65–7, 69, *see also*
credibility perceptions; social licence to
operate
Lenglat, Dominique 61
levels, social licence to operate (SLO)
43–5, 46–50, 51–8, 83–5, 102–12,
113–21, 123–8, 157–9
licenceSLO concepts 41–50, *see also* social
licence to operate
life expectancies 155
Lípez xviii, 5, 6, 70, 72, 76–7, 87, 122–3
'Lípez Health Network' 87, 93–4
listening assessments 104–12
literacy training 66–7, 84, 86, 133–4
lithium recovery projects 78, 81
'living well' model policies 35–6
llamas i, xviii, xx, xxii, 7–8, 9, 23, 56,
58, 66, 69–70, 90, 124, 131, 140–51,
154, 156; 2004 to 2006 construction
period 142–8; 2007 to 2009 transition
to operating mine period 144–8; 2015
situation 150–1, 154; background
xx, xxii, 7–8, 131, 140–51, 154, 156;
characteristics 141; cultural issues
140–1, 150; declining livestock trends
xviii; fencing decisions 148; historical
context 7–8, 140–1; husbandry essentials
141; notes kept by Thomson 142–8;
ownership marks 141, 150; pasture
improvement plans 142–3, 148; quinoa
149–50; relocation/resettlement
considerations 69, 90, 140, 141, 142–8;
roles 7–8, 140–51; statistics 141, 142–3;
territoriality xx, xxii, 140–8; trains 8,
141; water issues 142–8; women 131
Los Tres Gigantes 4–5, 8
loyalties 12–16, 17–20, 78

Maduro, Nicolas 158
majority influences, social licence to
operate (SLO) 45–6, 113–21
malnutrition 79
Mamani, Juan 49, 66–7
management consultants xvi–xvii, 66–7;
biases xvi–xvii
management teams xxi, 59–67, 68–9, 77–8,
87–97, 135
Mancomunidad de Lípez 122–3
Mao Zedong 158
maps of the mines 6–8, 9–10, 56–7
marital/family stresses 134, 136–8, 139, 154
marketing 20, 36

marriage analogy, communities 156
MAS–Movement towards Socialism 31,
35–7, 63, *see also* IPSP group; Morales,
Evo
mayors 126
media relations xxii, 29, 30–1, 45, 49–50,
52, 61, 104, 127, 138–9
Mejillones 6, 34, 62, 68
merchant banks 17
merchants, Uyuni 83
meritocratic principles 12–13, 14–15,
16–18, 20, 96, 123–4
Mesa, Carlos 35–6
Mesa de Plata silver mine xviii, 6, 8,
10–11, *see also* San Antonio de Lípez
metaphors i, 3, 41–6, 67
Mexico 35
micro-irrigation technologies 125
middle classes 81–2
military interventions 32, 34–5
Minera Manquiri 37
Minera San Cristobal (MSC), background
i, xvi–xvii, xix, xx, xxii, xxiii, 12, 13–23,
51–67, 68–80, 81–97, 103–21, 122–8,
132–9, 152–9; cleaner/safer practices
23; conclusions xxii, xxiii, 80, 152–9;
contracts 59–60, 157–8; formation
56–7; Job Fair in 2006 65–6, 86, 133–4,
144–5; justice/fairness principles 13–16,
96–7, 103–12, 138–9, 152–9; Morales
visit 78, 138–9; organisational structure
xvi, 49, 56–7, 59, 66, 78; overview
of the book xvi–xxiii; owners xvi, 37,
56–7, 59, 66, 78; security company uses
65; women support initiatives 138–9, *see
also* resource companies; San Cristobal
mine; Sumitomo Corporation
miners' union 22–4, 30–2, 88–94
mini-insurrection of 2010 85–6, 117, 118
Mining Water report (Moran) 76–7, 82–3
Ministry of Environment 104
Ministry of Labour 91–4
minority influences, social licence to
operate (SLO) 45–6, 113–21
MINTEC 25–7, 51–3
Misima Island, Papua New Guinea 103
mita taxes 5–6
mobile phones 84, 90
Molina, Jorge 75
monopolies 18–20, 95, *see also* rent-seeking
Moore, W.H. 42
Moral Tribes (Greene) 13
Morales, Evo xx, xxi, 12, 23–5, 28, 31,
34–7, 63, 65, 76, 78–9, 81–2, 138–9,

172 Index

159; ascendancy xx, xxi, 12, 34–7; cocaine 24–5, 34; election in 2006 xx, xxi, 12, 35–6, 65, 81–2; foreign investment attitudes 36–7; high hopes 23; Minera San Cristobal (MSC) 78, 138–9; women 138–9
Moran, Robert 76–7, 82–3
Moscoso, Fernández 53–4
Mothers Club membership 137
mules 7
mutual learning and influence concepts xvi–xix, 54, 65, 77, 104, 159

nationalisations xxii, 12, 17, 29–30, 32, 34–7, 74, 119, 123–4; oil and gas 36; risks in 2012 xxii, 12, 17, 119, 123–4
nationalism 35–7, 127
natural resources, geography 25–6, 154
neo-liberal reforms xx, 12, 21, 23–8, 29–31, 33–7, 63, 112, 119–20, 123–4; free market attitudes from 2013 119–20, 123–4; historical context xx, 23–8, 29–31; mainstream opposition 33–7; push back 29–31, 33–7
nepotism 15
Netherlands 16–17
New Economic Policy (NEP) 24
Newrest Catering Bolivia S.A. 135
Niltetsu Mining Consultants 77, 82–3
non-governmental organisations (NGOs) 75–7, 103
Nor Lípez 4–5, 8–9, 10–11, 26–7, 30–1, 70, 72, 75, 83–5, 95, 152–5
North, Douglass 16
Norway 19

objective perspectives, biases xvi–xvii, 97
occupations of mines xxi, 31–2, 86–97, 106, 116–17, 157, see also unrest
odds ratios 106–7
oil and gas 24, 27, 34–6
old-age benefits 27
Olivera, Oscar 75
open-pit mines 61–7, 68, 82–3, 90, 133–5, 139, 144–9, 158
operating mine period, 2007 to 2009 transition to operating mine period xix, xxi, 3, 48–50, 68–80, 144–8
opinion leaders, definition 110
Oruro 25–7, 29–30, 31, 149
Orvana Minerals 37, see also Don Mario mine
'outside workers' 86–7, 90, 96, 133
over-qualified applicants, jobs 156
overview of the book xvi–xxiii, 3

Pachamama earth goddess 30–1, 35–6
Pan American Silver 27–8, 37
participant field observation, 1994 to 2008 San Cristobal case study methods 48–50, 69
patents 18, 72
path dependence, definition 21
Patriotic Accord 25
paved highways 86, 88, 91–4, 124
Paz Estenssoro, Victor 24, 25, 28, 29
Paz Zamora, Jaime 25–6, 28, 29
People's High Command 34–5, see also Morales, Evo
percentile concepts 105–7
permits 18
Peru 5, 34, 141, 149
petitions 47
Petrobras 27
pickup trucks 65, 79, 153
Pilcomayo River 32–3
pipeline gas exports 34–5
pipeline rupture in 2008, clean-ups 78
Placer Dome Inc. 42, 102–3
plurinationalism 36–7
political context of the study xvii, xix, xx, xxi, see also Bolivian politics
political emergence from 2015, San Cristobal community 120–1
political science 17–18, 157–8
pollution 23, 31, 32–3, 52, 63, 69, 73, 75–6, 115–16, 124–6, 145–7, see also environmental issues
Popular Participation Act 26–7
Porco mine tailings spill unrest 32–3, 52
potatoes 4
Potosí 6–8, 19–28, 31, 37, 75, 85–6, 91–2, 117–19, 121, 127, 135–7, 149, 159; August 2010 march 85–6, 117; unrest 85–6, 91–2, 117, 118–19, 127, see also second-ring communities
Potosí silver mine 6–8, 19–20, 21–8, 37; historical resentments 21–3
poverty 9–10, 12–14, 21–5, 27–8, 79, 81–3, 134, 137, 152–3, 155, 158; conclusions 155, 158; life expectancies 155
power concepts xvii, 18–19, 35–6, 42–6, 65, 67, 117, 158
preconstruction period, 1994 to 2004 preconstruction period xix, xxi, 10, 48–9, 51–8, 60, 80, 132–4
prestige 9–10
privatisations 24–5, 27, 33–4
production statistics, San Cristobal mine 71–2

Index **173**

property rights 16–17, 18, 19
prophecies xviii, xix, xx, xxi, 3–4, 6–7, 10, 78–80, 134–5
Prophecy Development Corp. 11
Prospectors and Developers Association 46
Protestant Europe 16–18, *see also* England
protests xxi, 47–8, 62–3, 69, 82–3, 85
pseudo-CSR 126
psychological identification level, social licence to operate (SLO) 46–50, 54, 105–7, 115–16
public opinion, social licence to operate (SLO) 43–4, 102, 157–8
public parks 154
Pueblos Modelos (model communities) project 58
Pulacayo silver mine xviii, 6, 11

qualitative study methods xix, xx, xxi, xxii, 3, 106–7
quantification of levels, social licence to operate (SLO) 104–12, 113–21, 157–9
quantitative measures, stakeholder strategies from quantitative measures xix, xx, xxi, xxii, 3, 99–128
quantitative socio-political risk assessment techniques i, xiv, xvii, xix, xx, xxi, xxii, xxiii, 3, 101–12, 113–21, 127–8; background xxi, xxii, 101–12, 113–21, 127–8; changes in methods 111, 128; colour gradations 104–5, 113–17; concerns/priorities 107–9, 113–14, 115–19, 122–8; information types 101–2; overview xix, xx, xxi, xxii, xxiii, 3; stakeholder influences 109–12, 113–21; validation of the measures 106–7, 109, 127–8, *see also* interview data
quartile concepts 105–7
Quechua language 5, 27–8, 29–30, 49, 54, 66, 141
question types, interview data 103–10
questionnaires 102
quinoa xviii, 4, 58, 81, 120, 124–5, 131–2, 148–50, 152–4; burgeoning trends xviii, 120, 124–5, 148–9, 152–4; equipment agreement 148–50; llamas 149–50
Quiroga, Jorge 34
Quisbert Salinas, Francisco 30–1, 52, 61, 75

racism 60, 62
Radio Pio XII 29, 52
radio uses 29, 31, 52
rail blockades 84–5, 90

rail transport xxii, 6–10, 19–20, 57, 62, 83–4, 95, 118–19, 123–4, 144–5; maps 6, 9–10, 57; origins 8
Ramaditas 61, 86, 135
Ramos, Rodolfo 53, 58
re-negotiation of roles and rights xxi, 80, 81–97, 116–17, 120–1, 122–3, 126–7
recycling innovations, water issues 71–2
redistributive wealth activities 18–19, 35–7, 123, 127, 154
redundancies 96
references 160–4
referendums, oil and gas 35
regional concerns, water issues 74–7
regional unrest 74–7, 82–3, 116–19, 122–3
relationships xvi–xxiii, 3, 20, 47–58, 60–80, 81–97, 102–12, 114–21, 122–8, 134–9, 152–9; definition 159; overview of the book xvi–xxiii, 3; San Pedro de Quemes 83–5, 155; stakeholder networks xvii, xxi, xxii, 42–6, 101–11, 114–21, 126, 127–8, 136, 152–9; stakeholder relations strategies 107–11, 122–8; types xxiii, 159; universal qualities 104–5, *see also* social licence to operate; unrest
relocation/resettlement considerations xviii, xxi, 11, 26, 29, 52–6, 60, 69, 72–5, 86–7, 90, 96, 125–7, 132–3, 140–8; agreements 54–5, 60, 62, 72–4, 86–7, 125–7, 132–3, 140, 144–7, 148–50; background 52–6, 60, 72–5, 86–7, 96, 127, 132–3, 140–8; committees 53–6; construction dates 55–6; house designs 54–5, 72, 79, 80; llamas 69, 90, 140, 141, 142–8; water issues 72–4, 125–6
rent-seeking 13, 16, 18–20, 92, 95, 123–4; definition 18–19; prevention methods 19, *see also* 'curse of natural resources'; institutional theory; monopolies
Repsol 27
resentment discourses xx, 21–8, 29–31, 82–3, 89–90, 97, 133–4
resource companies, bullying allegations xvii, 60, 61–5; conclusions xxii, xxiii, 152–9; cultural challenges xvii, xviii, xix, xx, xxi, xxii, 12, 20, 53–4, 80, 153–7; foreign investment 24–7, 29–33, 36–7, 158; historical context 24–8, 29–33, 36–7, 131–4; overview of the book xvi–xxiii, 3; poor reputations xvii, *see also* Minera San Cristobal; San Cristobal mine; social licence to operate
respect 9–10, 52, 65, 67, 78–80, 159

174 Index

responsibilities 9–10, 13–16, 68–9, 78, 125–6, 158–9
retrospective from discovery to routine operations xix, xxi, 39–97
retrospective study method, social licence to operate (SLO) xxi, 41, 49–50
revolutions, 1952 revolution 23, 159; Brinton's theory 28; Glorious Revolution of 1688, England 16–17
Rio Grande community 57, 62, 67, 68–9, 78, 93, 118, 143
Rio Tinto 26, 33
risk assessments i, xiv, xvii, xix, xx, xxi, xxii, xxiii, 3, 75, 101–12, 113–21, 127–8
risk hotspots xix, xxii, 113–21
road accidents 86, 88, 127
road blockades xxi, 31–2, 34–5, 47–8, 62–5, 82–3, 84–5, 90, see also unrest
road transport xxi, xxii, 5, 9, 31–5, 58, 62, 79, 83–6, 95, 118–19, 123–4, 127, 133–9, 143, 148–9
Rodriguez, Eduardo 35
Roelants, Chantal 30, 52
royalties 23, 75, 83, 84, 122–3, 154–5
Russia 81

sabotage 48, 84
Sachs, Jeffrey 24–5
sacred stones xxi, 64–5
Salar de Uyuni 4–5, 6, 8, 10, 30–1, 70, 78, 124; description 8, 70
San Antonio de Lípez xviii, 6, 8, 10–11, see also Mesa de Plata silver mine
San Bartolome mine 37
San Cristobal community, 20th century decline 8–10; 2011 occupation of the mine xxi, 86–97, 106, 116–17, 157; background xvi–xviii, 3–20, 23–4, 28, 30–1, 41–67, 68–80, 86–97, 103–12, 113–28, 131–9, 140–51, 152–9; conclusions 152–9; empowerment processes 53–6; Foundation 55–6, 58, 94, 116, 140, 149; freehold purchases from the Spanish 5, 30; geography 4–6, 70–1, 154–5; health care xxi, 27, 72, 79, 87–90, 91–2, 93–4, 96, 116–17, 126–7, 138; historical background xxii, 3–11, 131–4; maps of the mines 6–8, 9–10, 56–7; origins 5; overview of the book xvi–xxiii, 3; political emergence from 2015 120–1; rail transport history 8, 144–5; re-negotiation of roles and rights xxi, 80, 81–97, 116–17, 120–1, 122–3; relocation/resettlement considerations xviii, xxi, 11, 52–6, 60, 72–5, 86–7,

96, 125–7, 132–3, 140–8; service sector 62; Spain 5–6, 7, 12, 159; water requirements 72–4, 124–6; 'window on the sea' accolade 7, see also individual topics; social licence to operate
San Cristobal mine, 1994 to 2004 preconstruction period xix, xxi, 10, 11, 48–9, 51–8, 60, 80, 132–4; 1994 to 2008 San Cristobal case study methods 48–50, 69, 101; 1994 to 2011 period xix, xxi, 10, 48–50, 51–8, 60, 69, 80, 101, 125, 132–9; 1995 mineral deposit discovery xxi, 7, 11, 23–4, 28, 31, 41, 51–2, 74, 132, 152–3, 155; 2004 to 2006 construction period xix, xxi, 49, 58, 59–67, 132–4, 139, 142–8; 2007 to 2009 transition to operating mine period xix, xxi, 3, 48–50, 68–80, 144–8; 2009 dust concerns xxii, 69, 115–16, 122–3, 125, 146; 2009 to 2015 quantitative study methods period xix, xx, xxi, xxii, 101–12, 113–21, 122–8, 153–4; 2009 water controversy xix, 70–7, 82–3, 115–16, 125; 2010 and 2011 conflicts/unrest xix, xxi, 16, 19–20, 23, 41, 80, 81–97, 116–17, 123–7, 157–8; 2011 occupation of the mine xxi, 86–97, 106, 116–17, 157; 2012 nationalisation risks xxii, 12, 17, 119, 123–4; agreements 54–5, 60–2, 65, 68–9, 72–4, 82–7, 93–4, 96, 125–7, 132–3, 140, 144–50; background xvi–xxiii, 3, 7, 10–20, 23–4, 37, 48–58, 59–67, 68–80, 81–97, 101–21, 131–9, 140–51, 152–9; benefits for the community 78–80; conclusions xxii, xxiii, 80, 152–9; contracts 59–60, 157–8; environmental permits 56–7; illegal bulldozer acts 62; map of operating area 56–7; overview of the book xvi–xxiii, 3; owners xvi, 37, 56–7, 59, 66, 78; production statistics 71–2; television documentaries 61; women xx, xxii, 9, 53, 60, 61, 62–3, 65–6, 67, 131–9, see also resource companies
San Pedro de Quemes 26–7, 83–5, 155, see also second-ring communities
San Vincente silver mine 27, 37
Sánchez de Lozada, Gonzalo (Goni) 24, 26–8, 30–2, 34–5, 37
Santa Cruz 25, 34, 36, 65, 86–7, 135
second-ring communities xxi, 82–3, 84–5, 97, 114–19; discrimination inequity/inequality viewpoints 97, 117, see also Potosí; San Pedro de Quemes

Index **175**

security company uses, Minera San Cristobal (MSC) 65
self-declared stakeholders, definition 43–4
Senge, Peter 108
service sectors 62
sextile concepts 105–7, 113–14, 116–17
shamanistic prophecies, supernatural/superstition beliefs xviii, xix, xx, xxi, 3–4, 6–7, 10, 78–80
sheep herds 144, 151
Shell 27
shift work 68, 138
Shinglespit Consultants Inc., Canada i
Siles Zuazo, Hernán 24
silver mines xviii, xx, 3–4, 5–11, 21–8, 29–33, 37, 51–8, 59–67, 68–80, 110, 124, 152–9; closures xx, 9–11, 24–5, 27–8, 29–32, 124, 155, 156; conclusions 152–9; *El Tío* xviii, 6–7, 10–11, 80, 151, 154; historical context 3–4, 5–11, 21–8, 32–3, 37, 131–4; maps 6–8, 9–10, 56–7, *see also* resource companies; San Cristobal mine
Simon Fraser University, Canada i
Sinchi Wayra 37
single parent families 67, 134, 137, 139, 154
SLSN 101–2
smugglers 85, 95, 108, 118–19
social capital xiv, 103–4, 126
social contract concepts 14–15, 157–8
The Social Licence to Operate (Black) 103
social licence to operate (SLO) i, xiv, xvii, xix, xx, xxi, xxii, xxiii, 3, 20, 41–50, 51–8, 60–80, 83–5, 86–7, 101–12, 113–21, 123–8, 152, 157–9; 1994 to 2008 San Cristobal case study methods 48–50, 69, 101; acceptance/tolerance 42–8, 50, 51, 58, 60–1, 66–7, 85, 105–7, 113–14, 116–17, 118–19, 121, 128; approval level 46–50, 52, 58, 59, 69, 78, 86–7, 105–7, 117, 119–21, 128; colour gradations 104–5, 113–17; components 46–50; concepts i, xvii, xix, xxi, xxii, xxiii, 3, 20, 41–50, 69, 101–2, 128, 152, 157–9; conclusions xx, xxii, xxiii; definitions 41–6, 102–3, 128, 157–8; entity types 157–8; focal organisation impacts 44–5; four-level model concepts 46–8; historical background 103; levels 43–5, 46–50, 51–8, 83–5, 102–12, 113–21, 123–8, 157–9; licenceSLO concepts 41–50; longitudinal quantitative methods xxi; measures xiv, xix, xx, xxi, xxii, 3, 41–50,

51–8, 101–12, 113–21, 127–8; overview i, xix, xx, xxi, xxii, xxiii; psychological identification level 46–50, 54, 105–7, 115–16; public opinion 43–4, 102, 157–8; quantification of levels 104–12, 113–21, 157–9; retrospective study method xxi, 41, 49–50; stakeholder networks xvii, xxi, xxii, 42–6, 101–11, 114–21, 126, 127–8, 152–9; stakeholder politics platforms 43–4; strategies that work xx, xxii, 107, 121, 122–8; three-level stair-step model concepts 46–7; validation of the measures 106–7, 109, 127–8; withdrawals xxi, 43, 45–50, 62–5, 105–7, 115–16, 123, 157–8; withholding issues 43, 45–50, 83–4, 105–7, 115–16, 118–20, 121; yacht-sailing analogy 128, *see also* communities; credibility perceptions; legitimacy perceptions; trust
Social Management Plan 72
social network analysis 109–11, 136, *see also* stakeholder networks
social norms/pressures 14–15, 63–5
social organisation 35–6
social responsibility 49, 68–9
social science concepts xvii, xix, 3
socialism 25–6, 30–1
socio-political conflicts xix, xx, 12–20
socio-political risk assessments i, xiv, xvii, xix, xx, xxi, xxii, xxiii, 12, 101–12, 113–21, 127–8, *see also* risk assessments
solar greenhouses 58
South Africa 81
Spain 5–6, 7, 12, 16–20, 21–2, 57, 81–2, 134, 159; English/Spanish institutional contrasts 16–18; First Inquisition witchcraft beliefs 134
spiritual enrichment xix, xx, 4–5, 16, 25, 30–1, 64–5, 76–7
sports facilities 154
Stakeholder 360 measure xiv, 103
stakeholder engagement plans *see* stakeholder relations strategies
stakeholder management i, xiv, xvi–xxiii, 12, 99–128, 152–9; overview of the book xvi–xxiii; strategies that work xx, xxii, 107, 121, 122–8
stakeholder networks xvii, xxi, xxii, 42–6, 101–11, 114–21, 126, 127–8, 136, 152–9; definition 109–10; inclusiveness considerations 110–11, 113–17
stakeholder politics platforms, social licence to operate (SLO) 43–4
stakeholder relations strategies 107–11, 122–8, *see also* relationships

176 Index

stakeholder strategies from quantitative measures xix, xx, xxi, xxii, 3, 99–128; limitations 127–8; overview xix, xx, xxi, xxii, 3

stakeholders, articulation problems 107–8; clusters 102, 110, 114–21; concerns/priorities quantification methods 107–9, 113–14, 115–19, 122–8; conclusions 152–9; definition 43–5; influence concepts 44–6, 65, 109–11, 113–21

start-up phase 3, 69–80, 144–5

stewardship 42, 127, see also social licence to operate

strategies that work xx, xxii, 107, 121, 122–8

street lights 154

strikes 24, 31–2, 48, 69, 89–91, see also unrest

subjective perspectives, biases xvi–xvii, 97

Sud López 10–11, 72

Sudan 18

Sumitomo Corporation xvi, 37, 66, 77, 78, 103, 134, see also Minera San Cristobal

supernatural/superstition beliefs xvii, xviii, xix, xx, 3–7, 10, 25, 30–1, 64–5, 76–80, 134–5, 141, 150, 154

supply chain relations 109

surveys 85

SUVs 65, 79, 153

taxes 5–6, 16–18, 27, 44, 75, 83, 84, 125

television documentaries 61

third-ring communities 114–16, 117

Thomson, Ian 41, 42, 46–8, 103, 104–5, 142–8

three-level stair-step model concepts, social licence to operate (SLO) 46–7

tin 24, 75

tobacco industry 157

Toldos silver mine 8, 51–2, 61, 144

tolerance, social licence to operate (SLO) 42–8, 50, 51, 58, 60–1, 66–7, 105–7, 113–14, 116–17, 118–19, 121, 128

tourism 58, 85, 154

traditional dress, Bolivia 30

training 55, 58, 66–7, 82–3, 86, 96, 119–20, 123–4, 132–4, 144, 149, 156

transformational relationships xvi–xxiii, 3, 20, 52, 159; overview of the book xvi–xxiii, 3

transport options xxii, 5, 7–10, 19–20, 31–5, 57, 58, 62–3, 79, 83–4, 118–19, 123–4, 133–9, 141

tribalism preferences 13–16, 110, 159, see also communities

truck metaphor, Consejo Consultivo leadership group 67

trucking cooperatives 95, 118–19

Trump, Donald 97

trust 43–4, 46–50, 52, 54, 56–7, 63–4, 92–3, 104–12, 152–3, see also social licence to operate

tyrants 128

Ugalde, Gaston 58

unions 22–4, 30–2, 34, 88–94

unrest xix, xxi, 16, 19–20, 23–4, 31–7, 47–8, 52, 55, 61–5, 69, 80, 81–97, 106, 115–17, 123, 150, 157–8; 2010 and 2011 conflicts/unrest xix, xxi, 16, 19–20, 23, 41, 80, 81–97, 116–17, 123–7, 157–8; Dialogue Table 93; health care 87–9, 91–2, 93–4, 96, 116–17, 126–7; hostages 84; income inequalities 82–3, 85–6, 96–7, 115–16, 120, 122–3, 124–6; mini-insurrection of 2010 85–6, 117, 118; occupation of 2011 86–97, 106, 116–17, 157; Pablo Calcina's death 86, 87–90, 127; Potosí 85–6, 91–2, 117, 118–19, 127; Potosí August 2010 march 85–6, 117; regional unrest 74–7, 82–3, 116–19, 122–3; San Pedro de Quemes 83–5, 155; smugglers 85, 95, 108, 118–19; strikes 24, 31–2, 69, 89–91; unions 88–94; water inequalities 82–4, 89–90, 122–3, 124–6; water issues xix, 33–4, 70–7, 82–5, 89–90, 115–16, 123; water privatisation 33–4, see also occupations of mines; protests; road blockades; sabotage; strikes

USA 11, 24–5, 26, 34–5, 37, 51, 60, 63, 97, 156

Usloque/Osloka (Aymara) community, historical context 5

Uyuni 4–8, 9–11, 30–1, 57–8, 61, 70, 83, 91, 94, 137, 143, 149

validation of the measures, social licence to operate (SLO) 106–7, 109, 127–8

value-added exports 23, 27, 34–5, 120, 125

Venezuela 18, 158

verbal abuses, women 133–4

vetoes, social licence to operate (SLO) 46

victimhood discourses xx

Vila Vila community 9–10, 56–9, 67–9, 72–7, 82–3, 86–8, 93–6, 131–2, 135, 137, 140, 150

village councils 44

'voice' codes 106–7, 109
volcanoes 11, 70

wages xxi, 15–16, 20, 62, 65, 78–86,
96–7, 115–16, 120–3, 124–6, 137–8,
155–6; fairness principles 15–16, 20,
96–7, 123–5; inequalities 82–3, 85–6,
96–7, 115–16, 120, 122–3, 124–6,
155–6; statistics 82–3, *see also* economic
benefits; jobs
War on Drugs 25, 34, *see also* drugs
Warhol, Andy 58
Washington Group 59–60, 62, 68, 69,
132–4, 139
waste water/sewage 54, 66, 69, 71–2,
73–4, 154
water issues xix, 4, 8, 33–4, 54–7, 58, 61–3,
66, 69–77, 82–5, 89–90, 115–16, 123–6,
145–8, 154–5; 2000 water controversy
33–4; 2009 water controversy xix, 70–7,
82–3, 115–16; background to the worries
33, 70–7, 82–3, 84–5, 89–90, 115–16,
123, 124–6; community requirements
72–4, 124–6; consumption at the mine
71–3, 75–6; corrosion issues 71; dams
33; droughts 75, 82–3, 147; education
initiatives 124–6; evaporation rates 70–2;
in-migration pressures 69, 72–4, 125–6;
innovations 71–2, 74, 124–6; llamas 142–8;
micro-irrigation technologies 125; price
increases 33; privatisations 33–4; quality
concerns 61, 63, 66, 69, 70–7, 115–16,
124–6, 145–7; recycling innovations
71–2; regional concerns 74–7; relocation/
resettlement considerations 72–4, 125–6;
San Pedro de Quemes 84–5; sources 4, 8,
58, 63, 66, 70–1, 72–4, 145–8; statistics
125–6; unrest xix, 33–4, 70–7, 82–5,
89–90, 115–16, 123; waste water/sewage
54, 66, 69, 71–2, 73–4, 154
water table concerns 73–7, 82–3
Water War in Cochabamba 75
Weber, Max 15
well-being 13–16, 42–50, 67, 155
western Bolivia, geography 25–7, 36, 70, 77

Wila Khara 56–7, 63, 66–7, 71, 73, 90,
140, 142–4, 146, 148–50
William III, King of England 17
'window on the sea' accolade, San
Cristobal community 7
wisdom 20
withdrawals, social licence to operate
(SLO) xxi, 43, 45–50, 62–5, 105–7,
115–16, 123, 157–8
withholding issues, social licence to operate
(SLO) 43, 45–8, 50, 83–4, 105–7,
115–16, 118–20, 121
women xx, xxii, 9, 53, 60, 61, 62–3,
65–6, 67, 131–9; 2016 situation 134–5;
abuses 133–5, 136, 139; advancement
restrictions 135–6, 139; background
xx, xxii, 61, 65–6, 131–9; community
perspectives on women in the
workplace 136–8; company support
initiatives 138–9; conclusions 139;
cultural issues 131, 134–9; day-care
centre facilities 137–8; First Inquisition
witchcraft beliefs 134; historical context
xxii, 131–4, 139; llamas 131; marital/
family stresses 134, 136–8, 139, 154;
Morales visit 138–9; overview xx,
xxii, 131–4; perspectives on women in
the workplace 135–9; pride 136, 139;
resentment issues 133–4; single parent
families 67, 134, 137, 139, 154; statistics
135–6; studies 135–9; work types
132–5, 138–9; work-family balance
problems 136–8, 139, *see also* jobs
word-of-mouth messages 114
work-family balance problems 136–8, 139
World Bank 42, 49, 143, 151
World People's Conference 76

yacht-sailing analogy, social licence to
operate (SLO) 128
YPFB state oil and gas company 36

z scores 106–7
Zeland Mines 26
zinc 27, 32–3, 51, 52, 68, 71, 110

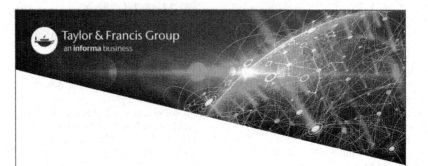